APR 03 2019

AMC'S BEST DAY HIKES
VERMONT

Four-Season Guide to 60 of the Best Trails
in the Green Mountain State

Second Edition

JEN LAMPHERE ROBERTS

D1063458

AMC's best day hikes in
Vermont.
HUDSON
PUBLIC LIBRARY

WITHDRAWN
FROM OUR
COLLECTION

HUDSON PUBLIC LIBRARY
3 WASHINGTON STREET
HUDSON, MA 01749
ADULT: 978-568-9644
CHILDREN: 978-568-9645
www.hudsonpubliclibrary.com

Appalachian Mountain Club Books
Boston, Massachusetts

AMC is a nonprofit organization, and sales of AMC Books fund our mission of protecting the Northeast outdoors. If you appreciate our efforts and would like to become a member or make a donation to AMC, visit outdoors.org, call 800-372-1758, or contact us at Appalachian Mountain Club, 10 City Square, Boston, MA 02129.

outdoors.org/publications/books-maps

Copyright © 2018 Jen Lamphere Roberts. All rights reserved.

Distributed by National Book Network.

Front cover photograph of the Long Trail, with Mount Abraham in the distance © Brian Mohr/EmberPhoto
Back cover photographs, from left, of Mount Hunger © Brian Mohr/EmberPhoto and near Pico Peak © Jerry and Marcy Monkman/EcoPhotography
Interior photographs © Jen Lamphere Roberts, unless otherwise noted
Maps by Ken Dumas © Appalachian Mountain Club
Book design by Abigail Coyle

Published by the Appalachian Mountain Club. No part of this publication may be reproduced or transmitted in any form or by any means, electronic or mechanical, including photocopying and recording, or by any information storage or retrieval system, except as may be expressly permitted by the 1976 Copyright Act or in writing from the publisher.

Library of Congress Cataloging-in-Publication Data
Names: Roberts, Jennifer Lamphere author.
Title: AMC's best day hikes in Vermont : four-season guide to 60 of the best
   trails in the Green Mountain State / Jen Lamphere Roberts.
Other titles:: Appalachian Mountain Club's best day hikes in Vermont
Description: Second Edition. | Boston, Massachusetts : Appalachian Mountain
   Club Books, [2018] | "Distributed by National Book Network"--T.p. verso. |
   Previous edition: 2013. | Includes index. |
Identifiers: LCCN 2018010385 (print) | LCCN 2018010959 (ebook) | ISBN
   9781628420791 (epub) | ISBN 9781628420807 (Mobi) | ISBN 9781628420784
   (paperback)
Subjects: LCSH: Hiking--Vermont--Guidebooks. | Walking--Vermont--Guidebooks.
   | Trails--Vermont--Guidebooks. | Outdoor recreation--Vermont--Guidebooks.
   | Vermont--Guidebooks. | Appalachian Trail--Guidebooks.
Classification: LCC GV199.42.V4 (ebook) | LCC GV199.42.V4 L35 2018 (print) |
   DDC 796.5109743--dc23
LC record available at https://lccn.loc.gov/2018010385

The paper used in this publication meets the minimum requirements of the American National Standard for Information Sciences-Permanence of Paper for Printed Library Materials, ANSI Z39.48-1984. ∞

Outdoor recreation activities by their very nature are potentially hazardous. This book is not a substitute for good personal judgment and training in outdoor skills. Due to changes in conditions, use of the information in this book is at the sole risk of the user. The author and the Appalachian Mountain Club assume no liability for accidents happening to, or injuries sustained by, readers who engage in the activities described in this book.

Interior pages and cover are printed on responsibly harvested paper stock certified by The Forest Stewardship Council®, an independent auditor of responsible forestry practices.

Printed in the United States of America, using vegetable-based inks.

6 5 4 3 2 1   18 19 20 21 22

MIX
Paper from responsible sources
FSC
www.fsc.org
FSC® C005010

Dedicated to all the little trekkers,
especially Indy, Max, Teddy, Finn, and Molly.

LOCATOR MAP

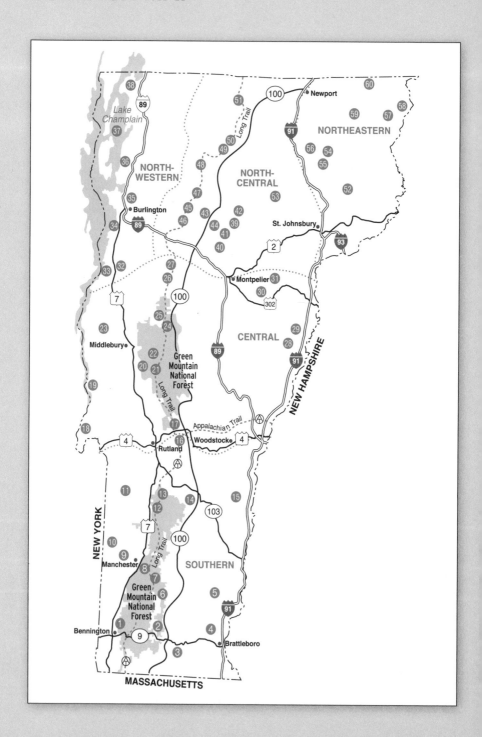

CONTENTS

NATURE AND HISTORY ESSAYS

AT-A-GLANCE TRIP PLANNER

TRIP NUMBER	TRIP NAME	LOCATION	DIFFICULTY	DISTANCE	ELEVATION GAIN
SOUTHERN VERMONT					
1	Bald Mountain	Bennington and Woodford	Moderate	7.4 mi from Bennington trailhead; 3.8 mi from Woodford trailhead; 5.6 mi end-to-end	2,099 ft from Bennington trailhead; 1,509 ft from Woodford trailhead; 2,099 ft end-to-end
2	Haystack Mountain (Wilmington)	Wilmington	Moderate	4.2 mi	1,025 ft
3	Mount Olga	Wilmington	Easy-Moderate	1.8 mi	520 ft
4	Black Mountain	Dummerston	Moderate	3 mi	875 ft
5	Putney Mountain	Putney	Easy	1.2 mi	140 ft
6	Grout Pond and Somerset Reservoir	Stratton	Easy	4.6 mi	250 ft
7	Bromley Mountain	Peru	Moderate	5 mi	829 ft
8	Lye Brook Falls	Manchester	Moderate	4.4 mi	740 ft
9	Mount Equinox	Manchester	Strenuous	6 mi	2,805 ft
10	Mount Antone	Rupert	Moderate	5.8 mi	800 ft
11	Haystack Mountain (North Pawlet)	Pawlet	Moderate	4 mi	770 ft
12	Little Rock Pond	Mount Tabor	Easy	4.8 mi	365 ft
13	White Rocks Ice Beds	Wallingford	Easy	1.8 mi	336 ft
14	Okemo Mountain	Mount Holly	Moderate-Strenuous	6 mi	1,950 ft
15	Mount Ascutney	Windsor	Strenuous	5.2 mi	2,450 ft
16	Pico Peak	Mendon and Killington	Strenuous	7.6 mi	1,600 ft
CENTRAL VERMONT					
17	Deer Leap	Killington	Easy-Moderate	2 mi	430 ft
18	Buckner Memorial Preserve	West Haven	Moderate	2.6 mi	240 ft
19	Mount Independence	Orwell	Easy-Moderate	3 mi	200 ft

Estimated Time	Trip Highlights	Fee	Good for Kids	Dog-Friendly	X-C Skiing	Snowshoeing
5.5 hrs from Bennington trailhead; 3.5 hrs from Woodford trailhead; 4.5 hrs end-to-end	Unusual cobble fields and white sands on summit ridge, views of southern Vermont			🐕		⛄
3 hrs	Views of Haystack Pond		👫	🐕		⛄
1.5 hrs	Loop hike, varied forests, fire tower	$	👫	🐕	🎿	⛄
2.5 hrs	Rare forest on ridge with blueberries					⛄
1 hr	Easy ridgeline walk, grassy summit		👫	🐕	🎿	⛄
2.5 hrs	Swimming in two lakes, easy hiking		👫	🐕	🎿	⛄
3.5 hrs	Pretty ridgeline forest hike, views		👫	🐕		⛄
3 hrs	125-ft waterfall in steep wilderness valley		👫	🐕	🎿	⛄
4.5 hrs	Views from pretty ridge trail on highest Taconic peak			🐕		⛄
4 hrs	Educational farm, parklike mature hardwood forests		👫	🐕	🎿	⛄
3 hrs	Panoramic views and diverse forests		👫			⛄
3.5 hrs	Loop around scenic pond with swimming		👫	🐕	🎿	⛄
1.5 hrs	Open hemlock forest, microclimate at rock slide		👫	🐕		⛄
4 hrs	Fire tower with views across southern Vermont			🐕		⛄
4 hrs	Waterfall, multiple viewpoints, fire tower			🐕		⛄
4 hrs	Open birch glade, views, historic camp			🐕		⛄
1.5 hrs	Rock outcrop, views		👫	🐕		⛄
2.5 hrs	Rare wildlife, open hickory forest		👫			⛄
2 hrs	Historic site, Lake Champlain views	$	👫	🐕	🎿	⛄

TRIP NUMBER	TRIP NAME	LOCATION	DIFFICULTY	DISTANCE	ELEVATION GAIN
20	Rattlesnake Cliffs and Falls of Lana	Salisbury	Moderate	4 mi	1,029 ft
21	Mount Horrid's Great Cliff	Goshen	Moderate	1.6 mi	620 ft
22	Robert Frost Trail	Ripton	Easy	1 mi	30 ft
23	Snake Mountain	Addison	Moderate	3.6 mi	900 ft
24	Sunset Ledge	Lincoln	Easy	2.2 mi	387 ft
25	Mount Abraham	Lincoln	Strenuous	5.2 mi	1,582 ft
26	Burnt Rock Mountain	Fayston	Strenuous	5.2 mi	2,090 ft
27	Camel's Hump (East and West Sides)	Duxbury and Huntington	Strenuous	7 mi east side; 5.3 mi west side	2,585 ft east side; 2,230 ft west side
28	Bald Top Mountain	Fairlee	Moderate-Strenuous	6.8 mi	1,320 ft
29	Wright's Mountain	Bradford	Easy-Moderate	2.7 mi	326 ft
30	Spruce Mountain	Plainfield	Moderate	4.4 mi	1,300 ft
31	Owl's Head	Peacham	Easy-Moderate	3.8 mi	370 ft
NORTHWESTERN VERMONT					
32	Mount Philo	Charlotte	Moderate	2.4 mi	580 ft
33	Williams Woods	Charlotte	Easy	1.2 mi	Minimal
34	Allen Hill	Shelburne	Easy	1.9 mi	120 ft
35	Colchester Pond	Colchester	Easy-Moderate	3.2 mi	150 ft
36	Eagle Mountain	Milton	Easy	2.1 mi	200 ft
37	Burton Island	Saint Albans	Easy	2.8 mi	Minimal
38	Missisquoi National Wildlife Refuge	Swanton	Easy	3 mi	Minimal
NORTH-CENTRAL VERMONT					
39	Worcester Range Skyline	Worcester and Middlesex	Strenuous	10.5 mi	3,350 ft
40	White Rock Mountain	Middlesex	Moderate-Strenuous	4.6 mi	1,558 ft
41	Mount Hunger	Waterbury Center	Moderate-Strenuous	4 mi	2,290 ft

Estimated Time	Trip Highlights	Fee	Good for Kids	Dog-Friendly	X-C Skiing	Snowshoeing
3.5 hrs	Waterfall, views, recreation hub		✔	✔		✔
1.5 hrs	Rare plants, views			✔		✔
45 mins	Frost poems throughout fields, woods, and swamp		✔	✔	✔	✔
2 hrs	Mature hardwood forest, cliff-top views		✔			✔
1.5 hrs	Ridgeline walk, views of Adirondacks		✔	✔		✔
3.5 hrs	Rare, above-treeline tundra plants; views			✔		✔
3.5 hrs	Boreal ridge, fun rock scrambles, views			✔		✔
6 hrs east side; 5.5 hrs west side	Iconic Vermont peak with rare tundra plants, views			✔		✔
4.5 hrs	Grassy summit, views of White Mountains		✔	✔		✔
1.5 hrs	Rock outcrop, views, vernal pool		✔	✔	✔	✔
3.5 hrs	Fire tower, views		✔	✔		✔
2 hrs	Open fern meadows, rocky outcrop with views	$	✔	✔		✔
2 hrs	Scenic hike beneath cliff, views on top	$	✔	✔	✔	✔
1 hr	Rare stand of mature, native forest; wildflowers		✔		✔	✔
1.5 hrs	Lake Champlain views, swimming		✔	✔	✔	✔
2 hrs	Pondside fields, woods, swimming, bird-watching		✔	✔	✔	✔
1 hr	Varied landscapes, tons of spring wildflowers		✔	✔	✔	✔
2 hrs	Shoreline loop hike with views and swimming	$	✔	✔	✔	✔
1.5 hrs	Bird-watching on flat walk through unusual peatland		✔	✔	✔	✔
8 hrs	Four peaks, remote forest ridge			✔		✔
3.5 hrs	Fun rock scrambling, unusual summit terraces, views			✔		✔
3.5 hrs	Steep ledges, bald summit, views			✔		✔

	TRIP NUMBER / TRIP NAME	LOCATION	DIFFICULTY	DISTANCE	ELEVATION GAIN
42	Elmore Mountain	Lake Elmore	Moderate	4.5 mi	1,145 ft
43	Wiessner Woods	Stowe	Easy	1.5 mi	100 ft
44	Stowe Pinnacle	Stowe	Moderate	2.8 mi	1,520 ft
45	Mount Mansfield's Chin	Underhill	Strenuous	6.2 mi	2,543 ft
46	Mount Mansfield's Forehead	Underhill and Stowe	Strenuous	5.2 mi	2,520 ft
47	Sterling Pond	Cambridge	Moderate	3.3 mi	1,320 ft
48	Prospect Rock	Johnson	Easy-Moderate	3 mi	540 ft
49	Devil's Gulch and Big Muddy Pond	Eden	Moderate	5.2 mi	1,000 ft
50	Belvidere Mountain	Eden and Lowell	Moderate-Strenuous	6 mi	2,050 ft
51	Jay Peak	Westfield	Moderate	3.4 mi	1,638 ft
NORTHEASTERN VERMONT					
52	Burke Mountain	Burke	Strenuous	6.2 mi	2,080 ft
53	Barr Hill	Greensboro	Easy	0.8 mi	120 ft
54	Mount Pisgah	Westmore	Moderate	4.8 mi	1,395 ft
55	Mount Hor	Sutton	Easy-Moderate	2.9 mi	601 ft
56	Wheeler Mountain	Sutton	Moderate	4.1 mi	870 ft
57	Conte Refuge	Brunswick and Ferdinand	Easy	1.1 mi from Nulhegan River trailhead; 3.9 mi from North Branch trailhead	120 ft from Nulhegan River trailhead; 90 ft from North Branch trailhead
58	Monadnock Mountain	Lemington	Moderate-Strenuous	5 mi	2,108 ft
59	Bluff Mountain	Island Pond	Moderate	3.3 mi	1,110 ft
60	Brousseau Mountain	Norton	Easy-Moderate	1.6 mi	590 ft

Estimated Time	Trip Highlights	Fee	Good for Kids	Dog-Friendly	X-C Skiing	Snowshoeing
3 hrs	Loop hike, fire tower, views, balanced boulder on ridgeline	$	🧍	🐕		🥾🥾
1 hr	Loop hike through varied forests		🧍	🐕	⛷	🥾🥾
2.5 hrs	Views from bald spot on mountainside			🐕		🥾🥾
4.5 hrs	Open ridgeline hike, alpine tundra, highest point in Vermont	$		🐕		🥾🥾
4.5 hrs	Loop hike, tundra, views			🐕		🥾🥾
3 hrs	Steep, scenic notch and high mountain pond		🧍	🐕		🥾🥾
2 hrs	Views from rock outcrop		🧍	🐕		🥾🥾
4 hrs	Rock scrambling in narrow ravine, pond shore, views from shelter		🧍	🐕		🥾🥾
4.5 hrs	Fire tower, views			🐕		🥾🥾
3 hrs	Open ridge and summit, views			🐕		🥾🥾
4.5 hrs	Mature open hardwoods, fire tower, views			🐕		🥾🥾
45 mins	Multiple viewpoints, loop hike		🧍		⛷	🥾🥾
3 hrs	High, rocky perches over scenic lake			🐕		🥾🥾
1.5 hrs	Ridge walk to varied views, including Lake Willoughby		🧍	🐕		🥾🥾
3.5 hrs	Cliff-top views			🐕		🥾🥾
45 mins from Nulhegan River trailhead; 2.5 hrs from North Branch trailhead	Two loops along remote river in boreal basin		🧍	🐕	⛷	🥾🥾
3.5 hrs	Fire tower view of valley and White Mountains			🐕		🥾🥾
2.5 hrs	Loop hike, steep ledges, views			🐕		🥾🥾
1 hr	Rocky outcrop, views		🧍	🐕		🥾🥾

ACKNOWLEDGMENTS

I had a tremendous amount of help putting this book together. Thanks to Kip Roberts, Julie Roberts, and my parents, Judy and Gary Lamphere, for the million things you four do all the time to support me and my projects. Thanks to Indy Roberts, Max Farnham, and Anna Wetherell for your energy and fun on the trail. Thanks to Silvia Cassano for so much good information, trail work, photos, and companionship on the trail.

Vermont is fortunate to have a huge number of smart, dedicated professionals working for the benefit of the state's natural places. I am fortunate to have benefited from their time and expertise to improve the descriptions in this book. Thanks to the following people for reviewing trips and helping update this second edition: Ellen McCarron, Diana Frederick, Susan Bulmer, Luke O'Brien, Louis Bushey, Jack Brooks, Barbara MacGregor, Jason Nerenberg, Rick White, and the staff of Vermont Department of Forests, Parks, and Recreation; Danna Strout, Holly Knox, Seth Coffey, and Ethan Ready of the U.S. Forest Service; Ilana Copel of the Green Mountain Club; Lynn McNamara of The Nature Conservancy; Rick LaDue of Equinox Preservation Trust; Kathryn Lawrence of Merck Forest and Farmland Center; Elsa Gilbertson of the Division of Historic Preservation; Maggie Stoudnour of Rivendell Trail Association; Nancy Jones of the Bradford Conservation Commission; Nick Warner of the Winooski Valley Park District; Geordie Heller of the Putney Mountain Association; Betsy Cieplicki of Shelburne Parks and Recreation; Kristen Sharpless of Stowe Land Trust; Chris Boget and Jeff O'Donnell of Lake Champlain Land Trust; Kym Duchesneau of the town of Milton; David Sausville and Amy Alfieri of the Vermont Fish and Wildlife Department; and Steve Agius of Silvio O. Conte National Fish and Wildlife Refuge.

And thanks, finally, to Shannon Smith, Larry Garland, Abigail Coyle, and Jennifer Wehunt at Appalachian Mountain Club Books for the opportunity to work on this project, for sharing their professional knowledge, and especially for their good-natured support and flexibility along the way.

INTRODUCTION

Vermont is named for its most defining feature: the Green Mountains. From border to border, the landscape is craggy, rumpled, and buckled. In some places, the stature and the sheer bulk of the mountains dominate the landscape; in other places, the hills roll more gently. Even the relatively level Champlain Valley is flat only in comparison with the rest of the state and is still hilly enough to have excellent hikes to peaks with long views.

The spine of the Green Mountains runs the length of the state, topped by the 270-mile Long Trail, the nation's oldest long-distance hiking trail. On either side of the high crest are lower parallel ridges called the First and Third ranges. The ancient Taconic Mountains roll across the southwestern corner of the state, while the northwest is dominated by the wide waters of Lake Champlain. Vermont's Northeast Kingdom is a highland of forests, cliffs, and lakes. The Connecticut River forms the state's eastern border, with the lower, rolling mountains of Vermont's Piedmont extending from there to the tall ridgelines in the center of the state. This widespread hilliness combined with Vermont's rural character encourages an outdoors culture—an appreciation for woods, undeveloped mountains, and the activities that happen in them: hiking, skiing, camping, paddling, fishing, and hunting.

All of these activities were practiced and perfected by Vermont's first settlers, the Abenaki. Part of the larger family called Wabanaki (People of the Dawnland), who moved into what is now the northeastern United States and southeastern Canada after the last ice age 12,000 years ago, the Abenaki settled from the shores of Lake Champlain eastward into the mountains. Today, the center of Abenaki culture in Vermont remains near the lake, in the northwestern corner of the state.

Although Vermonters have long appreciated the mountains and forests, hiking was not always as popular as it is today. The 1921 guide to the Long Trail begins with a lament that more hikers were not visiting: "The Green Mountains of Vermont have been sadly neglected, which is strange, as the entire range is within plain sight of the much frequented White Mountain and Adirondack Mountain groups and their noble skyline might well have inspired excursions into a virgin mountain region. This neglect lies with the people of the State who failed to make the mountains accessible or to give them due publicity." Today the mountains are probably Vermont's best-known feature, and hiking trails have made many of them accessible.

The hikes in this guidebook were chosen both for their remarkable features and for their representation of Vermont's different landscapes. They are spread across the state, including one on a Lake Champlain island that is accessible only by boat. They visit ponds, bogs, rivers, waterfalls, and interesting forests, as well as cliffs and ridgelines. The hikes vary in difficulty, but the majority are easy or moderate so that parents can keep up with their kids on the trail. Although I have seen children—even very young ones—on top of the highest Green Mountains, I mostly have been conservative and designated only the easier hikes with the good-for-kids icon (see "How to Use This Book," page xviii). Similarly, designating a hike as easy, moderate, or strenuous is necessarily a subjective activity, as is indicating the amount of time needed for a given trail. Hikers' perceptions of difficulty vary, and even the same hiker experiences a trail differently on different days, depending on level of energy, weather, mood, time of day, and a dozen other factors. Use your knowledge of your own pace and preferences along with the distance, elevation gain, and descriptions about the terrain to help you plan your hike.

Day-hiking is the perfect way to experience Vermont's special places. With a light pack containing a little food, some water, and a warm layer, hikers can explore woods, streams, waterfalls, and rocky summits for part of the day, then take a refreshing dip at a swimming hole or a state park beach and finish with a hearty meal in a nearby village. I can't think of a happier way to spend a day.

HOW TO USE THIS BOOK

With 60 hikes to choose from, you may wonder how to decide where to go. The locator map at the front of this book will help you narrow down the trips by location, and the At-a-Glance Trip Planner that follows the table of contents provides more information to guide you toward a decision.

Once you settle on a destination and turn to a trip in this guide, you will find a boldface summary up top, providing a brief overview of the hike's highlights. Below that, in a column to the right, you'll find the basics: location, difficulty rating, distance, elevation gain, estimated time, and maps. The difficulty ratings are based on the author's perception and are estimates of what the average hiker will experience. You may find hikes to be easier or more difficult than stated. The distance and estimated hiking time shown are for the whole trip, whether it's an out-and-back hike, a loop, or, in a couple cases, an end-to-end hike. The estimated time is also based on the author's perception. Consider your own pace when planning a trip. The elevation gain is calculated from measurements and information from U.S. Geological Survey (USGS) topographic maps, landowner maps, and Google Earth. Information is included about the relevant USGS maps, as well as where you can find trail maps.

Below those basics is a series of icons that indicate whether there are fees, whether the hike is good for kids, whether dogs are allowed, and whether cross-country skiing or snowshoeing is recommended. For those hikes with the good-for-kids icon, the author suggests an age range of children who might enjoy the hike, but of course children vary tremendously. These suggestions are based on children who are not athletic prodigies but whose families hike together regularly. Some of the hikes designated for kids visit waterfalls or cliff lookouts that are great rewards for the effort to get there but that can be hazardous. To determine whether a hike is appropriate for their family, parents ultimately will have to gauge their own children's levels of interest, motivation, and ability.

"Directions" explains how to reach the trailhead by car and includes global positioning system (GPS) coordinates for parking lots. Whether or not you own a GPS device, it is wise to bring an atlas, such as DeLorme's *New Hampshire and Vermont Atlas & Gazetteer* (2015), which shows small roads and forest roads in detail.

In "Trail Description," you will find detailed instructions on the given hike, including turn-by-turn directions. You will also learn about the natural and human history along the hike, as well as about flora, fauna, and any landmarks or objects you will encounter.

The trail maps that accompany each trip help guide you on your hike, but it is always wise to take an official trail map with you. Official maps are often—but not always—available online, at the trailhead, or at the visitor center. For each trip, see the listing of relevant maps included in the basic information. "Did You Know?" provides interesting facts about the area.

Each trip ends with a section called "More Information" that provides details about access times and fees, rules and regulations of the property on which the hike is located, and contact information for the place where you will be hiking. "Nearby" offers suggestions for places to continue the experience once you've finished the hike—including swimming, paddling, or mountain-biking destinations—and where to find the closest restaurants.

TRIP PLANNING AND SAFETY

You will be more likely to have an enjoyable, safe hike if you take proper precautions. Planning is the first step to a safe hike. Some of the trips ascend to bare, high-elevation summits where winds and low temperatures necessitate extra clothing. Other hikes visit clifftops or waterfalls where you'll need to use extra caution with children and dogs. Learn about the terrain you will travel through in order to pack the right gear and prepare for the experience. Allow extra time in case you get lost.

Pack as if you will be out on the trail for hours longer than you hope to be, and you will have the supplies you need to stay comfortable and well fed in case an injury or a lost hiker keeps you on the trail into the evening or even overnight. Before heading out for your hike, consider the following:

- Select a hike that everyone in your group is comfortable taking. Match the hike to the abilities of the least capable person in the group. If anyone is uncomfortable with the weather or is tired, turn around and complete the hike another day.
- Plan to be back at the trailhead before dark. Before beginning your hike, determine a turnaround time. Monitor your group's pace and progress, and turn around in time to get off the trail by dark, even if you have not reached your intended destination.
- Check the weather and assume it will be cooler and windier on the mountain than at the base. Weather conditions can change quickly, and any changes are likely to be more severe the higher you are on the mountain. In New England, planning for wet weather is always a good idea, regardless of the forecast.
- Bring a pack with the following items:
  - ✓ Water: Two quarts per person is usually adequate, depending on the weather and the length of the trip. You can carry less if you know you will be able to find water along the trail and if you bring a means of sterilizing found water, such as iodine, a filter, or a SteriPEN.
  - ✓ Food: Even if you are planning just an hour-long hike, bring some high-energy snacks such as nuts, dried fruit, or protein bars.
  - ✓ Map and compass: Make sure to pack a map of your route. As backup, you might take a photo of the map with your phone or camera and extra batteries for that device. A handheld GPS device may also be helpful but shouldn't take the place of a paper map. If you pack a compass, make sure you know how to use it.

- ✓ Cell phone: Be aware that cell-phone service is still unreliable in many parts of Vermont, and mountains may block signals even from nearby towers. Mute your phone while in the woods to avoid disturbing the backcountry experience for other hikers.
- ✓ Headlamp or flashlight, with spare batteries
- ✓ Extra clothing: rain gear, wool or fleece sweater, hat, and mittens
- ✓ Sunscreen
- ✓ First-aid kit, including adhesive bandages, gauze, nonprescription painkillers, moleskin, and any necessary prescription medication you would need if you are on the trail longer than expected
- ✓ Pocketknife or multitool
- ✓ Waterproof matches or a lighter
- ✓ Toilet paper and double plastic bag to pack it out; do not leave toilet-paper flowers strewn in the woods
- ✓ Whistle
- ✓ Insect repellent
- ✓ Sunglasses
- ✓ Binoculars (optional)
- ✓ Camera (optional)

- Wear appropriate footwear and clothing. Waterproof boots or sneakers equal dry feet and more comfortable, happy hiking. Wool or synthetic hiking socks will keep your feet drier than cotton and help prevent blisters. Cotton clothing, in general, absorbs sweat and rain, making it effective at helping cool you down but problematic or even dangerous if the weather conditions change. If you choose to wear cotton while hiking, bring a synthetic, wool, or silk layer to change into. Polypropylene, fleece, silk, and wool all wick moisture away from your body and keep you warm in wet or cold conditions. To help avoid insect bites, you may want to wear pants and a long-sleeved shirt.

- Vermont's woods are home to biting insects that can be a minor or a significant nuisance, depending on seasonal and daily conditions. West Nile virus and eastern equine encephalitis (EEE) virus can be transmitted to humans by infected mosquitoes and cause rare but serious diseases. Reduce your risk of being bitten by using insect repellent, wearing long sleeves and pants, and avoiding hiking in the early morning and in the evening, when mosquitoes are most active. A variety of options are available for dealing with bugs, ranging from sprays that include the active ingredient DEET, which can potentially cause skin or eye irritation, to more skin-friendly products.

- When you are ahead of the rest of your hiking group, wait at all trail junctions until the others catch up. This avoids confusion and keeps people from getting separated or lost.

- If downed wood appears to be purposely covering a trail, it probably means the trail is closed.
- When a trail is muddy, walk through the mud or on rocks, never on tree roots or plants. Water-resistant boots will keep your feet comfortable. Staying in the center of the trail will keep it from eroding into a wide hiking highway.
- Leave your itinerary and the time you expect to return with someone you trust. If you see a logbook at a trailhead, be sure to sign in when you arrive and sign out when you finish your hike.
- After you complete your hike, check for deer ticks, which can transmit numerous illnesses, including Lyme disease.
- Stay alert for poison ivy, particularly at lower elevations near water. To identify the plant, look for clusters of three leaves that shine in the sun but are dull in the shade. If you do come into contact with poison ivy, wash the affected area with soap as soon as possible.
- Wear blaze-orange items in hunting season. In Vermont, hunting begins in September; although most seasons end in December, some may extend later in winter. Yearly schedules are available at vtfishandwildlife.com and in flyers and brochures available at town halls, general stores, and other public areas.

Many trails are closed during mud season, and even if they are not, it's a good idea to avoid hiking when trails are especially susceptible to damage. Mud season is loosely defined as most of April and May—essentially, spring in Vermont—but in reality, mud season begins whenever the ground starts to thaw and lasts until the ground has dried out. The same conditions—saturated, partly frozen soils—can also occur in the late fall and during winter thaws. Mud season begins and ends earlier in the warmer valleys than on the cool mountain slopes; you may be able to stagger your hikes according to when the trails dry out. If muddy conditions lead you to begin hiking on the sides of the treadway, rather than in the middle of the trail, turn around.

Winter hiking can be an enjoyable way to experience the Green Mountains in their snowy splendor, but it requires extra gear and planning. Once the snow piles up, many trailheads are not accessible by car, so plan to hike farther than the distance shown in this guidebook. The presence of alpine ski areas may alter your route and your experience, particularly on Pico and Jay peaks. Skis with traction (wax, skins, or a pattern etched in the base) or snowshoes keep you more or less on top of the snow, letting you travel more efficiently without creating "postholes" by sinking into the snowpack. Snowshoeing is an easy activity for beginners to pick up, as it is simply walking. Skiing on ungroomed, backcountry trails requires considerable skill. Cross-country skiers should be aware that difficulty ratings given for hikes in this book do not apply to skiing, which is generally more challenging. All winter travelers need to bring more food and warm layers than they would in summer and exercise more caution; fewer daylight hours, colder temperatures, and slower travel times magnify any problems that may occur, such as getting lost or twisting an ankle. Prudent winter travelers do not go out alone. Make sure at least one person in the group has a sleeping bag; something to use for emergency shelter, such as a small tarp; and a camp stove. When properly prepared, winter hikers can safely and comfortably experience the deep quiet and spectacular beauty of Vermont's frozen landscape.

GREEN MOUNTAIN CLUB

The Green Mountain Club (GMC) is a nonprofit organization founded in 1910. GMC built and maintains Vermont's Long Trail, and the organization's advocacy and education efforts also safeguard Vermont's many other hiking trails. At sensitive, high-use areas, GMC sponsors caretakers who perform trail and shelter maintenance, provide first aid, and talk with hikers about fragile summit ecosystems, local regulations, and Leave No Trace principles. For more information, visit GMC headquarters in Waterbury Center or see greenmountainclub.org.

GREEN MOUNTAIN NATIONAL FOREST

Green Mountain National Forest encompasses more than 400,000 acres in southwestern and central Vermont, forming the largest contiguous public land area in the state. The forest includes eight federally designated Wilderness Areas and three nationally designated trails (the Appalachian Trail, the Long Trail, and the Robert Frost National Recreation Trail), as well as approximately 900 miles of multiple-use trails. For more information, visit www.fs.usda.gov/gmfl.

LEAVE NO TRACE

The Appalachian Mountain Club (AMC) is a national educational partner of Leave No Trace, a nonprofit organization dedicated to promoting and inspiring responsible outdoor recreation through education, research, and partnerships.  The Leave No Trace program seeks to develop wildland ethics: ways in which people think and act in the outdoors to minimize their impact on the areas they visit and to protect our natural resources for future enjoyment. Leave No Trace unites four federal land management agencies—U.S. Forest Service, National Park Service, Bureau of Land Management, and U.S. Fish and Wildlife Service—with manufacturers, outdoor retailers, user groups, educators, organizations such as AMC, and individuals.

The Leave No Trace ethic is guided by the following seven principles:

1. **Plan Ahead and Prepare.** Know the terrain and any regulations applicable to the area you're planning to visit, and be prepared for extreme weather or other emergencies. This will enhance your enjoyment and ensure that you've chosen an appropriate destination. Small groups have less impact on resources and on the experiences of other backcountry visitors.

2. **Travel and Camp on Durable Surfaces.** Travel and camp on established trails and campsites, rock, gravel, dry grasses, or snow. Good campsites are found, not made. Camp at least 200 feet from lakes and streams, and focus activities on areas where vegetation is absent. In pristine areas, disperse use to prevent the creation of campsites and trails.

3. **Dispose of Waste Properly.** Pack it in, pack it out. Inspect your camp for trash or food scraps. Deposit solid human waste in cat holes dug 6 to 8 inches deep, at least 200 feet from water, camps, and trails. Pack out toilet paper and hygiene products. To wash yourself or your dishes, carry water 200 feet from streams or lakes and use small amounts of biodegradable soap. Scatter strained dishwater.

4. **Leave What You Find.** Cultural or historical artifacts, as well as natural objects such as plants and rocks, should be left as found.

5. **Minimize Campfire Impacts.** Cook on a stove. Use established fire rings, fire pans, or mound fires. If you build a campfire, keep it small and use dead sticks found on the ground.

6. **Respect Wildlife.** Observe wildlife from a distance. Feeding animals alters their natural behavior. Protect wildlife from your food by storing rations and trash securely.

7. **Be Considerate of Other Visitors.** Be courteous, respect the quality of other visitors' backcountry experience, and let nature's sounds prevail.

AMC is a national provider of the Leave No Trace Master Educator course. AMC offers this five-day course, designed especially for outdoor professionals and land managers, as well as the shorter, two-day Leave No Trace Trainer course at locations throughout the Northeast.

For Leave No Trace information and materials, contact the Leave No Trace Center for Outdoor Ethics, P.O. Box 997, Boulder, CO 80306; 800-332-4100 or 302-442-8222; lnt.org. For a schedule of AMC Leave No Trace courses, see outdoors.org/education/lnt.

SOUTHERN VERMONT

From its southern border to Rutland, 60 miles north, Vermont is pretty consistently about 40 miles wide. Mountains and other large land features in the state tend to occur in swaths that trend north–south, and a lot of diverse landscape is packed in that 40-mile width of southern Vermont.

On the western side of southern Vermont, the Taconic Mountains spill north out of Massachusetts and reach their highest point at Mount Equinox (Trip 9), in Manchester. From there, the Taconics become progressively smaller and the peaks less frequent until they disappear altogether. The Taconics are part of the Appalachian Mountains, as the Green Mountains are, but their origins are different. In fact, the origin of the Taconic Mountains is somewhat mysterious. Their summits are made of older rock than their bases, which means that somehow older rock was pushed onto the younger mountains beneath them. How that happened continues to be a source of debate. The limestone so prevalent in the Taconic Mountains is easily eroded by trickling water, forming caves inside the mountains and rich soils outside them. These soils create spectacular spring wildflower displays, as well as providing a habitat for some rare plants. Caves support bat populations, and the many seeps, streams, and springs of these porous mountains attract an array of amphibians. Extensive forests provide homes to animals large and small, including black bears, bobcats, white-tailed deer, and songbirds.

Tidily defining the border between the Taconic and Green mountains is the long, narrow Vermont Valley. US 7 runs through this channel, as do the Battenkill River in the south and Otter Creek, Vermont's longest river, heading north. The valley is wide in some places, such as around Bennington, where it stretches over several miles, and constricted in others, such as at Emerald Lake, where the road and railroad squeeze past the water along the base of Mount Tabor.

Winter views of Pico Peak showcase Vermont's beauty
in the snowy months. Photo by Silvia Cassano.

The Green Mountains occupy the central part of southern Vermont, as well as the center of the state as a whole. Although their western edge at the Vermont Valley is steep and sudden, for the most part the southern Greens consist of high, rolling land that is more a plateau than a sharply defined range of mountains. Some geologists speculate that this relatively flat, high place is what was left after the peaks were pushed west to become the new tops of the Taconics. Other geologists disagree, but either way this terrain was historically difficult for humans to settle and remained largely the domain of wildlife.

Today the southern section of the Green Mountain National Forest boasts almost 60,000 acres of federally designated Wilderness. Managed to preserve their wild character, Wilderness Areas are home to large animals, including black bears, moose, and bobcats, that prefer extensive tracts of undeveloped forests, such as the deep woods east of Lye Brook Falls (Trip 8). Encircling the Peru Peak and Big Branch Wildernesses, the White Rocks National Recreation Area conserves the surrounding scenic terrain—including the gem of Little Rock Pond (Trip 12) and massive rock slides that created the White Rocks Ice Beds (Trip 13)—for hiking, camping, and snowmobiling. The Appalachian Trail and the Long Trail run together through the southern Green Mountains, paralleled by Catamount Trail, a cross-country ski trail open to the public. Historical remnants of previous activity, such as fire towers, ranger cabins, sawmills, and charcoal kilns, still remain in many places.

East of the high plateau of the Green Mountains, the landscape generally consists of lower hills carved by a maze of rivers, streams, and, historically, glaciers. This region is called the Piedmont—literally "foothills"—and has some of the warmest temperatures in Vermont, leading to natural communities on dry hilltops, such as Black Mountain (Trip 4), that don't exist in other parts of Vermont. Species that normally live farther south, such as pitch pine and red oak, make an appearance here, and the big mammals mostly do not. Most of the mountains are small in the Piedmont; one notable exception is the massive monadnock, Mount Ascutney (Trip 15), which towers over the region and has high-elevation forests with the associated plants and wildlife.

On the far eastern edge of southern Vermont, the Connecticut River flows through its own unique landscape of floodplains and natural shoreline communities that are unusual in Vermont. Technically, only the river's beaches are in Vermont, as the New Hampshire border extends to the low-water mark on the Vermont side. But the valley and its plants, animals, history, and recreation are very much a part of southern Vermont life.

1

BALD MOUNTAIN

Glastenbury Wilderness has many hidden secrets, including this unusual ridgeline peak with views across southern Vermont.

DIRECTIONS

To Bennington Trailhead

From the traffic light at US 7/South Street and VT 9/Main Street in downtown Bennington, go east on VT 9/Main Street 0.8 mile and turn left on Branch Street. Go 0.3 mile and turn right on North Branch Street. Go 0.5 mile and turn right onto an unmarked dirt road where North Branch Street curves sharply left. The trailhead parking area is immediately on the right (space for about 12 cars). *GPS coordinates:* 42° 53.40′ N, 73° 10.83′ W.

To Woodford Trailhead

From the traffic light at US 7/South Street and VT 9/Main Street in downtown Bennington, go east on VT 9/Main Street, which becomes Molly Stark Trail, for 3.9 miles then turn left onto Harbour Road. Go 0.8 mile and turn left onto an unmarked dirt road at a water tower. Park on the grass off the left side of the road (space for about 8 cars). *GPS coordinates:* 42° 54.38′ N, 73° 07.38′ W.

TRAIL DESCRIPTION

Bald Mountain (2,857 feet) is the southern sentinel of a ridgeline that marks the western edge of the 22,330-acre Glastenbury Wilderness. Bald Mountain Trail crosses the ridge west to east (or vice versa) and is a fun, 5.6-mile, end-to-end hike, if you can leave a car or a bike at the other end. You can also hike each approach separately as an out-and-back hike (described below). However, the main trail description for this hike is for the end-to-end trek.

LOCATION
Bennington and Woodford, VT

BENNINGTON TRAIL:
RATING
Moderate

DISTANCE
7.4 miles (round-trip)

ELEVATION GAIN
2,099 feet

ESTIMATED TIME
5.5 hours

WOODFORD TRAIL:
RATING
Moderate

DISTANCE
3.8 miles (round-trip)

ELEVATION GAIN
1,509 feet

ESTIMATED TIME
3.5 hours

BENNINGTON TO WOODFORD:
RATING
Moderate

DISTANCE
5.6 miles (end-to-end)

ELEVATION GAIN
2,099 feet

ESTIMATED TIME
4.5 hours

MAPS
USGS Bennington; www.fs.usda.gov/gmfl

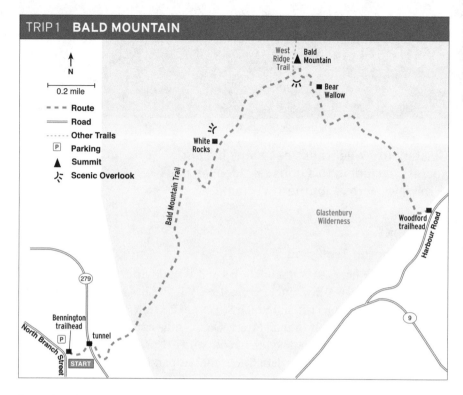

Bennington Trailhead

The western leg of the trail rises 3.7 rocky miles from Bennington to the ridge-line, passing the popular White Rocks lookout point at 2.9 miles. This hike is a bit more difficult than the hike up the other side of Bald Mountain from Woodford trailhead. Take this approach if you want a little challenge.

Woodford Trailhead

The eastern leg of the trail climbs more steeply to reach the ridge in 1.9 miles. For a peaceful round-trip hike, use this quieter, shorter eastern side.

For an end-to-end trek, either direction works; it's described west-to-east below. This route is best for kids 10 and older, given the distance and elevation gain.

Bennington to Woodford (end-to-end)

The Bennington side of Bald Mountain Trail starts with a staircase from the parking area, climbing past a kiosk and zigzagging through the brush of a power-line cut for 0.5 mile. Blue blazes on rocks mark the path in this open area. Before entering the woods, turn around for a view of Bennington Battle Monument soaring over the town. A sign here incorrectly indicates the West Ridge Trail junction on top of Bald Mountain as 4 miles away; it is actually 3.2 miles from this point.

Cross a wooded hillside and intersect with an eroded two-track in a gully. Turn right onto this trail and follow the two-track uphill, through the colorfully painted Free Expression tunnel beneath VT 279 and back across the power-line cut, entering woods on the far side. Blue blazes indicate the route across streams and past several unsigned intersections with old woods roads. At 1 mile, turn left off the two-track where it curves sharply to the right, continuing to follow the blue blazes. In another 0.3 mile, enter Glastenbury Wilderness.

The footing becomes challenging as the trail traverses soupy spots and long stretches of loose rock before finally rising onto the drier hillside where fir trees line the path. After a couple of switchbacks, openings appear in the woods where scree spills down the mountainside. At 2.9 miles, a massive pile of rocks appears to block the path, and a side trail leads left 100 feet. Follow it to White Rocks ledges for westward views across the Vermont Valley and Taconic Mountains.

The final 0.8 mile of climbing crosses several fields of loose rock (known locally as cobble) and ascends ledges before arriving atop the shrubby ridge amid spruces, blueberries, and surprising white sand from disintegrated quartzite. The highest point of Bald Mountain Trail (2,810 feet) is here at the junction of West Ridge Trail, and the view south is spectacular, if partially screened. The summit of Bald Mountain is 0.1 mile north on West Ridge Trail. The whole ledgy, shrubby area, with its various views, is worth exploring before descending.

Hikers encounter piles of quartzite and its sand high on the mountain. Photo by Silvia Cassano.

From the trail junction, continue east on Bald Mountain Trail toward Woodford. The white sand underfoot quickly gives way to conifer needles and duff. At 4 miles, an old sign for Bear Wallow marks a faint trail north to a seasonal spring. Continue steadily downward on Bald Mountain Trail, passing through a beautiful softwood forest, which gradually transitions to hardwoods and a wetter, wider path. At 5.3 miles, exit the Wilderness and bear right onto an old road, following it the final 0.3 mile to Harbour Road trailhead.

DID YOU KNOW?

Glastenbury Wilderness has featured prominently in many mysterious happenings and is well known for spooking hikers with unexplained sounds and eerie sensations. Look for books by Vermont writers Joe Citro and Tim Simard to scare yourself silly.

MORE INFORMATION

Glastenbury Wilderness is a place where human impact is kept to a minimum: Do not leave any personal property or use any wheeled device, such as a mountain bike or a wagon. Bald Mountain Trail and Glastenbury Wilderness are managed by Green Mountain National Forest, Manchester Ranger District, 2538 Depot Street, Manchester Center, VT 05255; 802-362-2307; www.fs.usda.gov/gmfl.

NEARBY

Swim, paddle, and camp at Woodford State Park, Vermont's highest-elevation state park at 2,400 feet. Head to downtown Bennington for food, shops, the Battle Monument, and the fabulous Bennington Museum.

2

HAYSTACK MOUNTAIN (WILMINGTON)

This pleasant cruise up a mellow ridge leads to a rocky top with views of nearby Haystack Pond and distant peaks.

DIRECTIONS

From the western junction of VT 100 and VT 9 in Wilmington, go west on VT 9 for 1.1 miles and turn right onto Haystack Road. (A large sign on the grass reads, "Chimney Hill.") Drive 1.2 miles and turn left onto Chimney Hill Road. Proceed 0.2 mile and turn right onto Binney Brook Road, which weaves past many turnoffs and ends after 1.1 miles at Upper Dam Road. Turn right and follow Upper Dam Road 0.3 mile (staying left at a junction, as marked) to park on the right shoulder (space for about 6 cars), where a gravel road heads uphill into the woods. *GPS coordinates: 42° 53.99′ N, 72° 54.66′ W.*

TRAIL DESCRIPTION

Haystack Mountain (3,410 feet) is a recognizable, pointed peak on the southern end of a ridge dominated by Mount Snow (3,586 feet) ski trails and its namesake ski area. The hike to Haystack's small, rocky summit traverses easy-to-moderate grades until the slightly steeper final 0.3 mile, making it a good hike for kids ages 6 and older.

From the roadside parking, follow the gravel two-track uphill into the woods and around a metal gate. Occasional blue plastic diamonds mark the two-track, which leads to Wilmington's water supply at Haystack Pond. Hiking among yellow birch and beech trees, you begin to hear Binney Brook as it tumbles through a ravine on your left. At 0.5 mile, where No Trespassing signs indicate the start of the Wilmington Watershed Protection Area and the brook flows through a large culvert under the road, turn

LOCATION
Wilmington, VT

RATING
Moderate

DISTANCE
4.2 miles

ELEVATION GAIN
1,025 feet

ESTIMATED TIME
3 hours

MAPS
USGS Mount Snow;
www.fs.usda.gov/gmfl

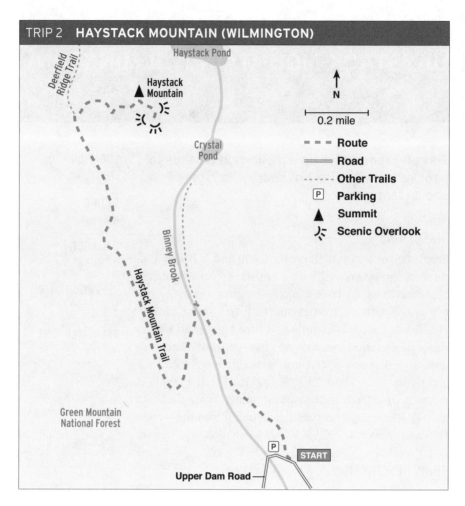

left onto a footpath. For the next 1.3 miles, Haystack Mountain Trail coincides with Deerfield Ridge Trail.

The narrow, rooty trail heads southwest to circle the end of the long ridge-line leading to Haystack's summit. Wood nettle, with its stinging hairs, spreads along the edges of the path as it rolls gently 0.3 mile from the two-track junction. The path then bends sharply back northwest and begins a moderate, steady climb across a rocky hillside. The climbing is pleasantly interrupted by level stretches and gradual pitches, and at 1.3 miles, a sharp S-curve brings you to the ridgeline. Lilies and ferns fill in the forest floor alongside rose twisted-stalk, with its flowers and berries dangling, hidden beneath its arched, leafy stem.

Passing through some wide muddy areas, Haystack Mountain Trail rounds the western side of Haystack's summit cone. At 1.8 miles, a wooden sign directs you to turn right off Deerfield Ridge Trail, which continues straight. Haystack Mountain Trail immediately moves from a northern hardwood forest on the ridgeline to a shady, tight boreal forest as you climb the summit knob. The path ascends switchbacks to a small, rocky opening at the summit. The view east is dominated by Haystack Pond in the basin below. Beyond that, the north–south valley carrying VT 100 is backed by rows of gentle, low hills. In the distant northeast, Mount Ascutney (3,130 feet) juts above the horizon, and far to the east, the large hump of Mount Monadnock (3,130 feet) rises over southwestern New Hampshire. Mount Snow's summit chairlift is just visible over the treetops to the north.

For views to the south and west, climb down through a narrow cleft in the rocks to another outlook, on the south face of the summit. This perch provides a great view of the 2,200-acre Harriman Reservoir (also called Lake Whitingham), the largest body of water within Vermont's borders. Built in 1923 to provide hydroelectric power, the lake is a dammed stretch of the Deerfield River. The Deerfield Valley village of Mountain Mills was abandoned to make way for the reservoir, and boaters today can occasionally spot the submerged foundation of the old mill. Another version of electrical production is visible to the west, where wind towers in Searsburg spin on top of a ridge. On a clear day, Massachusetts's highest point, Mount Greylock (3,491 feet), can be seen in the distant southwest.

Summit views from Haystack Mountain take in a broad sweep of southern Vermont, including the 8-mile-long Harriman Reservoir, frequented by bald eagles, loons, and paddlers seeking quiet water.

DID YOU KNOW?

Haystack Mountain's alpine ski area closed to the public in the early 2000s after 40 years of operation. It has since been transformed into a private recreation and vacation club.

MORE INFORMATION

Haystack Mountain is part of the Green Mountain National Forest, Manchester Ranger District, 2538 Depot Street, Manchester Center, VT 05255; 802-362-2307; www.fs.usda.gov/gmfl.

NEARBY

Swim and paddle on Harriman Reservoir, 3.5 miles south. Camp at Woodford State Park, which also has great swimming and paddling on a high-elevation lake, 6.4 miles west, or at Molly Stark State Park, 6.1 miles east (see Trip 3: Mount Olga). Food and shops are in Wilmington, 3.8 miles southeast.

3

MOUNT OLGA

The loop trail to Mount Olga's lookout tower is a pleasant ramble through a rich forest.

DIRECTIONS

From the junction of VT 9 and VT 100 in downtown Wilmington, drive 3.3 miles east on VT 9 to Molly Stark State Park on your right. A parking lot (space for about 20 cars) is near the park office. When the park is closed, park at the base of the entrance road and add 0.4 mile round-trip to the hike. *GPS coordinates:* 42° 51.29′ N, 72° 48.88′ W.

TRAIL DESCRIPTION

Mount Olga (2,418 feet) has all of the attractive features of a big mountain—including a variety of hiking terrains and terrific views—in a small package, making it a great destination for families or those with limited time. The trail on the north side of the loop is a little shorter (0.7 mile to summit) and therefore a little steeper—a better choice for the ascent. Descend on the more gradual, 1-mile trail that ends at the top of the campground. The southern side of the loop is good cross-country ski terrain, while the northern leg is more suited to snowshoes. Children as young as 5 will enjoy the accomplishment of summiting this small mountain.

Begin across the park road from the office, where Mount Olga Trail descends wooden steps to cross a stream. Follow blue blazes up a moderate climb, through a young forest of yellow birch, spruce, and fir. Where a rock wall ascends from the right, the trail turns sharply left and zigzags up a steep, rooty pitch. Mount Olga Trail climbs moderately for the first few tenths of a mile. Then, entering a spruce-fir stand, the trail levels and crosses more rolling terrain. Canada violets blossom in early spring in these

LOCATION
Wilmington, VT

RATING
Easy to Moderate

DISTANCE
1.8 miles

ELEVATION GAIN
520 feet

ESTIMATED TIME
1.5 hours

MAPS
USGS Wilmington;
vtstateparks.com/assets/
pdf/molly-stark-trails.pdf

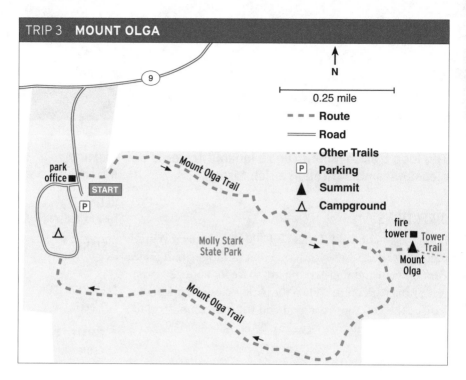

N

0.25 mile

- - - Route
=== Road
······ Other Trails
P Parking
▲ Summit
△ Campground

park office ■

START

P

△

Mount Olga Trail

Molly Stark State Park

fire tower ■ Tower Trail
▲ Mount Olga

Mount Olga Trail

9

damp woods, their white petals unfurling to reveal a yellow center and striking purple veins on the lowest petal.

Climbing moderately again, the trail leaves the coniferous forest and emerges into mixed deciduous woods. Ascend rock steps to a trail junction on the hillside, with ledges rising around you. Go left, climbing the 0.1-mile spur trail to a grassy summit area surrounded by tall trees.

From the cab, or lookout room, of Mount Olga's steel fire tower, Mount Greylock is visible to the southwest. To the northwest, Haystack Mountain's pointed peak (3,410 feet) juts from the prominent ridgeline leading north over Mount Snow (3,586 feet) and Stratton Mountain (3,940 feet). A small slice of Harriman Reservoir (Lake Whitingham) is visible, tucked into the hills directly west. Searsburg Wind Farm turbines sprout from the ridge just north of the reservoir. Far to the east, Mount Monadnock (3,130 feet) rises 2,000 feet higher than the New Hampshire hills surrounding it.

Go back down the summit spur trail (making sure not to descend a trail that heads east to Marlboro). Returning to the junction with Mount Olga Trail, head straight onto the southern leg of the loop, climbing over a little ridge before dropping downhill through a beech stand with remarkably twisted branches. After passing through a corridor between big rocks and crossing a stream on a low bridge, Mount Olga Trail curves to the right and begins a gentle downward grade, which it maintains for most of the remainder of the hike. If the leaves are off the trees, you can look back across the stream valley and see Olga's summit.

The deciduous woods here are rich with understory plants. In spring, look for tall, slender stalks of wild oats and trout lilies, as well as early yellow violets. Mats of evergreen partridgeberry and ferns spread across the forest floor. Shelf fungus and big, rectangular pileated woodpecker holes appear on rotting trunks. About 0.8 mile from the summit, the trail meets a rock wall and follows it to the campground. Emerge next to site 10, turn right (east), and follow the campground road back to the trailhead.

DID YOU KNOW?

Did you hear drumming resonating through Mount Olga's forests or see a striking red head on a large, dark bird? Pileated woodpeckers drum to mark their territory and to attract a mate. They excavate dead trees in search of delicious carpenter ants and other wood-boring insects and to make nests, leaving cavities that become shelters for other birds and small mammals.

MORE INFORMATION

Molly Stark State Park operates Memorial Day to Columbus Day; it is open for day use from 10 A.M. to official sunset. A day-use fee applies in summer. Off-season use is allowed; contact Vermont State Parks for more information: Molly Stark State Park, 705 Route 9 East, Wilmington, VT 05363; 802-464-5460 or 888-409-7579; vtstateparks.com.

NEARBY

Swim and boat in Harriman Reservoir, 5 miles west, or at the high-elevation Adams Reservoir in Woodford State Park, 13 miles west. The Southern Vermont Natural History Museum has year-round exhibits and seasonal events on the environment of this region, 1.5 miles east. Food and shops are along VT 9/VT 100 in Wilmington, 3 miles west.

Mount Olga's slopes burst with wildflowers: wild oats (pictured), trout lilies, and early yellow violets.

4

BLACK MOUNTAIN

Hike through a blueberry-filled forest to an unusual, rocky, woodland habitat on Black Mountain's summit, including a sprawling mountain laurel population.

LOCATION
Dummerston, VT

RATING
Moderate

DISTANCE
3 miles

ELEVATION GAIN
875 feet

ESTIMATED TIME
2.5 hours

MAPS
USGS Newfane

DIRECTIONS

From the junction of VT 30, VT 9, and US 5 in Brattleboro, head north on VT 30 (Linden Street becoming West River Road) for 4.3 miles. Turn right onto Green Iron Bridge and cross West River. At the end of the bridge, turn right onto Rice Farm Road and drive 1 mile to the trailhead parking area (space for about 5 cars) on the left, marked with a Nature Conservancy sign. *GPS coordinates:* 42° 54.68′ N, 72° 36.38′ W.

TRAIL DESCRIPTION

Black Mountain (1,279 feet) is a steep-sided, horseshoe-shaped mountain with a rolling, wooded summit ridgeline studded with granite outcrops. Its dry crest supports Vermont's only pitch-pine/scrub-oak woodland, a natural biosphere more commonly found along New England's coasts. The hike through Black Mountain Natural Area features frequent steep climbs, but the footing is not difficult, and the variety of landscapes is pleasantly distracting. White- and blue-painted blazes are left from earlier iterations of trails; follow the yellow and green plastic trail markers put in place by The Nature Conservancy (TNC).

Black Mountain Trail begins climbing northward from the parking lot, crossing the hillside on a grassy two-track speckled with wild strawberries and violets. At a metal gate, the trail enters the woods, rounds a switchback, and climbs onto a flat bench-like area. Tall pines make a shady path leading to a hallway of dense pine saplings. At 0.3 mile, after passing a TNC registration box fixed high

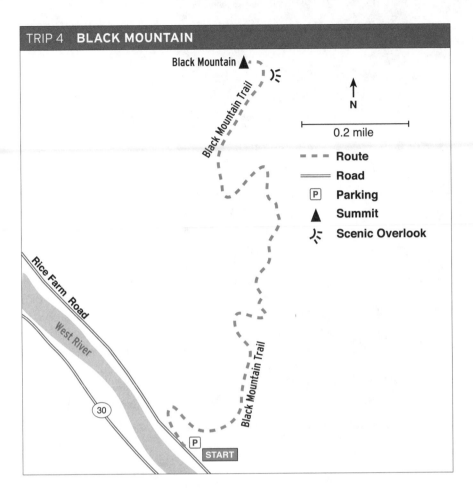

on a tree, Black Mountain Trail crosses a series of boardwalks that lead to a moderate climb across a rooty slope. Dwarf ginseng blooms in early summer here, with yellowish berries replacing the clusters of white flowers in mid- to late summer.

Now the trail begins a series of switchbacks up a steep hill. Black Mountain's steep sides are a result of its volcanic history. Unlike most Vermont mountains pushed up by tectonic-plate movement, Black is a granite pluton: the cooled, hardened magma from inside an ancient volcano that never erupted. Softer rocks surrounding it wore away over time, revealing the granite dome. As you climb, notice the change in the forest that occurs as the soils become thinner and more acidic on the upper mountain. Partway up this steep slope, red oaks and blueberries mix in with the beeches, pines, and hemlocks. As you hike higher, you'll see more blueberries and oaks and fewer—then no—beeches and hemlocks.

Climb several rock staircases onto a dry, ledgy plateau. Look for pileated woodpecker holes in the pines and spotted wintergreen with its pale stripe on dark, pointy leaves growing low among the blueberries on the forest floor.

Black Mountain treats hikers to a variety of forests, including dense pines, broadly spaced hemlocks, and beeches at middle elevations, with short, skinny scrub oaks and pitch pines across the summit.

Mounting this more moderate slope, you will zigzag through large beech trees and moss- and lichen-covered ledges to the base of another steep pitch, where switchbacks begin again.

You will ascend into a dry forest of scrub oak (endangered in Vermont), pitch pine, and the occasional red maple. The low canopy allows in a fair amount of sunlight, and blueberry bushes and granite ledges cover the ground between the small trunks. At about 1.1 miles, Black Mountain Trail begins its undulating course over the summit ridge. Continue northward, passing several stands of mountain laurel. In June, white-and-pink flowers blanket these evergreen shrubs in a stunning display.

Descending briefly, the trail arrives at a series of southeastern-facing ledges. Obstructed views through the branches reveal the tall point of New Hampshire's Mount Monadnock (3,130 feet) in the distance and rock slabs on the eastern half of Black Mountain in the foreground. The south-facing bowl within the horseshoe of Black Mountain captures solar heat, supporting plants that typically thrive 200 miles south of here. Follow the trail left, uphill to the highest ledge, surrounded by blueberries and wintergreen. Return downhill the way you came up.

DID YOU KNOW?

Pitch pines are adapted to wildfires. Their bark is heat resistant, and some of their pinecones do not open to disseminate seeds until they've been exposed to the heat of a fire.

MORE INFORMATION

Black Mountain Natural Area is limited to passive recreational activities, such as hiking, snowshoeing, bird-watching, photography, and nature study. Bicycles and motorized vehicles are not allowed. Service dogs are welcome; otherwise, dogs are not allowed. Do not remove plants, animals, artifacts, or rocks and do not build fires. The Nature Conservancy, 575 Stone Cutters Way, Montpelier, VT 05602; 802-229-4425; nature.org/vermont.

NEARBY

The West River has excellent paddling opportunities and a number of swimming holes, including one under the 267-foot-long West Dummerston Covered Bridge, the longest covered bridge open to traffic in Vermont, 2 miles north of the trailhead. (Before swimming, double-check the safety of swimming holes, as flooding may have altered the landscape.) Head to downtown Brattleboro, 6 miles south, for food and shopping. Camp at Fort Dummer State Park, 6.4 miles south, or Townshend State Park, 12.5 miles northwest.

Wild strawberries are some of the sweetest discoveries of summertime hikes in the Green Mountains.

5
PUTNEY MOUNTAIN

Walk through a variety of lovely forests on this loop hike to a grassy summit with views across southern Vermont and New Hampshire.

DIRECTIONS

From I-91, Exit 4, drive north 0.7 mile on VT 5 and turn left onto Westminster Road/Kimball Hill. After 1.1 miles, turn left onto West Hill Road and go 2.3 miles to Putney Mountain Road, on the right. Drive 2.2 miles to the trailhead parking area (space for about 15 cars) on the right. *GPS coordinates: 42° 59.78′ N, 72° 35.93′ W.*

TRAIL DESCRIPTION

Putney Mountain's open, fieldlike summit (1,666 feet) is the reward at the end of a pleasant ridgeline ramble. Kids ages 5 and older will have fun exploring interesting natural features described in a nature-trail guide available at the trailhead kiosk. Just beyond the kiosk, a trail junction marks the beginning and end of the loop hike. At the junction, go left onto West Cliff Trail and follow the yellow trail markers onto a shady hillside of mature hemlocks that effectively block the sun, leaving the understory sparse. Rock cairns, or piles of stones used to mark backcountry routes, have been artfully and frequently arranged along this stretch of trail. Note that these are placed by hikers and thus are not reliable trail markers; trust the yellow blazes on the trees instead. Step across small streams and the remnants of an old stone wall—evidence that this steep slope was previously cleared. At 0.7 mile, leave West Cliff Trail as it turns left and follow blue markers straight onto Summit Trail.

As soon as you start uphill on Summit Trail, the deep red-gold hues of the conifer forest recede, replaced by the light, airy white and green of a birch stand. Follow this

LOCATION
Putney, VT

RATING
Easy

DISTANCE
1.2 miles

ELEVATION GAIN
140 feet

ESTIMATED TIME
1 hour

MAPS
USGS Putney, USGS Westminster West; putneymountain.org/web/trails-maps

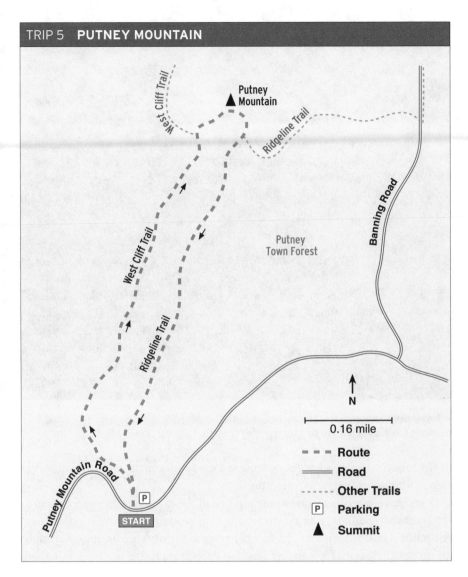

Putney
▲ Mountain

West Cliff Trail

Ridgeline Trail

Banning Road

West Cliff Trail

Putney
Town Forest

Ridgeline Trail

Putney Mountain Road

N

0.16 mile

- - - **Route**
═══ **Road**
- - - - **Other Trails**
P   **Parking**
▲   **Summit**

P

START

steep slope to the open summit of Putney Mountain. Small footpaths wander the grassy, shrubby area, looping and dead-ending, providing paths through the variety of plants, such as raspberry thickets, that colonize cleared forests at this latitude and elevation. Nubs and stripes of durable white quartzite jut out of the softer bedrock of gray phyllite.

Walk up to the height of land to see the rocky summit of New Hampshire's Mount Monadnock (3,130 feet), visible in the distance to the southeast. Turn around to see the long ridgeline of the Green Mountains to the west. The pointed peak of Haystack Mountain (3,410 feet) anchors the southern end of this chain, and the ski trails on Stratton Mountain (3,940 feet) are visible at the more northern end.

Putney Mountain's open slopes are the most important survey points in Vermont for monitoring migrating hawks on their flight path through the Connecticut and West River valleys.

The broad views and easy access make Putney Mountain a favorite observation site for autumnal hawk migrations.

From the height of land on the eastern side of the summit meadow, follow blue trail markers south, reentering the woods. After a short distance, you will meet Ridgeline Trail, which goes left (north) around Putney's summit and straight ahead (south) toward the parking area. Go straight on Ridgeline Trail, following white trail markers along the forested crest of the mountain. Shortly after crossing a stone wall, descend a ledge into a clearing. The enormous, oddly shaped white ash called the Elephant Tree, commemorated on Putney Mountain Association's logo, stood on the left side of this clearing for more than 200 years; its remains may still be evident.

Continue south along the rolling ridgeline, watching for white markers indicating the maintained Ridgeline Trail amid what is sometimes a maze of unofficial trails that wander across the open areas. Hikers create these informal trails by trying to avoid muddy spots, but doing so tends to enlarge the wet areas, trampling vegetation and increasing erosion. Walking through a puddle or rock-hopping across it causes less impact and requires less repair work than going around wet spots.

Water accumulates in shallow basins along this ridge, and at least one vernal pool, a seasonal breeding pond for amphibians, appears each spring near the trail and dries up in summer. Vernal pools have an important place in forest ecosystems, allowing tadpole and salamander larvae to hatch and complete their aquatic stage before maturing into terrestrial adults as the pool dries up.

Look for glacial striations, or scrapes and gouges left when mile-thick ice pushed over this ridge during the last ice age, as you descend a final ledge and arrive back at the junction of West Cliff Trail and the parking lot.

DID YOU KNOW?

The Putney Mountain Association, a membership-supported group that owns Putney's summit and maintains the trails, sponsors the annual Fall Putney Mountain Hawk Watch to gather data about raptor migration patterns.

MORE INFORMATION

Camping and fires are not permitted on Putney Mountain. Mountain biking is permitted, but motorized vehicles are not, except as needed to make the trails accessible to people with disabilities. Snowmobiles are permitted in winter. Putney Mountain Association, P.O. Box 953, Putney, VT 05346; putneymountain.org.

NEARBY

West Dummerston's historic covered bridge spanning the West River on VT 30 is a popular spot to picnic and swim. A few restaurants and a food co-op are found in Putney, near the junction of Westminster Road and VT 5, with more dining options 10 miles south in Brattleboro.

6

GROUT POND AND SOMERSET RESERVOIR

Pack your tent, canoe, and hammock. Once you find your way to the prettiest pond in Vermont, you'll want to set up camp and stay awhile.

DIRECTIONS

From VT 100 in West Wardsboro, take Stratton-Arlington Road 6.2 miles west to Grout Pond Road on the left. (From East Arlington, follow Old Mill Road east, which turns into Kansas Road. After crossing a bridge over US 7, go 0.4 mile farther and turn right onto Kelley Stand Road. Go 11.2 miles east to Grout Pond Road on the right.) Follow Grout Pond Road 1.2 miles through its campground and past the boat launch to the trailhead parking lot (space for about 20 cars). *GPS coordinates*: 43° 02.83′ N, 72° 57.10′ W.

TRAIL DESCRIPTION

Grout Pond and Somerset Reservoir are nestled between low hills in a remote section of the high, rolling plateau that characterizes the southern Green Mountains. Their clear waters offer refreshing swimming and long views over the otherwise thickly forested region. A trailhead at the north end of Grout Pond provides access to a network of rambling trails, including the long-distance Catamount Trail (often used for skiing), numerous loops through the forest, and a pedestrian route to the pond's appealing shoreline campsites. Kids of all ages will enjoy the flat first leg of this hike along Grout Pond's shore, and after that the rolling terrain is best-suited to kids 4 and older. The route described below follows close along the water on the east side of Grout Pond then descends to the edge of Somerset Reservoir before returning to finish the loop on the hillside above Grout's western shore. It is one of many options in the immediate area, and if you are lucky enough to be able to stay a few days, you can explore them all. Bring

LOCATION
Stratton, VT

RATING
Easy

DISTANCE
4.6 miles

ELEVATION GAIN
250 feet

ESTIMATED TIME
2.5 hours

MAPS
USGS Stratton Mountain; www.fs.usda.gov/gmfl

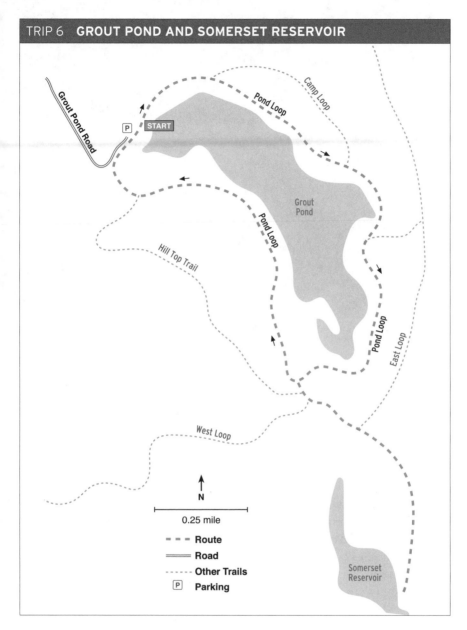

footwear that will allow you to enjoy encountering the inevitable muddy areas in this soggy landscape.

From the trailhead kiosk on the edge of the parking lot, descend a short distance to a T junction and go left on Pond Loop. Follow blue diamond markers along a wide gravel trail as it curves around the top of the pond, which is not quite visible through the foliage. Catamount Trail enters from the left via a spur trail to East Loop, and shortly after that, at 0.2 mile, the narrow Camp Loop Trail departs to the left. Stay on Pond Loop and round a curve to a long, flat

Skis or snowshoes allow hikers to stay on top of the fluffy, white stuff and experience the magnificent beauty of Vermont's backcountry in winter. Photo by Jerry Monkman.

straightaway with the first views of the pond. Campsites on the right provide access to the shoreline at regular intervals as you head southeast. Ski trails on the north slope of Mount Snow are visible over the treetops at the end of the pond. The trail narrows and rises away from the pond near campsite 10, traversing bog bridges, stepping-stones, and turnpikes—or gravel-filled wooden boxes—in this wet area. Pass the southern end of Camp Loop on your left and at 0.9 mile arrive at a trail junction. East Loop goes left, away from the pond; go right, continuing through thick woods on Pond Loop and Catamount Trail. Raspberries, ferns, and hobblebushes crowd the trail edges, and moss grows thickly beneath bog bridges as you round the muddy southern end of Grout Pond. Cross the dark, tumbling outlet stream on a wide bridge and weave through a pretty wetland on bog bridges before arriving at a four-way trail junction at 1.7 miles.

Straight ahead, Hill Top Trail climbs to the ridge. Pond Loop, your eventual return route, turns right here, and extends 0.9 mile back to the campground. Before taking Pond Loop back, turn left and follow Catamount Trail southbound on a wide swath through the woods. In 500 feet, West Loop departs to the right; bear left to continue on the two-track, part of the big East Loop, following blue diamond markers and descending through the forest. A bridge leads you back across a lower stretch of Grout Pond's outlet stream. Then, at 2.1 miles, East Loop goes left. Stay straight on Catamount Trail 0.4 mile more, through rolling terrain to a descent that brings you alongside an arm of Somerset Reservoir.

At a point where Catamount Trail turns sharply left and climbs away from the water, an informal path goes straight to the shoreline at a nice spot for a picnic with a view south. This is a good turnaround point, although you can continue to follow Catamount Trail south along the water as far as you like before turning around (you'll reach the south end of the lake in about 6 more miles). The 1,568-acre Somerset Reservoir is fed by the remote headwater streams of the Deerfield River, and although it is difficult to access, with only one long dirt road to the dam on the southern tip, mercury and acidity have impaired the health of aquatic wildlife. Swim and enjoy the peaceful surroundings, but don't fish for your dinner here.

Hike back the way you came down, returning to the four-way junction of Pond Loop and Hill Top Trail. Go straight on the western leg of Pond Loop and climb a gentle grade through pretty, open hardwoods. Nettle fills in the gaps between widely spaced yellow birch, maple, and beech trunks, and the pond waters are distantly visible through their branches. The trail gradually rises and descends numerous times as it crosses the hillside, finally rising to exit the woods next to a campsite where Hill Top Trail also ends. Go straight on a dirt road between two more campsites and arrive at Grout Pond Road. Turn right to return to the trailhead.

DID YOU KNOW?

Grout Pond's outlet stream is stained dark brown by tannins, a substance that leaches from plants into the soil and water. Tannins are recognizable in the dry, astringent feeling you get biting into a tart apple or sipping black tea or red wine.

MORE INFORMATION

Grout Pond's primitive campsites are first come, first served and have no fee, although the Forest Service is considering charging for camping starting in 2018. Camping is allowed only at designated sites. The campground is open year-round, but Grout Pond Road is not plowed; a winter lot is at the top of the road. Dogs must be leashed in Grout Pond Recreation Area. Green Mountain National Forest, Manchester Ranger District, 2538 Depot Street, Manchester Center, VT 05255; 802-362-2307; www.fs.usda.gov/gmfl.

NEARBY

The West River, renowned for paddling, offers good swimming holes and camping at Jamaica State Park, 14 miles northeast. Food and lodging are in Dover, 11 miles southeast, and in Arlington, 15 miles west. Mount Snow in Dover has mountain-bike trails and lessons for all abilities, from guided cross-country tours to a lift-served, downhill bike park.

BROMLEY MOUNTAIN

A long, breezy ridge provides a gradual ascent to Bromley's open summit and views across southern Vermont.

DIRECTIONS

From Londonderry, follow VT 11 west 4.3 miles and bear right onto Main Street. After 0.3 mile, make a hairpin right turn onto Hapgood Pond Road. Go 1 mile and bear left onto North Road. Go 0.8 mile and turn left on Mad Tom Notch Road. Go 2.1 miles and park in the lot on the left, just beyond (west of) the Appalachian Trail/Long Trail crossing (space for 12 cars). *GPS coordinates*: 43° 15.46′ N, 72° 56.32′ W.

TRAIL DESCRIPTION

Unlike the popular front-side route up Bromley Mountain (3,275 feet) from VT 11, the north approach to the summit is a quiet walk up a remote and beautiful ridgeline. The top is developed, but the grassy summit meadow and long views created by the ski trails are a worthwhile silver lining. Planning is underway to rebuild a summit observation tower that was removed in 2012 after 50 years of New England weather weakened its wooden supports beyond repair.

From the parking area, head east (right) on Mad Tom Notch Road 100 feet to the Appalachian Trail/Long Trail (AT/LT) crossing. A trailhead kiosk is on the left; to begin up Bromley Mountain, turn right off the road, following the white blazes southbound into the woods.

The first 0.3 mile is a flat walk through a pretty forest, with bog bridges crossing persistently wet areas and hobblebushes sprawling across the understory. The climb begins gradually through beech and birch trunks, intermittently rising, leveling out, descending a short way, then

LOCATION
Peru, VT

RATING
Moderate

DISTANCE
5 miles

ELEVATION GAIN
829 feet

ESTIMATED TIME
3.5 hours

MAPS
USGS Peru, USGS Danby

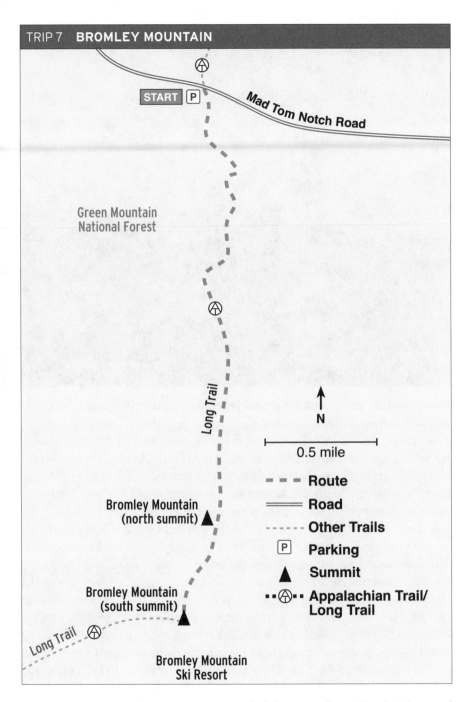

Mad Tom Notch Road

START   P

Green Mountain
National Forest

Long Trail

N

|———————————————|
0.5 mile

- - - Route
=== Road
····· Other Trails
P   Parking
▲   Summit
··Ⓐ··   Appalachian Trail/
Long Trail

Bromley Mountain
(north summit) ▲

Bromley Mountain
(south summit) ▲

Long Trail Ⓐ

Bromley Mountain
Ski Resort

rising again. At 1 mile, you enter a tunnel of short maples, yellow birches, and beeches, marking your arrival on a thickly forested ridgeline that you will follow to the top.

Bromley Mountain's grassy summit provides 360-degree views of southern Vermont.

The ridge eases into a higher elevation spruce-fir forest as it gradually climbs, the footing becoming rocky and rooty. At 2 miles, a remarkable ledgy boulder sits in the middle of your path, marking the north summit of Bromley (3,150 feet). From here, the trail descends 125 feet over a quarter mile and then rises in one final sustained pitch to the open south summit of Bromley Mountain.

A chairlift tops out on the far side of the summit area, and a ski-patrol hut hunkers next to the treeline. Wide swaths of grassy ski trails descend in several directions. To the west, the wooded edges of Run Around ski trail frame the pointy Mount Aeolus (also known as Green Peak, 3,210 feet) across the Vermont Valley. Looking south over Upper Twister ski trail, you can trace the general route of the AT/LT as it crosses the low land and then ascends Stratton Mountain (3,940 feet), with the mountain's northern-facing ski trails distinctly visible. Turning around, you can do the same looking north over Styles Peak (3,370 feet) and Peru Peak (3,429 feet). Far to the north, the AT/LT crosses the tall Coolidge Range, recognizable as a distant row of pointed summits. Killington Peak (4,219 feet) and Pico Peak (3,930 feet, Trip 16) are at the northern end of that range. After descending from Pico, the two long-distance hiking trails split: the LT continuing north to the Canadian border and the AT veering northeast toward its ultimate destination, Katahdin, in Maine.

Return downhill the way you hiked up.

DID YOU KNOW?

Nearby Stratton Mountain provided creative inspiration that led to the birth of long-distance hiking in the United States. James P. Taylor dreamed up the Long Trail in 1909 while sitting in a tent on the mountainside, waiting for rain to clear, and folklore has it Benton MacKaye conceived the Appalachian Trail while perched in a tree on the summit.

MORE INFORMATION

Bromley Mountain is in the Green Mountain National Forest, Manchester Ranger District, 2538 Depot Street, Manchester Center, VT 05255; 802-362-2307; www.fs.usda.gov/gmfl. The Long Trail is maintained by the Green Mountain Club, 4711 Waterbury–Stowe Road, Waterbury Center, VT 05477; 802-244-7037; greenmountainclub.org.

NEARBY

Paddle, swim, picnic, and explore the woods and wetlands of the lovely Lowell Lake State Park, a free day-use site in Londonderry, 12 miles east. Food and lodging are available in Londonderry; in Peru, 3.5 miles south of the trailhead; and in Manchester, 15 miles southwest.

THRU-HIKING

"No person should attempt to tramp The Trail without a light axe, and a good compass." So advised the 1921 edition of the *Long Trail Guide*. Hiking was not novel in America at that time, but the idea of a long-distance hiking trail was. The Green Mountain Club (GMC), formed in 1910 to create better access to the mountains, began cutting the Long Trail (LT) that same year. By 1920, the trail extended almost 200 miles, from Johnson, Vermont, to the Massachusetts border. Long-distance hiking in America had begun.

The LT now extends the length of Vermont, 272 miles, and was likely an inspiration for the 2,180-mile Appalachian Trail (AT), which was born as a proposal in an architectural journal in 1921. Today the AT and LT share their corridors for 105 miles in southern Vermont, and hiking either one end-to-end has become a badge of fortitude.

The two long-distance trails have developed similar subcultures of ambitious hikers striving to walk great distances over rugged terrain, and there are as many ways to hike as there are adventurous spirits to try it. Thru-hikers complete the trail in one long walk, while section hikers cover the distance in smaller chunks over a longer time. Some hikers adopt ultralight practices, forgoing luxuries to shave weight: going without a sleeping bag in warmer months, for instance, or cutting the handle off a toothbrush if you're really counting ounces. Others travel old-school style, wearing wool and leather. Some people hike barefoot, and one man who is blind completed the AT with a Seeing Eye dog. Slack-packers carry just water and snacks along the trail, heading to town at day's end for dinner, a shower, and a bed. Some thru-hikers are purists, resisting the urge to blue-blaze—that is, to skip a section of the AT proper by hiking a blue-blazed side trail and then rejoin it later on, perhaps after a pizza and a beer and a pint of ice cream. Others view the hike as a series of experiences linked by the general route of the trail but not bound to it. (Bill Bryson's book *A Walk in the Woods* [Broadway, 1999] is a humorous example of this philosophy.) However it's tackled, the challenge of a thru-hike requires as much emotional stamina as it does physical, and for most who complete it, the hike is transformational.

8

LYE BROOK FALLS

A magnificent 125-foot waterfall hides deep in a narrow wilderness valley just outside one of Vermont's most-visited towns.

DIRECTIONS

From the junction of US 7 and VT 11/VT 30 in Manchester, head east on VT 11/VT 30 for 0.5 mile. Turn right on East Manchester Road and go 1.2 miles. Turn left on Glen Road, which quickly forks. Stay right on Lye Brook Access Road and drive 0.4 mile to the road's end, at the Lye Brook Wilderness parking area (space for about 20 cars). *GPS coordinates:* 43° 09.55′ N, 73° 02.50′ W.

TRAIL DESCRIPTION

From bustling Manchester Village, Lye Brook Valley appears as an intriguing, narrow slice in the steep wall of eastern mountains. The valley provides access to the 18,122-acre Lye Brook Wilderness, a high forested plateau laced with streams, ponds, and bogs. On the way to these upland wilds, Lye Brook Falls, one of the highest waterfalls in Vermont, plummets down the wall of the valley. Lye Brook Trail alternately climbs and then crosses level stretches; it is most likely to be enjoyed by kids ages 8 and older. It is also fun terrain for a cross-country ski adventure.

Lye Brook's trailhead kiosk, detailing this unique Wilderness Area, is a few steps into a dim hardwood and hemlock forest. Beyond the kiosk, go left at the junction of several trails—mostly informal exploratory paths around the river and parking area—and ascend along the edge of Lye Brook's ravine. The wide path and the woods surrounding it are bursting with rocks, although you shortly cross onto smoother ground. Lye Brook Trail continues this pattern of alternating between very rocky and very smooth terrain the whole way to the Falls Trail junction.

LOCATION
Manchester, VT

RATING
Moderate

DISTANCE
4.4 miles

ELEVATION GAIN
740 feet

ESTIMATED TIME
3 hours

MAPS
USGS Manchester;
www.fs.usda.gov/gmfl

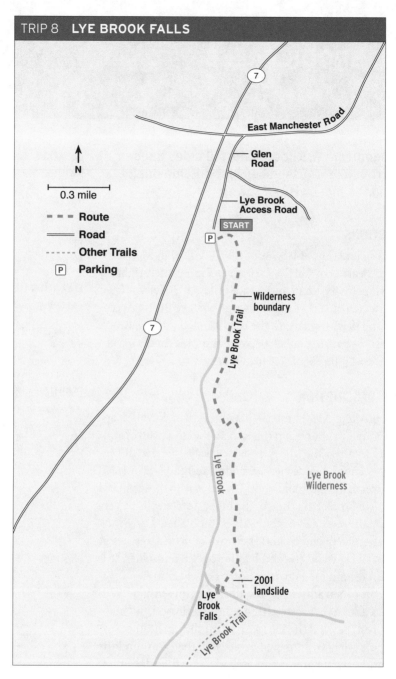

N

0.3 mile

- - - Route
——— Road
······ Other Trails
P Parking

7

East Manchester Road

Glen Road

Lye Brook Access Road

START

P

Wilderness boundary

Lye Brook Trail

7

Lye Brook

Lye Brook Wilderness

2001 landslide

Lye Brook Falls

Lye Brook Trail

Leveling out, the trail passes a hiker register box (use it!) and briefly follows the straight corridor of a former railroad bed before arriving at the Wilderness Area boundary. Continuing in a southwesterly direction across a gentle slope, Lye Brook Trail crosses a wide tannic stream on rocks. Climbing gradually, you will pass a small stand of brilliantly white, smooth gray birches on the left.

You will step easily across several small streams before entering a steeper, narrower section of Lye Brook valley at 1 mile. Curving left, Lye Brook Trail begins to climb a moderate pitch, entering a hemlock stand. Lye Brook drops away to the right, deep in its ravine. Curving north and then back to the south again, the trail climbs steadily for 0.6 mile over alternately rocky and then smooth, gravelly ground before leveling across the steep hillside high above Lye Brook.

At 1.8 miles, Lye Brook Falls Trail diverges to the right, while Lye Brook Trail continues uphill to the left. Head right, following the narrow path to the falls as it crosses a rocky sidehill, gradually descending past dripping ledges and more rock-filled stream gullies. At 2.1 miles, cross a 2011 landslide path, now revegetating. This dramatic slide, 60 feet across and about 500 feet long, was the result of heavy rains during Tropical Storm Irene, whose floods rearranged the landscape of many southern Vermont valleys.

The approach to Lye Brook Falls, 0.1 mile past the landslide, is a little unclear, as multiple trails spiderweb off the main path. Staying high, head left for the best view of the cascade. The steep edges of the stream's ravine are unprotected (*Caution:* Lye Brook Falls spills down a narrow rock chute for at least 125 feet; some estimates put it at 160 feet) before twisting and turning through boulders

Lye Brook Wilderness has ponds, waterfalls, and thousands of acres of quiet woods to explore and enjoy.

in the streambed below. The winter landscape here is a marvel of frozen sheets of ice draped over the rocks and hanging from the sides of the ravine.

Return to the trailhead the way you hiked in.

DID YOU KNOW?

Can you identify different types of waterfalls within Lye Brook Falls? A plunge exists where water drops over an edge and loses contact with rock. A horsetail happens where the waterfall contacts the rock for part of the drop then plunges off it. A fan occurs when water spreads horizontally across rock as it descends.

MORE INFORMATION

Lye Brook Wilderness is within the Green Mountain National Forest, Manchester Ranger District, 2538 Depot Street, Manchester Center, VT 05255; 802-362-2307; www.fs.usda.gov/gmfl.

NEARBY

Benson Hole is an informal swimming spot with a great view of Mount Equinox, just downstream from Glen Road's bridge over Bromley Brook, 0.4 mile from the trailhead. Swim, paddle, and camp at Emerald Lake State Park, 8 miles north, off US 7. Food and shops are in Manchester, 2.5 miles west.

9

MOUNT EQUINOX

A long, boreal ridgeline with incredible views is a well-deserved reward at the top of this challenging hike up the highest peak in the Taconic Mountains.

DIRECTIONS

From the junction of VT 7A and VT 11/VT 30 in downtown Manchester, head south on VT 7A for 1.2 miles. Turn right onto Seminary Avenue and follow it 0.2 mile to its end, where it bends left and becomes Prospect Street. Take the second right onto West Union Street and go 0.2 mile to the end of the public road. The parking lot (space for about 10 cars) is on the right. *GPS coordinates:* 43° 09.73′ N, 73° 04.93′ W.

This parking area fills quickly during peak season, and cars parked along West Union Street will be ticketed; find additional parking behind the Equinox Hotel on VT 7A or behind Burr and Burton Academy at the junction of Seminary Avenue and Prospect Street.

TRAIL DESCRIPTION

Mount Equinox (3,839 feet) steals the show in the Battenkill Valley, towering impressively over the village of Manchester. Its very steep sides support diverse natural communities, including rich northern hardwood forests and fen on the lower mountain, an old-growth red spruce/yellow birch stand on the midmountain, and boreal forest and calcareous outcrops on the upper mountain. The range of habitats led to conservation of much of the eastern slope in the 1990s, with the Equinox Preservation Trust (EPT) organized to manage it. Blue Summit Trail, formerly called Burr and Burton Trail, is the only route on the mountain that EPT designates double black diamond (most difficult), due to its relentlessly steep climb to the

LOCATION
Manchester, VT

RATING
Strenuous

DISTANCE
6 miles

ELEVATION GAIN
2,805 feet

ESTIMATED TIME
4.5 hours

MAPS
USGS Manchester; equinoxpreservationtrust.org/mapdown.php; equinoxmountain.com/mountain_trailmap.php

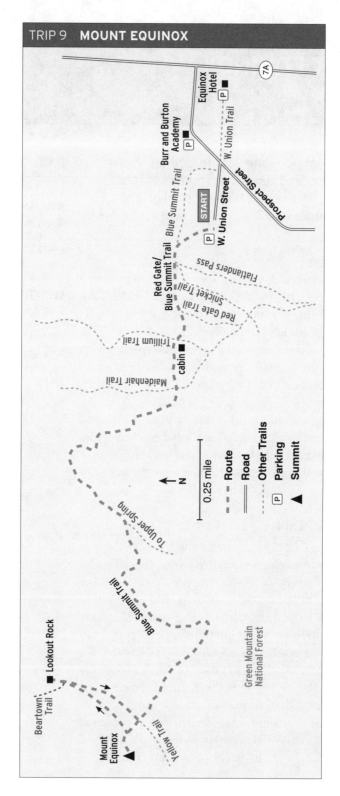

ridgeline at 2.1 miles, at which point the pitch lessens for the final 0.5 mile to the summit. Another 0.5 mile of gently sloped trail leads along the crest to Lookout Rock. Given this hike's steep climbs, traction devices, such as Microspikes, would be a smart addition to your gear between November and May.

Pass through the parking-area gate and begin your hike on Red Gate Trail. After a kiosk, Blue Summit Trail (still called Burr and Burton Trail on the signpost) joins from the right. Together, the two trails follow a gravel two-track past Flatlanders Pass and Snicket Trail. Following a moderate climb, the two trails separate at a fork at 0.3 mile. Go right on Blue Summit Trail and pass through private land where Trillium Trail crosses next to a small cabin.

Blue Summit Trail reenters EPT land at 0.7 mile, at the crossing of Maidenhair Trail, and the grade steepens. For the next 0.8 mile, the two-track jogs back and forth across the mountainside, maintaining a steep rise on every leg. The steady climb passes through beech, red oak, and bitternut hickory, with pale jewelweed, hobblebush, and a variety of ferns and wildflowers spreading across the angled slopes. In spring, look for bloodroot, hepatica, lady's slipper, and trillium; in summer, you may see Herb-Robert, as well as whorled aster.

At about 1.5 miles, you will cross a very steep rock band where thin yellow-birch saplings line the trail like sentries, and small spruces crowd along

Wildlife sighting! A luna moth caterpillar searches for a suitable place to make its cocoon.

the narrow shelf; here you will arrive at a junction. The two-track continues to Upper Spring; go right to remain on Blue Summit Trail, leaving the road for a rugged footpath, and continue up steeply for 0.6 mile more.

The grade eases, and the forest becomes more boreal at 2.1 miles, where an enormous yellow birch growing next to a large fir marks your arrival on the ridge. Climbing directly up a moderate slope, you will arrive at Yellow Trail (your return path) at 2.4 miles. If you want to skip the developed summit with its cars, roads, and building, head right (northeast) on Yellow Trail 0.5 mile to reach Lookout Rock. To continue to the top, stay straight, pass a cell tower station, and go left (west) where a wide path leads right (northeast) to Lookout Rock. Climb the last 0.1 mile to the summit, where the Saint Bruno Scenic Viewing Center is open 9 A.M. to 4:15 P.M. daily between Memorial Day and November 1; there is no shelter on the summit in the coldest months of the year. Carthusian Monks own 7,000 acres of the western side of Mount Equinox, including the road and summit, and manage the trails along the ridgeline. Views from the top are expansive, reaching across four states on a clear day.

To go to Lookout Rock, follow Blue Summit Trail the way you ascended and stay left at the cell-tower junction, following a wide rocky path. Yellow Trail becomes visible, paralleling your route before eventually merging with it. Beartown Trail drops off the ridgeline to the left just before you arrive at Lookout Rock's bench with its bird's-eye view of Manchester.

To descend, follow Yellow Trail back through the forest below the ridgeline and meet Blue Summit Trail in 0.5 mile. Turn left and go down the way you hiked up.

DID YOU KNOW?

The Taconic Mountains are so steep because the lower slopes are composed of soft rock that erodes more readily than the rock forming the upper slopes, thus washing away what once were more gradual hillsides.

MORE INFORMATION

Most of the trails and the eastern side of the mountain are managed by Equinox Preservation Trust, P.O. Box 986, Manchester, VT 05254; 802-366-1400; equinoxpreservationtrust.org. Summit trails are managed by Mount Equinox Skyline Drive, 1A Saint Bruno Drive, Arlington, VT 05250; 802-362-1114; equinoxmountain.com.

NEARBY

Benson Hole is an informal swimming spot on Bromley Brook near Glen Road bridge, 2.8 miles east of the Mount Equinox trailhead. Camp, swim, and paddle at Emerald Lake State Park, 10 miles north. The Battenkill River has many scenic paddling stretches. Food and shops are abundant in Manchester.

10

MOUNT ANTONE

Wander through a working farm and beautiful hardwood forests on your way to a grand vista on Mount Antone.

DIRECTIONS

From the junction of VT 30 and VT 315 in East Rupert, follow VT 315 west 2.6 miles to the height of land. Turn left and follow the 0.5-mile driveway to the Merck Forest and Farmland Center's parking area (space for about 100 cars). *GPS coordinates:* 43° 16.46′ N, 73° 10.45′ W.

TRAIL DESCRIPTION

Climbing Mount Antone (2,600 feet) at Merck Forest and Farmland Center is a pleasantly different kind of hiking experience. The nonprofit center uses its 3,160 acres of farm and forest to demonstrate sustainable agriculture, and the public is invited to observe, participate, or simply explore the landscape on 30 miles of trails. No fee is charged, but donations for upkeep of the trails are appreciated. Mount Antone is steep but not terribly high, with an amazing picnic spot on its wide, grassy shoulder. Kids ages 8 and older will enjoy the hike, if you can get them past the farm animals. Dogs need to be leashed near the visitor center and farm.

Next to the parking area, the visitor center has maps and restrooms, among other offerings. Go around a gate and walk 0.3 mile on a dirt road to the field that is the hub of farm activities. Animals graze along the road, and a large sugarhouse and barn invite further exploration. Continue straight through a four-way junction of dirt roads, descending between open fields on Old Town Road. Climbing from the low spot, Wildlife Trail heads right

LOCATION
Rupert, VT

RATING
Moderate

DISTANCE
5.8 miles

ELEVATION GAIN
800 feet

ESTIMATED TIME
4 hours

MAPS
USGS Pawlet;
merckforest.org/cms/
TrailMap.pdf

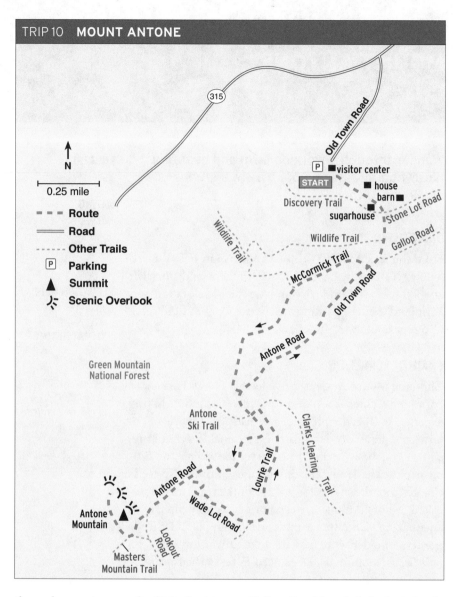

N

0.25 mile

- - - Route
═══ Road
- - - Other Trails
P Parking
▲ Summit
⅄ Scenic Overlook

Green Mountain
National Forest

315

Old Town Road

P ■ visitor center
START ■ house
Discovery Trail barn ■
sugarhouse Stone Lot Road

Wildlife Trail Gallop Road

Wildlife Trail

McCormick Trail

Old Town Road

Antone Road

Antone
Ski Trail

Clarks Clearing Trail

Lourie Trail

Antone Road

Wade Lot Road

Antone
Mountain

Lookout
Road

Masters
Mountain Trail

through a pasture, and a little farther on, Gallop Road heads left. At 0.6 mile into your hike, turn right onto McCormick Trail.

Drop across the hillside through birches and maples. Leveling out through widely spaced hardwoods, McCormick Trail passes through ferns and jewel-weed that create a meadow across the forest floor. At the lowest point, Wild-life Trail joins from the right, and McCormick Trail begins a moderate climb that becomes steep as it curves left and follows the edge of a ravine. Reaching the top of a ridge, the trail descends for a short distance to meet Antone Road in a clearing at 1.5 miles. Bear right across this small field and head south on Antone Road.

Antone Ski Trail diverges to the right next to a little cabin, and Clarks Clearing Trail heads left next to sap lines strung in sugar maples. Stay straight on Antone Road for a steep 0.3-mile climb to the mountain ridge. The grassy two-track switches back and forth a few times, but some pitches are simply straight up. Arriving on top, Antone Road rolls along the high land, passing the top of Antone Ski Trail on the right and then Wade Lot Road, your return route, on the left at 2.2 miles. Pass Lookout Road and climb a rocky, rooty pitch to a four-way junction at 2.5 miles. Turn right to continue on Antone Road and ascend the last 0.2 mile to the summit.

A small clearing provides a window northeast, back to where you started. For a really spectacular view, go 350 feet down the far side of the summit to a grassy field with a bench under an oak tree. A northern panorama stretches across the horizon, from the Champlain Valley in the northwest over the diminishing Taconics and tall Green Mountains to the big, 160-year-old barn anchoring Merck's farm fields.

Return 0.6 mile along Antone Road and turn right down Wade Lot Road. This curving, grassy two-track drops steeply through one of the most beautiful

Sugarhouses, like this one at Merck Forest and Farmland Center, are shacks where maple sap is boiled and reduced to syrup. Maple syrup ranges in color and flavor depending on when it's collected.

forests on the property, with ferns and grass spread beneath widely spaced hard-wood trunks. Ned's Place, a camping cabin, is visible downhill to the right.

At 3.6 miles, turn left onto Lourie Trail and continue through the same lovely forest until, curving north around the mountain, the woods fill with shrubby saplings. Blackberries, raspberries, and purple-flowering raspberries (also called thimbleberries) line the path as it crosses the steep mountainside before arriving at Clarks Clearing Trail at 4.3 miles. Go left onto Clarks Clearing Trail for a short distance to the junction of Antone Road. Turn right on Antone Road and retrace your steps to the meadow at the top of McCormick Trail. From there, follow Antone Road's gradual descent for 0.4 mile to Old Town Road. Go left on Old Town and return downhill 0.6 mile to the barn and sugarhouse. Retrace your steps to the parking lot.

DID YOU KNOW?

In 1850, most of the forest on this property was pasture cleared for sheep, with only the mountaintops remaining forested. See historical photos of the changing landscape at the visitor center.

MORE INFORMATION

Open dawn to dusk, seven days a week, year-round. Merck Forest and Farmland Center, P.O. Box 86, Rupert, VT 05768; 802-394-7836; merckforest.org.

NEARBY

Camping is available here on the property or at Emerald Lake State Park, which also has swimming and paddling, 14.5 miles east. The Battenkill River has scenic paddling 20 miles southeast. Restaurants are available in Dorset, 5 miles east, with more options in Manchester, 11 miles southeast.

11

HAYSTACK MOUNTAIN (NORTH PAWLET)

A lesser-known gem, Haystack has hillsides rich in biodiversity, as well as panoramic views from its cliffy summit.

DIRECTIONS

From the junction of VT 30 and VT 133 in Pawlet, head north on VT 30 for 1.7 miles and turn right on Waite Road. Go uphill (with the obligatory stop on the way to photograph Haystack's cleft south face) for 1.2 miles and park in the dirt pullout on the left at the bottom of Tunket Road (space for about 8 cars). Do not drive up or block the private Tunket Road. *GPS coordinates*: 43° 22.65' N, 73° 09.89' W.

TRAIL DESCRIPTION

Haystack Mountain (1,730 feet) is the southernmost of the striking Three Sisters in the North Pawlet Hills, jutting startlingly from the rolling farmland and beckoning hikers with its low, attainable summit and a rocky top that promises breezes and fabulous views. Like many of its Taconic Mountain siblings, Haystack is short but wickedly steep, and this trail goes almost straight up. You'll work for this summit, but it will be worth the effort. This is a good hike for kids ages 7 and older. Other than service animals, dogs are not allowed in the North Pawlet Hills Natural Area, and it's best to check with Vermont Audubon for closures related to peregrine falcon nesting season before heading up Haystack.

Start by walking uphill between cow pastures on the jewelweed-lined Tunket Road (do not drive on this privately owned road). Stay straight uphill when a wide driveway departs to the left; the road becomes rougher and enters woods. Shagbark hickories are easy to recognize here, with their scruffy, peeling trunks. At the top of the hill, an open

LOCATION
Pawlet, VT

RATING
Moderate

DISTANCE
4 miles

ELEVATION GAIN
770 feet

ESTIMATED TIME
3 hours

MAPS
USGS Wells

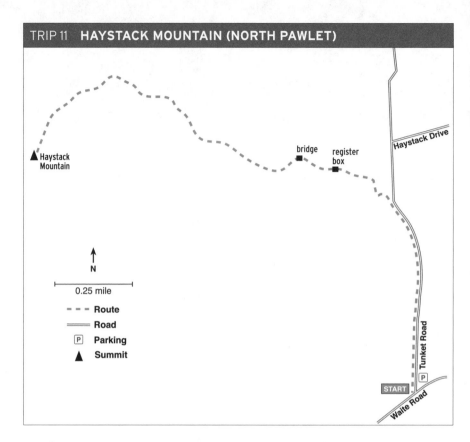

Haystack Drive

bridge   register box

▲ Haystack Mountain

↑
N

0.25 mile

— — — Route
════ Road
P   Parking
▲   Summit

Tunket Road

START

Waite Road

meadow permits a view north to Bald Hill, the tallest of the Three Sisters at just over 2,100 feet.

At 0.6 mile, at the end of the meadow, turn left off the road and follow green and white The Nature Conservancy (TNC) trail markers across the grass and into a conifer stand. Descend to a register box and then continue downhill to cross a stream, at 1 mile, on a bridge built by the Vermont Youth Conservation Corps in 2017. Ascend a rooty slope from the stream and begin a steady climb through hardwoods. The open understory is due to the relatively warm climate (for Vermont) and shallow soils, which combine to provide droughtlike conditions. The trail rises persistently until a relocation of the route at 1.7 miles provides welcome switchbacks through the woods. The respite is short, however, and soon you're climbing steeply again.

As you gain the ridgeline, the trees are noticeably smaller and widely spaced, and blueberries fill in the understory. This dry oak woodland is rare in Vermont, though fairly common here in the Taconics. The trail crosses many ledges and passes through a slight depression before ascending the final pitch to Haystack's grassy, rocky, open summit. Mettowee Valley farmlands stretch from the base of the North Pawlet Hills. The darkly forested Taconic Mountains march south, while the ridge of Green Mountains fills the eastern horizon. Far to the northeast, the prominent point of Killington (4,219 feet) is visible in the Coolidge Range. Foothills of the Adirondacks are visible to the northwest. Look north to see Haystack's two northern sisters, Middle Mountain and Bald Hill.

The top of Haystack Mountain was privately owned until 2012, when a local group formed the Friends of Haystack organization to buy the summit and keep it open to hikers and conserved to protect its natural communities. Vermont Land Trust and TNC work together to manage the landscape as part of the North Pawlet Hills Natural Area.

Keep an eye out for peregrine falcons while you're taking in the view. The cliffs you're sitting on make good hunting territory for these predators, and the birds sometimes nest here as well. Other animals that call the North Pawlet Hills home are bobcats, turkeys, deer, and grouse.

Return downhill the way you hiked up.

DID YOU KNOW?

Haystack is within the Slate Valley, a 24-mile-long, 6-mile-wide region along the Vermont–New York border that produces most of the colorful roofing slate sold in the United States. A quarry in nearby Granville, New York, is distinctly visible from the summit.

Views all around from Haystack's summit make this a perfect option for families with children.

MORE INFORMATION

North Pawlet Hills Natural Area is limited to passive recreational activities, such as hiking, snowshoeing, bird-watching, photography, and nature study. Bicycles and motorized vehicles are not allowed. Service dogs are welcome; otherwise, dogs are not allowed. Be aware that hunters may be in the area October 1 to December 31 and in May; find hunting season information at eregulations.com /vermont/hunting/. Remove no plants, animals, artifacts, or rocks; do not build fires. Camping is not allowed. The Nature Conservancy, 575 Stone Cutters Way, Montpelier, VT 05602; 802-229-4425; nature.org/vermont.

NEARBY

Some food is in Pawlet, with more options in the college-campus town of Poultney, 12 miles north. Swim, paddle, and camp at Lake Saint Catherine State Park, 9 miles north. The Slate Valley Museum in Granville (wheelchair-accessible) has exhibits, including the massive machinery of quarrying and artistic works inspired by the rock and the industry. It is open Tuesday through Saturday year-round. Slate Valley Trails provides a network of single-track and gravel-road mountain bike rides, as well as more walking trails in this region.

12

LITTLE ROCK POND

A gentle valley hike leads to a fun loop trail around a beautiful pond with lots of swimming spots.

DIRECTIONS

About 17 miles south of Rutland, crossroads between Danby and Mount Tabor meet US 7. From US 7, turn east onto Brooklyn Road/Forest Road 10 at an industrial-looking lot next to the railroad. Go 3.1 miles up this winding mountain road to the Appalachian Trail/Long Trail parking lot (space for about 20 cars) on the right. (Winter hikers: Park at the USFS Mount Tabor Work Center on Forest Road 48, 0.4 mile along Brooklyn Road from US 7.) *GPS coordinates:* 43° 22.36′ N, 72° 57.76′ W.

TRAIL DESCRIPTION

The clear waters of Little Rock Pond (1,854 feet) gather in a pretty basin along the high crest of the Green Mountains. The hike follows gradual grades along a stream then circles the berry-lined pond, passing some beautiful swimming spots. All of these factors make this a great hike for kids ages 7 and older, but they also make Little Rock Pond a popular area. If solitude is your goal, head to the pond in the cooler seasons when its beauty is possibly even more luminous.

Cross Forest Road 10 from the parking area and follow the white-blazed Appalachian Trail/Long Trail (AT/LT) north. For 0.2 mile, the trail rises moderately along the wide, rocky Big Branch. Curving west, the path leaves the river and settles into the gentle, almost level pitch it maintains the rest of the way to the pond. The waters of Little Black Brook become audible in the ravine on your left before they become visible at 0.6 mile, when you cross the stream on a narrow metal I-beam. Small cascades tumble

LOCATION
Mount Tabor, VT

RATING
Easy

DISTANCE
4.8 miles

ELEVATION GAIN
365 feet

ESTIMATED TIME
3.5 hours

MAPS
USGS Danby,
USGS Wallingford

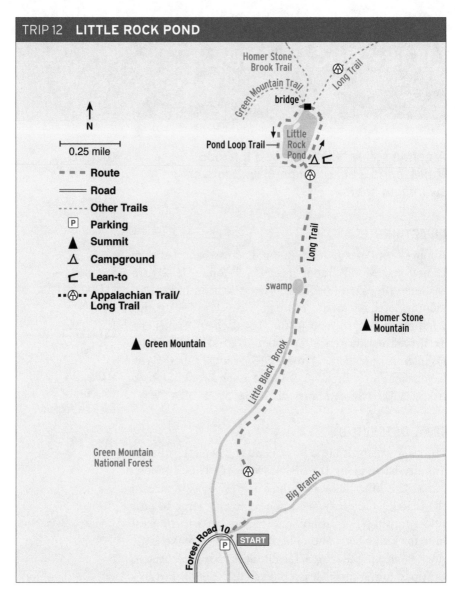

downhill as you follow the left bank 0.2 mile then cross it again on large rocks. Hobblebushes, Indian cucumbers, blue cohosh, and blue-bead lilies sprout from the mossy ground alongside the trail.

Bog bridges and chunky rock underfoot characterize the second half of the 2-mile hike to the pond. At 1.5 miles, skirt the right side of a small swamp and climb a little higher on the hillside. A final, long string of bog bridges leads to the T intersection at the shore of the pond at 2 miles. Go right, past the camping area with its large shelter, built in 2010 to replace the Lula Tye Shelter and the old Little Rock Pond Shelter, both of which were removed.

Continue on the AT/LT along the rocky eastern shore of the pond. As you round the north end, openings in the trees provide access to the water and views of Homer Stone Mountain (2,503 feet) to the east and Green Mountain (2,509 feet) above the western pond edge. Around the swampy area at the pond's outlet, where Pond Loop Trail breaks off from the AT/LT, lady's slippers bloom in early summer. After the pouch-like flower has shriveled, a single nodding leaf remains atop the tall stalk with two large ribbed leaves at ground level. Go left on the blue-blazed Pond Loop/Green Mountain Trail and cross a bridge over the outlet, passing Homer Stone Brook Trail. Follow the shoreline into shady hemlocks, and climb to the junction where Pond Loop Trail diverges from Green Mountain Trail. Staying left on Pond Loop Trail, descend along the narrow channel separating the mainland from a small island. A great place to picnic and swim is on your left, across from the southern tip of the island. A wide ledge eases into the water, and blueberry bushes grow abundantly beneath white pines.

Continuing south, cross an inlet stream and clamber over rocks before climbing to the top of the little rock of the pond's name. Watch kids and dogs here, as the trail edges close to the drop of this small cliff. Cross the swampy pond inlet in the final 0.2 mile to the AT/LT junction. Return to the trailhead the way you walked in.

Little Rock Pond is one of the sweetest stops for thru-hikers on the Appalachian Trail and Long Trail.

DID YOU KNOW?

The camping area at Little Rock Pond has attracted people since the ancestors of the Wabanaki and Mahican moved into the Green Mountains, shortly after the last ice age. An archaeological excavation at the campsite between 2009 and 2012 found evidence that this area may have been used as far back as 11,000 years ago, "when they could have still heard the glaciers calving," the lead archaeologist noted.

MORE INFORMATION

Green Mountain National Forest, Manchester Ranger District, 2538 Depot Street, Manchester Center, VT 05255; 802-362-2307; www.fs.usda.gov/gmfl. Appalachian Trail/Long Trail and Little Rock Pond Campsite are maintained by the Green Mountain Club; 4711 Waterbury–Stowe Road, Waterbury Center, VT 05677; 802-244-7037; greenmountainclub.org. Camping fee is $5 per person between Memorial Day and Columbus Day weekends.

NEARBY

If backcountry camping isn't on your agenda, Emerald Lake State Park has car camping, as well as swimming and paddling, 7.5 miles south. General stores have limited food along US 7 in either direction; restaurants and shops are in Manchester, 17 miles south, and Rutland, 20 miles north.

13

WHITE ROCKS ICE BEDS

Hike to the foot of a giant rock slide, where pockets of ice remain through the summer, releasing a cold stream and cool breezes on even the hottest days.

DIRECTIONS

From the junction of US 7 and VT 140 (School Street) in Wallingford, follow VT 140 east for 2.1 miles. Bear right on Sugar Hill Road and take the next right onto Forest Road 52 (White Rocks Picnic Road). Follow it 0.5 mile to its end in the trailhead parking lot (space for about 25 cars). Winter hikers: Park alongside the road at the gate and add 0.4 mile round-trip to the hike. *GPS coordinates:* 43° 27.05′ N, 72° 56.61′ W.

TRAIL DESCRIPTION

The steep northwestern side of White Rocks Mountain (2,682 feet) is eroding in a series of dramatic rock slides easily viewed from a nearby ridge. After a short climb to the lookout, descend to the foot of one of the slides to experience the microclimate created by sheltered ice beds slowly melting deep within the rocks. This hike ascends and descends in both directions and is fun for kids ages 5 and older. The rocky outcrops atop the lookout ridge are particularly amusing places for kids to explore—with supervision, as there are some cliffs—and are far more appealing picnic spots than the tables next to the parking lot. Dogs must be leashed.

From the parking area, Keewaydin Trail departs east, and Ice Beds Trail goes southwest onto a low ridge. Follow the blue blazes of Ice Beds Trail into a hemlock forest. A rocky ridge descends toward you through the trees, with many unofficial trails created by explorers looking for views. Ice Beds Trail crosses the base of the rocks to rise

LOCATION
Wallingford, VT

RATING
Easy

DISTANCE
1.8 miles

ELEVATION GAIN
336 feet

ESTIMATED TIME
1.5 hours

MAPS
USGS Wallingford;
www.fs.usda.gov/gmfl

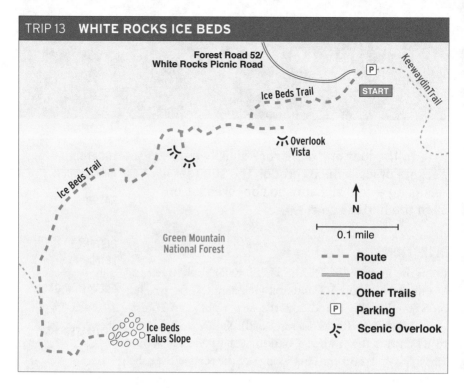

TRIP 13 WHITE ROCKS ICE BEDS

Forest Road 52/
White Rocks Picnic Road

Ice Beds Trail

Keewaydin Trail

START

P

Ice Beds Trail

Overlook
Vista

N

0.1 mile

Green Mountain
National Forest

- - - Route
==== Road
----- Other Trails
P Parking
Scenic Overlook

Ice Beds
Talus Slope

gradually along the right slope. A series of switchbacks then climbs the steep pitch to arrive at a T junction on top of the rocky crest at 0.2 mile. Go left to Overlook Vista, where a low rock wall and blueberry bushes line the edge of a cliff. A narrow valley separates the outlook from steep talus slopes on White Rocks Mountain. A sharp escarpment descends from its pointy peak to the valley, and conifers rim the rock slides.

Follow the path back to the junction and go straight to continue along Ice Beds Trail, which immediately scrambles up a ridge bristling with rock. After 0.1 mile from the junction, the trail encounters a wall of ledge and turns sharply right to descend off the ridge. Before going down, climb onto the wide, smooth ledge and take in the view south and west. The western slope of White Rocks Mountain is now visible, dominated by an enormous rock slide that tumbles about 1,000 feet from the summit cliffs to the trees in the valley below. The Vermont Valley stretches south, with Otter Creek—the longest river within Vermont, at 112 miles—snaking northward along the bottom. A limestone quarry is visible along the valley floor, and the Taconic Mountains stack up along the southern and western horizons.

Return to the trail and descend into the wooded valley. The route can be challenging to follow through the hemlocks, because there is almost no undergrowth to define the path; keep an eye out for blue blazes. As you drop over the left side of the ridge, the footpath arrives at a dirt road. Go left on the road to continue along Ice Beds Trail, heading downhill into a thicker, more diverse forest, including some very tall hobblebushes. Cross the wide stream and the flat valley floor, trending left as a rocky hillside rises steeply on the right. Bog bridges extend over damp ground before the trail begins to gradually rise. The open white slope of talus becomes visible through the trees, and the air turns noticeably cooler. Feel the stream running out of the base of the slide; the ice beds hidden in the rocks produce an achingly cold rivulet of 35 to 40 degrees Fahrenheit. Ice Beds Trail ends at the bottom of the slide, but steep eroded bootleg trails ascend the right side, and the jumble of boulders calls to be climbed. Use caution scrambling around here and don't assume the rocks are stable.

When you've finished exploring, return to the trailhead the way you hiked in.

DID YOU KNOW?

In a rock slide, the size of the rocks differs from the top to the bottom. The momentum of large rocks carries them farther, and they end up lower on the slope, while smaller rocks are more easily stopped by obstacles and remain higher on the slide.

Hemlock bark, buds, and needles are porcupines' favorite winter food.

The white rocks spilling down their namesake mountain were once sand on an ocean floor. Squeezed and heated to become quartzite, they can be found all along the western edge of the Green Mountains.

MORE INFORMATION

Robert T. Stafford White Rocks National Recreation Area is within the Green Mountain National Forest, 231 N. Main Street, Rutland, VT 05701; 802-747-6700; www.fs.usda.gov/gmfl.

NEARBY

Swim, paddle, and camp at Emerald Lake State Park, 16 miles south. Mill River's Clarendon Gorge is a popular swimming hole 6 miles northwest. Restaurants and shops are in Wallingford, 2.5 miles west.

14

OKEMO MOUNTAIN

A historical fire tower on this big peak gives a 360-degree view across all of southern Vermont.

DIRECTIONS

From the junction of VT 100 and VT 103, go west on VT 103 for 2.8 miles and turn left on Station Road. Go 0.7 mile and cross active railroad tracks. Turn left and proceed about 500 feet to the end of the road at the Healdville Trail parking area (space for about 6 cars). *GPS coordinates: 43° 25.95′ N, 72° 45.70′ W.*

TRAIL DESCRIPTION

Okemo Mountain (3,339 feet) is the name often used for Ludlow Mountain due to the so-named ski area on the mountain's eastern side and the 7,323-acre state forest encompassing most of the peak. The hiking trail on its western side, built by youth crews in the early 1990s, is a steady climb for the first half and a cross-mountain trek for most of the second.

Leaving the parking area, walk parallel to the train tracks for a short distance then curve right, following blue-blazed Healdville Trail uphill. Catamount Trail shares the path for a little way then breaks off at a wide wooden bridge. Healdville Trail starts out wide and mostly smooth as it climbs alongside a stream then becomes narrower and rockier. Pretty cascades tumble down on your right, while rose twisted-stalk, blue and white cohosh, trillium, and Indian cucumber line the sides of the trail.

At 0.8 mile, cross a plank bridge and continue up the valley 0.2 mile more. Then a hard-left bend begins a series of switchbacks that lead you up through a northern hardwood forest and among glacial erratics for almost 0.5 mile.

LOCATION
Mount Holly, VT

RATING
Moderate to Strenuous

DISTANCE
6 miles

ELEVATION GAIN
1,950 feet

ESTIMATED TIME
4 hours

MAPS
USGS Mount Holly; vtstateparks.com/assets/pdf/okemo_sf_trails.pdf

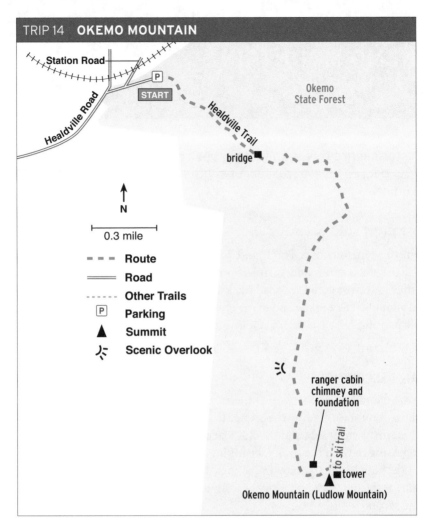

Station Road

Healdville Road

P

START

Healdville Trail

Okemo
State Forest

bridge

N

0.3 mile

- - - Route
=== Road
----- Other Trails
P Parking
▲ Summit
⅃ᔓ Scenic Overlook

ranger cabin
chimney and
foundation

to ski trail

tower

Okemo Mountain (Ludlow Mountain)

A final push straight up the moderate pitch brings you to the cross-mountain section of trail at 1.6 miles.

Walk south over undulating ground high on the mountainside, and cross muddy areas on wide, flat step stones. At 2.4 miles, a small outlook opens to the north and west. Coolidge Range, including Killington Peak (4,219 feet), Vermont's second highest, extends north. To the west, a gap allows VT 103 and the railroad to pass out of the Green Mountains and into the Vermont Valley, beyond which the Taconic Mountains rise. The Taconics were pushed up millions of years before the Greens and have weathered into steep-sided, round-topped humps that extend from the Champlain lowlands south along the Vermont–New York border and through western Massachusetts and Connecticut (where they are generally lumped in with the neighboring Berkshire Mountains).

Continue across the mountain, climbing moderately as the forest becomes more boreal, with bunchberry and Canada mayflower growing beneath paper birch, spruce, and fir. About 0.25 mile below the summit, Healdville Trail curves left and climbs steeply, skirting a tall rock ledge and winding through a damp boreal forest. Look for the ghostly Indian pipe sprouting from the shady forest floor here. Arriving on the summit ridge, descend gradually to a stone chimney in a clearing, backed by the moss-covered foundation of the former forest ranger cabin. Continue 25 feet farther to the summit spur trail on the right. Follow this spur trail up a short rocky pitch to the fire tower.

The roofed cab of the tower provides an immense view over southern Vermont. Beyond the chairlifts and slopes of the Okemo ski area, Ludlow Village extends east along the valley. The massive ridge of Mount Ascutney (3,099 feet) dominates the northeastern horizon. Lake Ninevah rests in a high basin to the north, with Salt Ash Mountain (3,286 feet) and the Coolidge Range beyond it. Due west, White Rocks National Recreation Area covers the high ground, with its scenic hikes to White Rocks Ice Beds (Trip 13) and lovely Little Rock Pond (Trip 12). South Mountain (3,179 feet) is the appropriately named bump close by to the south, with Bromley Mountain (Trip 7) and Stratton Mountain (3,940 feet) in the southwest beyond it.

Return downhill the way you hiked up.

That cute, blaze-orange critter creeping across the forest floor is a red eft, the juvenile stage of the eastern newt. Its color is a warning to predators that toxins make it an unsavory snack.

DID YOU KNOW?

The 4.5-mile auto road up Okemo Mountain and the fire tower and ranger cabin were built in the 1930s by Civilian Conservation Corps crews. The auto road can be biked or driven in summer, but it's the mountain's longest ski trail in winter.

MORE INFORMATION

Healdville Trail is open to foot travel only. It is closed during mud season, from snowmelt to around the third week in May. Okemo State Forest, Vermont Department of Forests, Parks and Recreation, 100 Mineral Street, Suite 304, Springfield, VT 05156; 802-289-0603; vtstateparks.com.

NEARBY

Swim, picnic, hike, and rent a camping cabin at Camp Plymouth on Echo Lake, 8 miles north, where group camping is available. Individual campsites are available at Gifford Woods State Park, 25 miles north; Ascutney State Park, 27 miles east; or Emerald Lake State Park, 27 miles southwest. Food and shops are in Ludlow, 5 miles east.

Looking more fungus than plant, clusters of Indian pipe pop up from leaf litter throughout summer.

15

MOUNT ASCUTNEY

Cascades and lookout ledges provide scenic rest spots along this challenging hike to the top of southeastern Vermont's most recognizable landmark.

DIRECTIONS

From the junction of US 5 and VT 44 in Windsor, follow VT 44 west for 3.3 miles. Make a left hairpin turn onto VT 44A (Back Mountain Road) and travel 0.2 mile to an Ascutney State Park parking lot (space for about 10 cars) on the right, marked by a small sign, Windsor Trail Parking, on the opposite side of the road. *GPS coordinates: 43° 27.42′ N, 72° 25.33′ W.*

TRAIL DESCRIPTION

Mount Ascutney (3,099 feet) towers over the hills of the Connecticut River valley, its granite and syenite dome—once the magma inside a volcano—more durable than the landscape around it and therefore slower to wear down. The steep sides of the mountain have long drawn adventurers whose marks remain: an auto road (still in use), ski area (closed), and stone hut (now just a foundation). Five hiking trails ascend from points around the dome and converge along the summit ridgeline. Windsor Trail ascends the northeast side, climbing steadily and often steeply past numerous points of interest on its way to an observation tower for spectacular views over the treetops.

From the parking area, follow a mowed path uphill through a field and enter the woods on a white-blazed trail. Pass through hardwoods and sumac to enter a dim hemlock stand, where the trail comes alongside a steep ravine. Windsor Trail follows the right side of this stream valley for about a mile, climbing steadily. Hemlocks give

LOCATION
Windsor, VT

RATING
Strenuous

DISTANCE
5.2 miles

ELEVATION GAIN
2,450 feet

ESTIMATED TIME
4 hours

MAPS
USGS Windsor, VT-NH

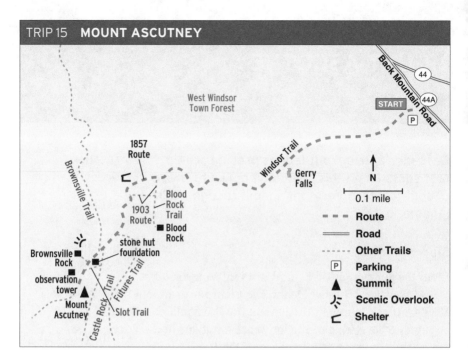

West Windsor
Town Forest

START

44

44A

1857
Route

Windsor Trail

Gerry
Falls

N

0.1 mile

Brownsville Trail

Blood
Rock
Trail

1903
Route

Blood
Rock

stone hut
foundation

Brownsville
Rock

Rock

observation
tower

Mount
Ascutney

Castle Rock Trail

Futures Trail

Slot Trail

- - - Route
=== Road
----- Other Trails
P Parking
▲ Summit
⦚ Scenic Overlook
⌐ Shelter

way to hardwoods as you ascend, and views of Mountain Brook become more common as the ravine becomes less deep. At 0.8 mile, a side trail leads left to a view of the long, cascading tumble of Gerry Falls. Use caution on the slick ledges if you explore along the stream.

After ascending a short, steep distance above the falls, cross the stream with the help of ropes strung at hand height between trees and continue ascending over slippery slab. Windsor Trail zigzags across Mountain Brook several more times and then heads right to cross a hillside littered with large chunks of rock. A steep, rocky climb leads to the junction of two sections of Windsor Trail at 1.6 miles: The 1857 route leads right, and the 1903 route goes left. (The two legs rejoin in 0.2 mile.) Go right on the 1857 route. After 0.1 mile, the open front of a log shelter appears, jutting from the steep hillside. The trail veers left, climbing close to the impressive stone chimney as it ascends the slope above. A couple of switchbacks bring you to the upper junction with the 1903 route. Stay right.

Climb over roots and mossy rocks for 0.2 mile to reach the junction of Futures Trail on your left. Go right for 0.2 mile more, ascending switchbacks to a bore-al-forest ridge and a little rock-walled bowl in the mountainside. Castle Rock Trail departs left; stay on Windsor Trail and climb a short pitch to the right, meeting Brownsville Trail at the top. Stay left and climb another 0.1 mile to arrive at the stone-hut foundation, 2.3 miles into the hike. From the right side of the clearing, walk 200 feet down a spur trail to find wide western views from Brownsville Rock.

Continuing along the ridge on Windsor Trail, pass Slot Trail on the left and climb a small slope to the observation tower at 2.5 miles. From its open platform, you can see across New Hampshire and Vermont, north into Quebec and south into Massachusetts. The Connecticut River slips in and out of view between the hills, and if you're lucky, you may see a hang glider launching from the southwest side of the mountain. The southern view is dominated by a cell tower rising from the trees around Ascutney's true summit, 0.1 mile farther along the trail.

Return downhill the way you ascended. For variety, go right onto the 1903 route, which has the same mileage as the 1857 route. Blood Rock Trail extends south 0.3 mile from the 1903 route to a nice view east and north from an uncomfortably angled slope above a cliff. (The origin of the ominous name of the outlook is less dramatic than you might guess: According to the Dartmouth Outing Club, a climber cut his hand trying to carve his initials in the rock.) If you check out the view from Blood Rock, add 0.6 mile to your total trip distance.

DID YOU KNOW?

According to Frank H. Clark's book *Glimpses of Ascutney* (1905), the mountain's original road and stone hut were built in 1825 in anticipation of a visit by the

Mount Ascutney's many trail networks, deep woods, ravines, and high summit ridge make it a premier destination for hikers, skiers, mountain bikers, and hang gliders.

French general Lafayette. Due to a change in his travel itinerary, Lafayette never ascended the mountain.

MORE INFORMATION

Windsor Trail is maintained by Ascutney Trails Association, P.O. Box 147, Windsor, VT 05089; ascutneytrailsassociation.org.

NEARBY

Take a dip in the Black River's Twenty Foot Hole, 10 miles west, off Tyson Road in Reading. Camp at Mount Ascutney State Park, 2.5 miles south, where less ambitious hikers can drive the auto road to within an easy mile of the summit. For food, head into Windsor, 4 miles northeast.

16

PICO PEAK

Traverse rich hardwoods full of wildflowers, open birch glades, and a boreal ridgeline on this loop hike around the peak.

DIRECTIONS

From the junction of US 4 and VT 100 in Killington, head west on US 4 for 2.3 miles to the parking lot at the Appalachian Trail/Long Trail crossing (space for about 25 cars) on the left. *GPS coordinates: 43° 39.97' N, 72° 50.96' W.*

TRAIL DESCRIPTION

Sometimes you hike for big views, and sometimes you hike just because the trail is lovely. This loop falls in the latter category. The western slope of Pico Peak (3,930 feet) hosts one of the sweetest stretches of the Long Trail. Its airy forests, diverse wildflowers, and undulating terrain almost mask the fact that you're ascending one of Vermont's tallest peaks (seventh highest, precisely). Pico's actual summit is less lovely, heavily developed, and with limited views. This loop hike combines the Appalachian Trail/Long Trail (AT/LT) and its former route, Sherburne Pass Trail, to circle Pico's summit, taking in the outstanding beauty on the shoulders of this big mountain and bypassing the top. (Peakbaggers can climb a 0.4-mile spur trail to the true summit.) The hike can be done in either direction. I prefer the longer climb up the AT/LT because it's an enjoyable ascent through distractingly beautiful terrain. Near the end of the loop, food and drink await at the Inn at Long Trail before the final 0.8-mile road walk downhill.

From the parking lot, the AT/LT and Catamount Trail follow a path alongside US 4 for a short distance before turning left to enter the woods. After crossing a bridge, Catamount Trail departs to the right; stay left and begin a gentle climb. Flat stretches roll out between moderate

LOCATION
Mendon and Killington, VT

RATING
Strenuous

DISTANCE
7.6 miles

ELEVATION GAIN
1,600 feet

ESTIMATED TIME
4 hours

MAPS
USGS Pico Peak

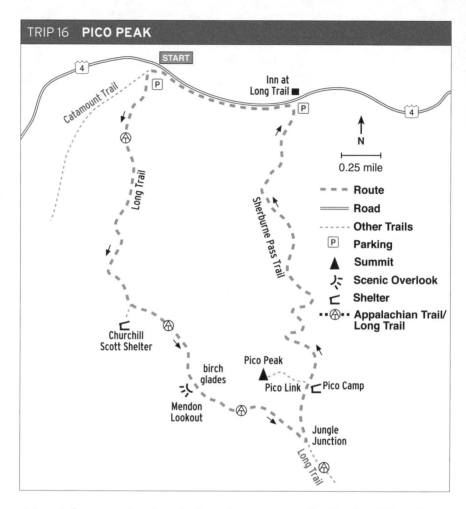

START

4

Catamount Trail

P

Long Trail

Inn at
Long Trail ■

P

4

N

0.25 mile

- - - **Route**
=== **Road**
···· **Other Trails**
P **Parking**
▲ **Summit**
⅄ **Scenic Overlook**
⊏ **Shelter**
··⊛·· **Appalachian Trail/
Long Trail**

Sherburne Pass Trail

Churchill
Scott Shelter

birch
glades

Pico Peak
▲

Pico Link

Pico Camp ⊏

Mendon
Lookout

Jungle
Junction

Long Trail

rising pitches as you head south along the mountainside. Blue-bead lily, trillium, and false Solomon's seal grow amid ferns and hobblebush. The trail descends gradually into a damp area covered with thick clumps of jewelweed, blue cohosh, and Canada violets. From the moist slope, the trail climbs into a drier hardwood forest where the trees are widely spaced and the undergrowth is low. Watch for stinging wood nettle but also the delicate Virginia waterleaf and sweet cicely.

Saplings again thicken the understory as you crest the hillside, and the AT/LT curves sharply left to mount the ridge. Indian cucumber's double-decker leaves rise on tall stems from club moss as you wind uphill through erratic boulders. Bending right again, the trail flattens across a bench then drops steeply into a gully to cross a stream before climbing switchbacks out the other side.

At 1.9 miles, a short spur trail leads right to Churchill Scott Shelter and marks the beginning of one of the more interesting sections of this hike. Paper birch now starts to dominate the forest, and as the trail ascends onto a high shoulder of the mountain, the entire forest becomes white trunks. Ferns wave in the breeze between the widely spaced trees, and Mendon Lookout, on the right, provides an obstructed view west to the Taconics.

Rather suddenly, the AT/LT leaves the paper birches and enters a spruce-fir forest. It rolls gently uphill to its highest point, 3,550 feet, and follows the contour of the hillside briefly before descending to Jungle Junction at 3.8 miles. The AT/LT southbound goes right here; turn left onto Sherburne Pass Trail. A flat, 0.4-mile walk through boreal woods and across a ski trail leads to the historical Pico Camp, which perches on the hill, its windows affording views of Killington (4,219 feet) and Ascutney (3,099 feet) peaks. (Behind the cabin, Pico Link leads steeply up an eroded trail to the summit.)

For 0.5 mile from Pico Camp, Sherburne Pass Trail crosses the hillside; it then descends briefly on a ski trail and reenters the woods. From here, the descent is rocky, rooty, and mostly moderate with some steep eroded pitches. At 5.5 miles, a small stream magnified by Tropical Storm Irene gouged a massive gully in 2011. Continue downhill, passing a bootleg trail on the left at 6 miles and skittering down bedrock to a flat, straight exit from the woods into the parking lot across from the Inn at Long Trail. Turn left on US 4 and descend 0.8 mile to the trailhead.

Pico Camp provides a welcome shelter and a great view south in any season. Photo by Silvia Cassano.

DID YOU KNOW?

The rich woods on the west side of Pico support many plants with edible and medicinal properties, such as sarsaparilla, blue-bead lily, Indian cucumber, jewelweed, bunchberry, and nettle. To learn more, consult a reputable field guide to edible plants.

MORE INFORMATION

The Long Trail, Sherburne Pass Trail, and their shelters are maintained by the Green Mountain Club, 4711 Waterbury–Stowe Road, Waterbury Center, VT 05677; 802-244-7037; greenmountainclub.org. Part of Pico's hillside is in the Green Mountain National Forest, 231 N. Main Street, Rutland, VT 05701; 802-747-6700; www.fs.usda.gov/gmfl.

NEARBY

Camp in an old-growth forest at Gifford Woods State Park on VT 100, 3 miles northeast. Chittenden Reservoir has paddling and swimming with spectacular mountain views, 11 miles northwest. Trails around the reservoir are good for cross-country skiing, as is Catamount Trail. In addition to the restaurant at the Inn at Long Trail, more food options are found along Killington Road, 2.5 miles east, and on US 4 and in downtown Rutland, 8 miles west.

CENTRAL VERMONT

Vermont meteorologists often refer to changes in the weather happening north or south of Route 2 or Route 4, because these corridors approximately define the geography of central Vermont. From Lake Champlain to the Connecticut River, the broad middle of the state is about 60 miles wide and stretches about 55 miles north to south. The Green Mountains dominate this section, with their highest spine running just west of the center and parallel ranges descending on either side toward the eastern and western lowlands.

Lake Champlain forms the western border of the state here, but it is not the broad, dark expanse that usually comes to mind when the lake is mentioned.

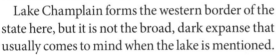

Instead, it looks more like a wide river along the shore of central Vermont, stretching about 2 miles across near Vergennes and narrowing to a snaky channel at its southern tail, where it slips by the cliffs of Buckner Preserve (Trip 18). Champlain's waters, which support a variety of native and introduced plants and animals, are an important migratory stopover for many birds. The rolling expanse of the Champlain lowlands is the "banana belt" of Vermont, warmer and more fertile than most of the rest of the state, and consequently has an ecological and human history that is intertwined as far back as the departure of the last glacier, 11,000 years ago. The Taconic Mountains so prominent in southern Vermont extend northward into the Champlain Valley with occasional cliffy prominences, such as Snake Mountain (Trip 23), but for the most part they are overshadowed by the dominance of the surrounding farmland and the much more eye-catching Green Mountains to the east and Adirondacks across the lake. The state's longest river, Otter Creek, and the wide, turbid Dead Creek flow north side by side through the southern Champlain lowlands, draining the valley into the lake and providing miles of shoreline and wetland habitats, as well as paddle-craft recreation.

East of the Champlain lowlands, the front range of the Green Mountains rises steeply, making a dramatic departure from the relatively flat valley floor. From there, mostly parallel ranges stack up to the east, covering the middle of the state with a wide swath of high land. The northern half of the Green Mountain

National Forest encompasses a large chunk of this landscape, accompanied by numerous state forests. Breadloaf, Bristol Cliffs, and Joseph Battell Wilderness Areas protect more than 41,000 acres of forest and crag, including the rare plants of Mount Horrid's Great Cliff (Trip 21). Moosalamoo National Recreation Area supports a wide variety of activities on almost 16,000 acres near Lake Dunsmore, such as watching hawk migrations from Rattlesnake Cliffs (Trip 20). The Appalachian Trail and the Long Trail part ways below Deer Leap (Trip 17), and the latter continues north parallel to the ski-specific Catamount Trail. In the northern part of central Vermont, two peaks, Mount Abraham (Trip 25) and Camel's Hump (Trip 27), are high enough to support small above-treeline areas where rare arctic plants grow.

The smaller Braintree and Northfield mountain ranges—both part of the third range of the Green Mountains—run parallel east of the big peaks, giving way to the unorganized hills of the Piedmont in eastern central Vermont. Although the Piedmont summits are smaller and less popular with hikers than the main range of the Green Mountains, there are some lovely small peaks, such as Wright's Mountain (Trip 29), and a few notable larger ones, such as Spruce Mountain (Trip 30) in the Granite Hills. Appropriately named, as their provenance is closer to the granitic White Mountains of New Hampshire than the Green Mountains, some Granite Hills reach more than 3,000 feet and provide a large area of prime recreation in Groton State Forest.

The big, placid Connecticut River forms the eastern border of Vermont. The water mostly snakes through floodplain fields in central Vermont and then slowly backs up behind Wilder Dam in White River Junction. Hikers on Bald Top Mountain (Trip 28) get a good overview of the region known as the Upper Valley, a place defined by the geography of the river more than by the state line dividing it.

17

DEER LEAP

This short hike to a rocky promontory gives close-up views of the Coolidge Range towering over Sherburne Pass.

DIRECTIONS

From the junction of VT 100 and US 4 in Killington, follow US 4 west 1.5 miles to a parking area (space for 30 cars) on the left, across from the Inn at Long Trail. *GPS coordinates:* 43° 39.84′ N, 72° 49.94′ W.

TRAIL DESCRIPTION

Where US 4 crosses the height of land at Sherburne Pass, Deer Leap's cliffs seem to rise straight out of the Inn at Long Trail. Getting to the cliffs involves circling behind the outcrop and approaching from the more gradual northern side. Although earlier generations of hikers scaled the steeps more directly, that route is no longer available due to erosion and danger, as well as to its more recent preservation as Abenaki sacred space. The Sherburne Pass and Deer Leap Mountain trails to the outlook have rocky, uneven footing, but the short distance and gradual rise make the hike suitable for children ages 5 and older who can reliably understand the safety precautions needed at the top. The 100-foot drop from the edge of the cliff appears suddenly; bring a leash for your dog.

From the parking area, Sherburne Pass Trail extends on both sides of US 4; it is the renamed former route of the Appalachian Trail (AT) and Long Trail (LT). Cross US 4 to the northern trailhead on the far right side of the Inn at Long Trail. At first, the blue-blazed Sherburne Pass Trail parallels the road below, gaining elevation gradually as it crosses jumbles of rocks along the hillside. At 0.3 mile, a gentle left curve steers the route deeper into the woods. Climbing easily through an open hardwood

LOCATION
Killington, VT

RATING
Easy to Moderate

DISTANCE
2 miles

ELEVATION GAIN
430 feet

ESTIMATED TIME
1.5 hours

MAPS
USGS Pico Peak;
www.fs.usda.gov/gmfl

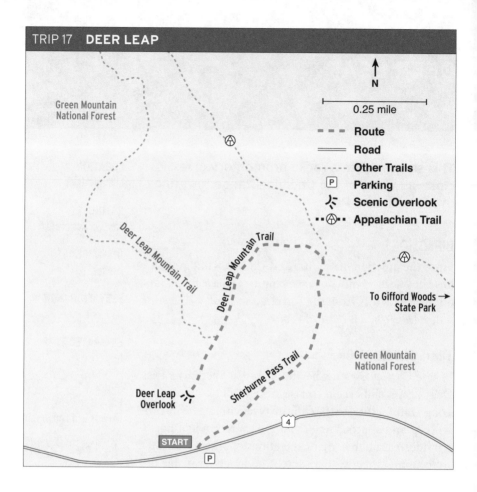

Green Mountain
National Forest

N

0.25 mile

- - - Route
=== Road
----- Other Trails
P Parking
Scenic Overlook
Appalachian Trail

Deer Leap Mountain Trail

Deer Leap Mountain Trail

To Gifford Woods →
State Park

Green Mountain
National Forest

Sherburne Pass Trail

Deer Leap
Overlook

4

START

P

forest, Sherburne Pass Trail arrives at a junction at 0.5 mile. The AT north to
Maine heads right; stay straight, following the white-blazed southbound AT for
200 feet across a flat bench then turn left onto Deer Leap Mountain Trail, once
again following blue blazes.

The route now curves south toward the cliffs, climbing a hardwood hillside.
As the trail levels out on top of this knoll, it enters an enchanting forest of widely
spaced spruce and paper birch trunks. Weaving between them, cross the flat top
of the hill and descend over rooty, rocky ground. Look for birch roots arching
out of the dirt; their bark is surprisingly black, with striking red stripes. Paper
birch is distinguishable from its yellow and gray relatives by its sheets of peeling bark. Paper birch is often called white birch—a name also used sometimes
for gray birch—or canoe birch, since its bark is used to construct traditional
Abenaki boats.

The woods become thick with spruce and fir as you descend from the knoll
to a trail junction. Deer Leap Mountain Trail curves sharply downhill on your
right. Stay straight on Deer Leap Overlook Spur, continuing over rocky terrain.

A boardwalk and wooden steps facilitate the last, steep descent to the overlook. Keep children and dogs close as you leave the woods; the edges of Deer Leap are steep.

Dominating the view across Sherburne Pass are the ski trails and wooded slopes of Pico Peak (3,930 feet). Over Pico's eastern shoulder, the top of the ski trails at Killington are visible farther south. Killington Peak (4,219 feet) is the second tallest in Vermont and anchors the Coolidge Range, a section of the Green Mountains stretching south from US 4, connecting the southern and northern tracts of the Green Mountain National Forest. Catamount Trail, a winter-travel version of the Long Trail, parallels the combined route of the AT and LT through the Coolidge Range, although it stays at lower elevations.

Nearby in the west, Blue Ridge Mountain (3,259 feet) rises in a solitary hump. US 4 curves between Blue Ridge and East Mountain (2,350 feet) as the road descends toward Rutland in the Vermont Valley, a long, narrow lowland running north–south between the Green and Taconic mountains.

Return downhill the way you hiked up.

Deer Leap's overlook gives hikers a view of majestic Coolidge Range, including Pico Peak.

DID YOU KNOW?

"One could do worse than be a swinger of birches." In his poem "Birches," Robert Frost described the remarkable flexibility of birch trunks and a couple of reasons—factual and fanciful—why you may see them arched, their branches sweeping the forest floor.

MORE INFORMATION

Deer Leap is within the Green Mountain National Forest, 231 N. Main Street, Rutland, VT 05701; 802-747-6700; www.fs.usda.gov/gmfl.

NEARBY

Camp in an old-growth forest at Gifford Woods State Park on VT 100, 2 miles northeast (or hike there on the AT from Sherburne Pass Trail). Chittenden Reservoir has paddling and swimming with spectacular mountain views, 12 miles northwest. Trails around the reservoir are good for cross-country skiing, as is Catamount Trail. In addition to the Irish pub at the Inn at Long Trail, there are restaurants, grocery stores, and shops along Killington Road, 1.5 miles east, and on US 4 and in downtown Rutland, 9 miles west.

18

BUCKNER MEMORIAL PRESERVE

This loop hike follows cliffs through a parklike forest that is home to rare species and overlooks the southern reach of Lake Champlain.

DIRECTIONS

Although the trailhead is in Vermont, you must drive through New York to reach it. Traveling west on US 4, 5.1 miles after entering New York from Vermont, cross railroad tracks. Take the second right after the tracks (0.2 mile west of them) onto NY 9A, which is not well marked. Go 0.9 mile, to the end of the road, and turn left onto NY 9. Drive 0.2 mile and take the first right onto NY 10/Doig Street. After 0.5 mile, where NY 10 curves right, bear left onto an unmarked dirt road and follow it 0.1 mile over the Poultney River, reentering Vermont. After crossing the bridge, go left on Galick Road and follow it 0.7 mile to a small pullout (space for about 3 cars) at Tim's Trail on the right. *GPS coordinates:* 43° 34.41′ N, 73° 24.26′ W.

TRAIL DESCRIPTION

The Helen W. Buckner Memorial Preserve at Bald Mountain sits on an ecologically rich peninsula of Vermont that dips into New York, defined by the Poultney River and a long, narrow arm of Lake Champlain. The 4,010-acre preserve provides a habitat for a wide array of rare and uncommon species: 11 animals, 18 plants, and 15 natural community types. Some species are notable for their general rarity, such as peregrine falcons and bald eagles; others are rare or unusual elsewhere in Vermont, with this landscape representing the very northern extent of the habitat of chestnut and bur oaks, timber rattlesnakes, and five-lined skinks—Vermont's only lizard.

LOCATION
West Haven, VT

RATING
Moderate

DISTANCE
2.6 miles

ELEVATION GAIN
240 feet

ESTIMATED TIME
2.5 hours

MAPS
USGS Whitehall, NY

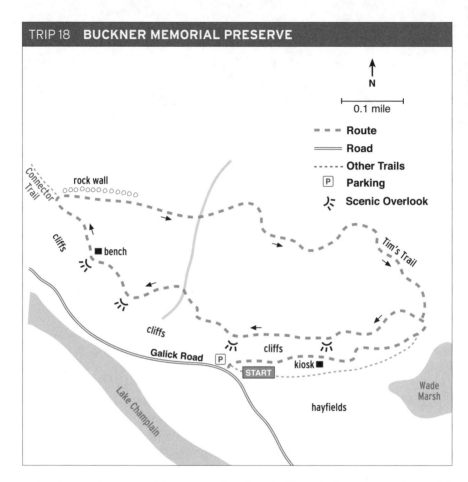

On the southern tip of the peninsula, a band of low cliffs supports a beautiful dry oak/hickory/hop hornbeam forest that is unusual in Vermont. Tim's Trail explores the talus slope beneath the cliffs before climbing through a variety of forest types on top. Southern-facing outcrops are the preferred basking spots for reptiles that need to absorb solar heat; watch for snakes as you walk. Rattlesnakes are reserved unless they are stepped on or intentionally harassed and will not strike unless they feel threatened. The land's owner, The Nature Conservancy (TNC), recommends the following precautions: wearing long pants and ankle-high boots; inspecting the ground before you sit; and, if you encounter a rattlesnake, backing away slowly and giving the snake a 20-foot berth. Other than service animals, dogs are not allowed on the Buckner Preserve. The interesting terrain and likelihood of spotting a variety of animals makes this hike appealing for kids ages 6 and older.

Begin the hike following green and yellow TNC markers along talus slopes at the base of the cliffs. A kiosk with brochure maps is located 0.2 mile down the trail. At 0.4 mile, the trail curves right and appears to go both directions on a two-track. To the right, the mowed path goes back to the parking lot along the edge of the field. Go left over bog bridges to the intersection of the two ends of Tim's Trail loop. Go left on the southern leg and climb for a short distance to arrive on top of the cliffs, where grasslike sedges spread beneath widely spaced, shaggy trunks of hickory, hop hornbeam, cedar, and oak. Climbing along the edge of the cliffs, you will pass viewpoints overlooking Wade Marsh in the field below, as well as the Champlain Canal and Whitehall, New York, in the distance. Use caution moving around the edge of the cliff.

After passing directly above the trailhead at 0.8 mile into your hike, Tim's Trail turns sharply right, crosses an open area, and descends into a dim hemlock forest. Cross a small stream and resume climbing through a wide hickory meadow, entering an area where tree trunks are scorched from a 2012 fire. A bench at 1.2 miles looks out over steep mountainsides that drop dramatically to Lake Champlain's South Bay.

From here, the trail rises 0.1 mile to the junction with Connector Trail on the left. Turn right to stay on Tim's Trail, and follow an impressive stone wall downhill, passing eventually into a thicker mixed forest with beech and hemlock. For 0.9 mile from the Connector Trail junction, Tim's Trail descends through a varied forest and crosses two small streams. Joining a two-track, it curves around the edge of a deep ravine and drops back to the loop junction.

Northern leopard frogs may leap out of your path atop the cliffs of Tim's Trail.

Return across bog bridges and follow either the trail along the base of the cliffs or the parallel path along the field edge to the trailhead.

DID YOU KNOW?

Leopard frogs may jump out of your path as you hike here. Many of these spotted amphibians recently have been noted for their missing or deformed legs. Biologists have been studying them, using short aluminum fences you may notice along the field wetlands.

MORE INFORMATION

The Nature Conservancy owns the preserve: 575 Stone Cutters Way, Montpelier, VT 05602; 802-229-4425; nature.org/vermont.

NEARBY

Paddle on the Poultney River, 0.7 mile east. Camp, swim, and paddle at Bomoseen State Park, 15 miles northeast. A limited selection of food is available in Whitehall, New York, 2.5 miles south. More options are along VT 4A in Castleton, 14 miles east.

19

MOUNT INDEPENDENCE

Interpretive panels help you imagine the fort that once stood on this hill as you wander through regrown forest and fields, toward views across Lake Champlain.

DIRECTIONS

Go west on VT 73 from its junction with VT 22A in Orwell. After 0.3 mile, when VT 73 curves right, stay straight on Mount Independence Road. After 4.7 miles, stay on Mount Independence Road around a sharp left turn uphill, toward the parking area (space for 100 cars) for Mount Independence State Historic Site. *GPS coordinates:* 43° 49.07′ N, 73° 23.08′ W.

TRAIL DESCRIPTION

In 1776, Mount Independence (302 feet) was cleared of trees, topped with a star-shaped fort, and covered with buildings to support American soldiers. Today the only building on the reforested hill next to Lake Champlain is the boat-shaped Visitors Center Museum, with a swooping roofline and curved walls. The terrain is mild, with gentle elevation changes, appropriate for hikers of varying ages and abilities.

To start, stop by the museum to purchase an entry ticket ($5 per adult; no fee for children ages 14 and younger) and pick up an interpretive map. Checklists of the mountain's birds and wildflowers are also available. Find the Baldwin trailhead to the left of the building. Named for the chief engineer of the Mount Independence defenses, this wide, compacted path is suitable for outdoor wheelchairs. Baldwin's diary provided important clues about this American fortification. You will ascend gradually through open grass and enter the forest, where loose strips of bark on hop hornbeam and shagbark hickory make it seem like the trees are shedding.

LOCATION
Orwell, VT

RATING
Easy to Moderate

DISTANCE
3 miles

ELEVATION GAIN
200 feet

ESTIMATED TIME
2 hours

MAPS
USGS Ticonderoga NY-VT; handout maps at museum

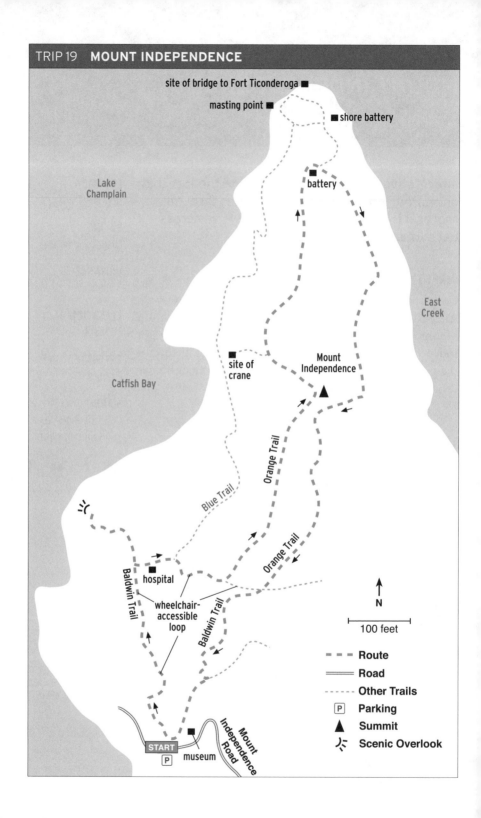

site of bridge to Fort Ticonderoga ■

masting point ■

■ shore battery

■ battery

Lake
Champlain

East
Creek

■ site of
crane

Mount
Independence
▲

Catfish Bay

Orange Trail

Blue Trail

Orange Trail

Baldwin Trail

■ hospital

wheelchair-
accessible
loop

Baldwin Trail

N

100 feet

START
P
museum

Mount
Independence
Road

- - - **Route**
═══ **Road**
····· **Other Trails**
P **Parking**
▲ **Summit**
ツ **Scenic Overlook**

Baldwin Trail flattens as it heads north along the ridge and, after a short distance, comes to a fork. Go left to a viewing area on a promontory. Look for bald eagles soaring over the lake here. While still endangered in Vermont, bald eagles are slowly returning to nest.

The reconstructed walls of Fort Ticonderoga are visible across the narrow stretch of Lake Champlain. When the British came to attack in autumn 1776, the sight of the combined fortresses caused them to retreat. They returned the next summer and took over Mount Independence, but when they learned of the British general John Burgoyne's surrender in Saratoga that autumn, they burned all the buildings to the ground and abandoned the fort.

Return to the Baldwin Trail fork and go left, heading east to the middle of the peninsula. Pass Blue Trail on the left; a short distance farther, turn left onto the wide, grassy Orange Trail. This tree-lined swath leads along the height of land to a grassy clearing at the summit of Mount Independence, the center of the former star fort. The path continues northwest into a deciduous forest dotted with historic sites and to a clearing at the tip of the peninsula. Cannons were aimed at the lake from this high point. Return to the head of the clearing, where Orange

Just across Lake Champlain (and the Vermont–New York state line) is Fort Ticonderoga: a large, eighteenth-century, star-shaped fort built by the French during the Seven Years' War.

Trail continues left, back into the forest. You immediately arrive at a fork. Go right to return south toward the museum, gradually climbing the side of Mount Independence, surrounded by red oak, white pine, and eastern red cedar.

Orange Trail ends at a T junction with Baldwin Trail. Go right and immediately left, downhill on the return leg of Baldwin Trail. Descending through the woods, you will pass the former locations of a storehouse and a blockhouse. A spur trail leads left; stay straight to return to the grassy field next to the museum.

DID YOU KNOW?

More than 300 shipwrecks are scattered along the bottom of Lake Champlain, including at least two near the bridge that once connected Mount Independence and Fort Ticonderoga. The Lake Champlain Underwater Historic Preserve provides public access for divers who want to explore the wrecks, and it protects the artifacts from anchor damage and looting.

MORE INFORMATION

Camping and overnight parking are not allowed. Pets must be leashed. Digging, collecting any materials (including plants), and using metal detectors are all forbidden. The grounds of Mount Independence State Historic Site are open year-round; in winter the parking lot is not plowed, and parking on the edge of Mount Independence Road is prohibited by the town. The museum is open from Memorial Day through mid-October, 9:30 A.M. to 5 P.M. daily; trail fees are charged during operating hours. Mount Independence State Historic Site Administrator, 8149 VT 17W, Addison, VT 05491; 802-759-2412 or 802-948-2000 in season; historicsites.vermont.gov/directory/mount_independence.

NEARBY

Half Moon State Park, 23 miles southeast in Hubbardton, has paddling and swimming. Some food can be found in Orwell, 7 miles east, or in Benson, 12 miles south, with more options in Brandon, 19 miles east. The Lake Champlain Maritime Museum in Vergennes, 37 miles north, has full-size replicas of Colonial-era vessels on the lake, as well as a shipwreck tour.

20

RATTLESNAKE CLIFFS AND FALLS OF LANA

Tall waterfalls, exceptional views from a rocky promontory, and a wide array of activities within the 20,000-acre Moosalamoo National Recreation Area make this a hike not to miss.

DIRECTIONS

From the junction of US 7 and VT 125 south of Middlebury, follow US 7 south for 3.1 miles. Turn left onto VT 53 (Lake Dunmore Road) and go 4 miles to the Silver Lake parking area on the left (space for about 25 cars). *GPS coordinates:* 43° 54.01′ N, 73° 03.85′ W.

TRAIL DESCRIPTION

Rattlesnake Cliffs hover high above Lake Dunmore, providing views across the water to the Taconic and Adirondack mountain ranges. On the way up, a short side trail leads to an overlook of the spectacular Falls of Lana. The Moosalamoo National Recreation Area is a hub of recreation activities, providing places to hike, mountain bike, camp, cross-country ski, and even pick wild berries. The particular habitat needs of peregrine falcons and bluebirds, along with those of many other wildlife species, are supported within Moosalamoo. Rattlesnake Cliffs may be closed March 15 to August 1 if peregrine falcons are nesting in the area; check with Audubon Vermont (vt.audubon.org) or Green Mountain National Forest (www.fs.usda.gov/gmfl) for details. Kids ages 8 and older will enjoy the hike to Rattlesnake Cliffs, but keep in mind that both the outlook and the Falls of Lana have unprotected ledges.

From the parking area, start up the wide Silver Lake Trail. You may share this path with mountain bikers or the occasional utility truck. At 0.3 mile, the penstock (water pipe) from the power-generating impoundment of Silver

LOCATION
Salisbury, VT

RATING
Moderate

DISTANCE
4 miles

ELEVATION GAIN
1,029 feet

ESTIMATED TIME
3.5 hours

MAPS
USGS East Middlebury; www.fs.usda.gov/gmfl

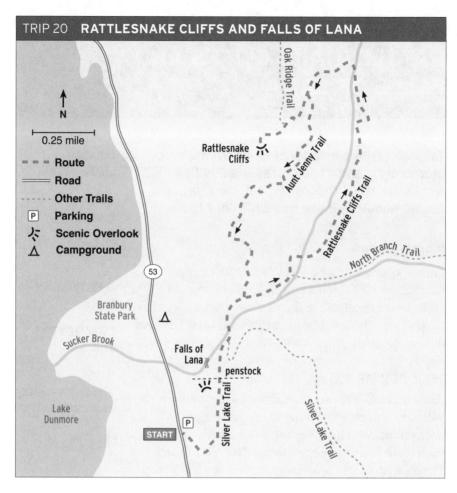

N

0.25 mile

- - - **Route**
—— **Road**
------- **Other Trails**
P **Parking**
☀ **Scenic Overlook**
△ **Campground**

Oak Ridge Trail

Rattlesnake Cliffs

Aunt Jenny Trail

Rattlesnake Cliffs Trail

North Branch Trail

53

Branbury State Park

Sucker Brook

△

Falls of Lana

penstock

Silver Lake Trail

Silver Lake Trail

Lake Dunmore

P

START

Lake passes overhead in a clearing. For a view across the gorge to the Falls of Lana, head 300 feet down the penstock's corridor to a fenced opening on the right. To continue uphill, pass under the penstock and follow Silver Lake Trail along the upper section of Sucker Brook as it tumbles toward the falls. The side of the brook is well worn by explorers looking for views of the falls; use caution if you venture downhill here.

With pretty cascades on the left and a tall mossy ledge on the right, Silver Lake Trail proceeds upstream to a trail junction at 0.5 mile. Turn left onto North Branch Trail. Cross Sucker Brook on a wide bridge and continue upstream on its left bank. At 0.7 mile, Aunt Jenny Trail forks to the left; this will be your return route. For now, stay right on North Branch Trail, climbing moderately for 0.2 mile through a young stand of birches speckled with hemlock saplings. At the next junction, turn left onto Rattlesnake Cliffs Trail.

Climb away from the river for a short distance then return to cross it on a bridge. The trail rises steeply out of the gorge, curving left at the top of the hill and paralleling the stream high above it. Hemlocks give way to a mixed-hardwood forest on the steady ascent. Watch for blue trail blazes at a sharp right curve away from the stream valley, where a bootleg trail continues straight uphill. Rattlesnake Cliffs Trail wends its way back to cross two branches of the stream and then crosses the hillside, passing the top of Aunt Jenny Trail. The trail narrows and scoots around rocks and logs before climbing a series of wooden steps through scrubby beech trees.

The remarkable Falls of Lana tumble in several tiers, with the uppermost pictured here.

Views appear intermittently through the branches on your left as you arrive at the junction of Oak Ridge Trail on your right. Stay left, descending slightly as you edge around the height of land to another junction. Rattlesnake Cliffs Trail makes a sharp left and heads downhill. From the southern-facing cliffs, Silver Lake shines in its high bowl, held back from tumbling into the valley by the thin wall of Chandler Ridge (1,500 feet). The Green Mountains rise above Silver Lake to the east, and Lake Dunmore stretches south to Fern Lake.

Exit the cliff area the way you came, returning to the intersection with Aunt Jenny Trail. Turn right onto Aunt Jenny Trail and follow blue blazes down the ridgeline. Turning right on a flat bench, follow a short section of old road then descend on a foot trail again through red oaks and beeches. A few white oaks mix with red where a discontinued trail heads uphill to the right. Aunt Jenny Trail edges around the top of a steep, hemlock-filled ravine that drops to Lake Dunmore then rejoins North Branch Trail. From here, hike out the way you came in.

DID YOU KNOW?

Loons nest on Lake Dunmore and Silver Lake. If you're lucky, you may hear their haunting vocalizations. The four distinct calls of the loon are the yodel, the tremolo, the wail, and the hoot. The yodel is a male's territorial call, while the tremolo—sometimes referred to as a "laugh"—is a warning or alarm. The long notes of the wail and the quiet hoot help the birds locate one another.

MORE INFORMATION

The Moosalamoo National Recreation Area is within the Green Mountain National Forest, Rochester Ranger District, 99 Ranger Road, Rochester, VT 05767; 802-767-4261. Moosalamoo is managed in partnership with the nonprofit Moosalamoo Association, P.O. Box 148, Brandon, VT 05733; moosalamoo.org.

NEARBY

The best recreation options around are right here in the Moosalamoo National Recreation Area and Branbury State Park. Excellent mountain-bike trails and campsites ring Silver Lake. Restaurants, grocery stores, shops, and cultural attractions are in downtown Middlebury, 8 miles northwest, and to a lesser degree in Brandon, 8 miles south.

21

MOUNT HORRID'S GREAT CLIFF

Rare plants and wide views await hikers on this rugged clifftop in the Joseph Battell Wilderness.

DIRECTIONS

US 7 and VT 73 coincide through the village of Brandon. From the southern junction of these two roads, head east on VT 73 for 7.7 miles to the U.S. Forest Service Brandon Gap parking area (space for 20 cars) on the right. *GPS coordinates:* 43° 50.382′ N, 72° 58.114′ W.

TRAIL DESCRIPTION

Mount Horrid's Great Cliff (2,860 feet) supports a remarkable diversity of life, including rare and uncommon plants, as well as peregrine falcon nesting sites. Some years, depending on where the falcons nest, the cliffs may be closed between March 15 and August 1 to protect the chicks. Check with Audubon Vermont (vt.audubon.org) or the Green Mountain National Forest (www.fs.usda.gov/gmfl) for details. The hike to the cliffs is relatively short but steep and rocky. Use caution on the cliff; the edge is sudden and unprotected.

From the parking area, cross VT 73 and follow a dirt path through chokecherries to a signed intersection and a kiosk. Beyond the signs, you enter the Joseph Battell Wilderness, an L-shaped tract bounded by Brandon Gap to the south and Middlebury Gap to the north. While the north–south leg of the L surrounds the Long Trail, the east–west leg of this Wilderness Area encompasses Monastery Mountain (3,224 feet) and Philadelphia Peak (3,203 feet), which together make up the longest roadless and trailless ridgeline in the Green Mountain National Forest. (*Note:* Wilderness Areas are designated by the U.S. Congress to provide retreats from civilization, where humans are visitors, and nature takes precedence. Natural

LOCATION
Goshen, VT

RATING
Moderate

DISTANCE
1.6 miles

ELEVATION GAIN
620 feet

ESTIMATED TIME
1.5 hours

MAPS
USGS Mount Carmel

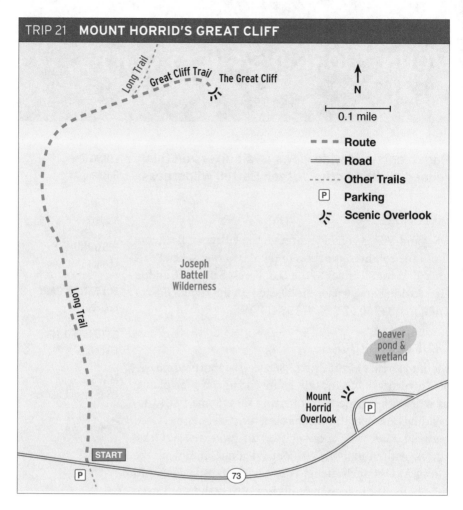

Long Trail

Great Cliff Trail   The Great Cliff

N

0.1 mile

= = = Route

===== Road

------ Other Trails

P   Parking

Scenic Overlook

Joseph
Battell
Wilderness

beaver
pond &
wetland

Long Trail

Mount
Horrid
Overlook

P

START

P   73

conditions dominate the character of the landscape, so travel may be slower as you encounter downed trees, few signs, or a lack of bridges across streams. This section of trail to the Great Cliffs, however, has clear signage at the single junction and no large streams to cross.)

Blazed in white, this route is part of the Long Trail (see "Thru-Hiking," page 30). The hike starts steeply on a rock-choked path through boulders and skinny striped maples (also called goosefoot maples for their large leaves' resemblance to webbed feet). The trail switches back and forth across the steep slope as it ascends from the road and then heads up the west side of the hill.

The climb moderates as the trail crosses to the east side of the hill and follows a smooth bedrock path through a grassy birch forest. After a short distance, the Great Cliff rises from the soil on your right, and the climbing gets steep again. Multiple rock staircases pass the ledge and ascend to the junction of the Long Trail and Great Cliff Trail. Go right onto the blue-blazed Great Cliff Trail, which climbs a short distance before flattening out. Exiting the forest, you pass through a band of ferns and goldenrod before stepping onto a narrow ledge with an uneven surface. Between the rocks, in pockets where soil has accumulated, mats of three-toothed cinquefoil grow.

Directly in front of you, a ridge running east–west rises steeply, cresting into several summit points; Goshen Mountain (3,292 feet) is the peak on the right. In the southeast, Round Mountain (3,342 feet) lifts its pointed summit skyward before sloping north over Corporation Mountain (3,142 feet). If you're lucky, you might spot a beaver or a moose in the wetlands directly below your perch.

Seventeen rare, threatened, or endangered plants have been reported on Mount Horrid over the years, many of them on and around Great Cliff. Sitting on the lookout, you are amid a number of interesting species. Northern single-spike sedge (sometimes called Scirpus-like sedge in Vermont) is rare in the state but widespread on Great Cliff. Among the common American mountain ash growing around Great Cliff is some uncommon showy mountain ash, with more rounded leaf tips and larger fruit. The best treat to stumble across may be blueberry bushes. Black bears, finding a good habitat in the remoteness of Joseph Battell Wilderness, would agree.

Return the way you hiked up.

Overlooking nearby Round Mountain, Mount Horrid's Great Cliff supports rare plants.

DID YOU KNOW?

The black bear is the smallest of the three North American bear species (brown and polar being the other two) and the only kind living in Vermont. While you are unlikely to see one of these elusive creatures, if you do, alert it to your presence by clapping, waving your arms, and talking then back away slowly.

MORE INFORMATION

No personal property may be left in the Joseph Battell Wilderness, and motorized or wheeled devices of any kind are not allowed. Green Mountain National Forest, 99 Ranger Road, Rochester, VT 05767; 802-767-4261; www.fs.usda.gov/gmfl. The Long Trail is maintained by the Green Mountain Club, 4711 Waterbury–Stowe Road, Waterbury Center, VT 05677; 802-244-7037; greenmountainclub.org. Audubon Vermont (vt.audubon.org) and the Vermont Fish and Wildlife Department (vtfishandwildlife.com) provide peregrine-falcon-related trail-closure information.

NEARBY

Branbury State Park on Lake Dunmore, 10.8 miles northwest, offers swimming and paddling. Both Brandon, 7.5 miles west, and Rochester, 9.9 miles east, have restaurants and shops.

22

ROBERT FROST TRAIL

This winding path through woods, wetlands, and berry fields is adorned with posted poems inspired by these landscapes.

DIRECTIONS

From the junction of US 7 and VT 125 south of Middlebury, head east on VT 125 for 6.2 miles. The trailhead parking area (space for about 10 cars) is on the right. *GPS coordinates: 43° 57.48′ N, 73° 00.67′ W.*

TRAIL DESCRIPTION

Two connected trail loops wander through varied landscapes that inspired the poet they honor and that, in turn, are augmented by his poems, mounted on posts throughout. Interpretive signs identify plants, while occasional benches offer the opportunity to linger along this short hike. The first loop, 0.3-mile, is wheelchair accessible, and the entire route is friendly to all ages of hikers. The Robert Frost Trail is a great place to explore on skis, with rolling terrain and a connector trail leading to Water Tower Trails, a series of cross-country ski loops. Dogs must be leashed.

From the cluster of signs near the bathroom at the trailhead, go right into the trees along a wide gravel path. After a short distance, past a bench and the first poem, the path becomes an elevated boardwalk traversing a wetland thick with alders. "A winter garden in an alder swamp," begins the poem posted here. Robert Frost (1874–1963), the winner of four Pulitzer Prizes, spent time almost every year from 1921 to 1963 in Ripton, and many of his poems include references to the local landscapes. Curving left, the walkway returns to gravel and meets a spur trail that leads to the second loop. The universally-accessible path curves

LOCATION
Ripton, VT

RATING
Easy

DISTANCE
1 mile

ELEVATION GAIN
30 feet

ESTIMATED TIME
45 minutes

MAPS
USGS East Middlebury;
www.fs.usda.gov/gmfl

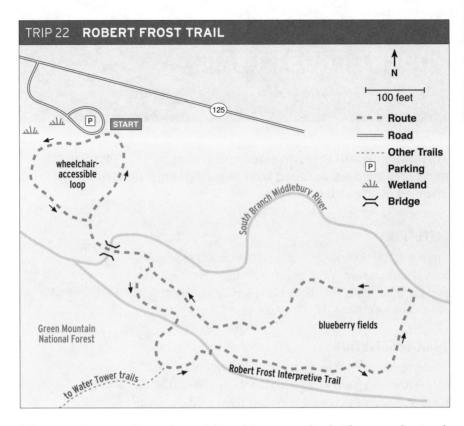

left; to continue on the trail, go right, taking a wooden bridge over the South Branch of the Middlebury River.

At the end of the bridge, enter a dim hemlock grove on a more natural footpath. The trail curves left, rising gently into a pine forest where it meets the second loop in a small clearing, where one of Frost's most famous works, "The Road Not Taken," is posted. Go right, away from the river. Trout lilies and ferns cover the forest floor between birches and spruces, and hobblebushes spread their large leaves alongside the path. Cross a small stream on a low bridge to reach a large wooden interpretive sign, where the poem "Nothing Gold Can Stay" accompanies a description of the fleeting woodland wildflowers found here: trillium, wood anemone, bunchberry, and spring beauty. From this panel, the path climbs gradually to a junction with a trail leading to Water Tower Trails. This junction has the highest elevation of the hike, and Robert Frost Trail now bends left and returns downhill, crossing the small brook a little farther upstream.

The path curves right to follow the stream through varied woods, with a beaked hazelnut tree identified alongside a gray birch and a muscly looking blue beech. (Also called ironwood, this tree is actually a member of the birch family.) Of the birch, Robert Frost observed: "The only native tree that dares to lean, / Relying on its beauty, to the air. / (Less brave perhaps than trusting are the fair.)"

The first loop of Robert Frost Trail is universally accessible and passes through an alder swamp, much like the one memorialized in Frost's poem posted on the boardwalk railing.

The trees give way to shrubs as you enter fields at the far eastern end of the trail loop. Blueberries and huckleberries attract many animals, including humans, to this open area, which the U.S. Forest Service maintains through prescribed burns. A bench and a rumination from the poem "The Black Cottage" are situated with a view north across fields and river to the steep slope of Breadloaf Mountain (3,835 feet). With almost 25,000 wooded and formerly logged acres, the Breadloaf Wilderness surrounding its namesake peak supports black bears and moose in considerable numbers.

Head downhill through the fields and curve left along the bank of the Middlebury River. An interpretive sign and the poem "The Last Mowing" address the succession of fields and forests before you arrive back at the beginning of this loop. Go right, retracing your steps to the shorter hiking loop on the other side of the river. There, go right to finish the hike on a gravel path leading to the parking area.

DID YOU KNOW?

Robert Frost taught on the nearby campus of Middlebury College's Bread Loaf School of English for 42 years, and the college maintains his Ripton farm as a National Historic Landmark.

MORE INFORMATION

The trail is in the Green Mountain National Forest, 231 N. Main Street, Rutland, VT 05701; 802-747-6700; www.fs.usda.gov/gmfl.

NEARBY

Swim, hike, mountain bike, and camp at Branbury State Park and the adjacent Moosalamoo National Recreation Area, 10 miles southwest. Food and shops are in Middlebury, 10 miles northwest.

23

SNAKE MOUNTAIN

Hike through a mature forest—rare in the Champlain lowlands—to panoramic views of Lake Champlain and the Adirondacks from summit cliffs.

DIRECTIONS

Follow VT 22A south 2.9 miles from its junction with VT 17 and turn left onto Wilmarth Road. Go 0.5 mile to a T intersection at Mountain Road. Turn left, toward a parking lot (space for 10 cars) on the left. *GPS coordinates:* 44° 02.57′ N, 73° 17.31′ W.

TRAIL DESCRIPTION

Snake Mountain's serpentine ridge slithers north–south through farmlands along Lake Champlain. The 1,287-foot mountain's sudden rise from the surrounding lowlands creates an island of mature hardwood forest in the midst of open fields and gives hikers an extraordinary view of the broad Champlain Valley. The Nature Conservancy's 81-acre Wilmarth Woods protects the forest on the mountain's west side, and Vermont Fish and Wildlife Department's 1,215-acre Snake Mountain Wildlife Management Area (WMA) conserves wildlife habitats along its crest. Some of the summit area may be closed to hikers if peregrine falcons are nesting; check with Audubon Vermont (vt.audubon.org) for current information. Dogs must be under direct control of their owners on Snake Mountain, and hunting is encouraged in the WMA, so wear orange during open seasons; find hunting season dates at vtfishandwildlife.com/hunt/seasons. This short hike is fun for kids ages 8 and older.

A metal gate across from the end of Wilmarth Road marks the Snake Mountain trailhead; cross a clearing beyond it and enter the woods on a wide trail heading east.

LOCATION
Addison, VT

RATING
Moderate

DISTANCE
3.6 miles

ELEVATION GAIN
900 feet

ESTIMATED TIME
2 hours

MAPS
USGS Snake Mountain

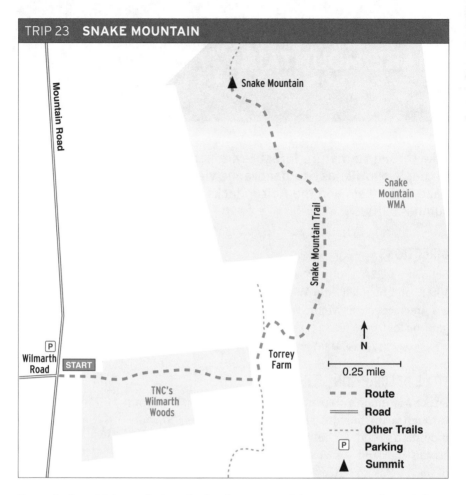

Snake Mountain

Snake Mountain Trail

Snake
Mountain
WMA

Mountain Road

Wilmarth
Road

START

P

Torrey
Farm

TNC's
Wilmarth
Woods

N

0.25 mile

- - - **Route**

====== **Road**

------ **Other Trails**

P **Parking**

▲ **Summit**

From the late 1700s until 1992, this land was part of the 200-acre Wilmarth family farm. This particular area was a woodlot and a shady cow pasture; today it is one of the largest stands of mature mesic red oak/northern hardwood forest in the Champlain lowlands. The trail passes through large beech and maple trees, some of which are 150 years old and host breeding cerulean warblers. Look for the bright-sky-blue back of the male and the more muted turquoise back of the female as they flit through the upper canopy, foraging for insects from spring through midsummer.

Snake Mountain Trail rises gradually on a rutted track. At 0.7 mile, the trail turns abruptly left at a T junction (no signs or blazes). You will encounter few directional signs on Snake Mountain, and logging activities may change the appearance of trail junctions; when in doubt, search for the most worn footpaths and for piles of brush or rows of rocks across one trail, providing a vague suggestion to choose the other path.

Heading north, Snake Mountain Trail climbs more steeply. After a very short distance, stay right at an unmarked fork, following red and blue blazes uphill.

The trail now heads eastward, entering the Snake Mountain Wildlife Management Area. Because the mountain is a small, rocky refuge of upland forest in an otherwise heavily farmed part of Vermont, it provides important wildlife habitats, including a white-tailed deer wintering area and a wetland near the summit known as Cranberry Bog. Signs indicate closed or sensitive areas to avoid. The trail turns north again and follows Snake Mountain's central ridgeline to the summit.

The hike becomes rolling and pleasant, passing several unmarked trail junctions. At a final junction, stay left, heading toward open sky along the western edge of the ridge. Snake Mountain Trail exits the woods and arrives on a concrete pad that once supported the Grand View Hotel.

The views south, west, and north are jaw-dropping. Immediately beneath you, a patchwork of farmland spreads in all directions, cut by the muddy, tree-lined bends of Dead Creek as it makes its way north to join Otter Creek before emptying into Lake Champlain. Across the lake, the foothills of the Adirondacks rise from the water, while the high peaks cut a jagged line across the sky. If you visit in autumn, Snake Mountain's quartzite cliffs provide an excellent seat from which to watch hawk migrations.

Return to the trailhead the way you climbed up.

Snake Mountain, like so many Taconic peaks, seems to pop straight up from Champlain Valley farmland, giving a big, dramatic view in exchange for a relatively small hiking effort.

DID YOU KNOW?

About 10,000 years ago, Snake Mountain was an island in the Champlain Sea, a temporary arm of the Atlantic Ocean. Marine life, such as seals and beluga whales, swam here, leaving behind skeletons that gave nineteenth-century settlers their first clues to the valley's oceanic past.

MORE INFORMATION

The first 0.5 mile of Snake Mountain Trail is managed by The Nature Conservancy's Vermont Chapter, 575 Stone Cutters Way, Montpelier, VT 05602; 802-229-4425; nature.org/vermont. Bicycles, motorized vehicles, camping, and fires are not allowed in Wilmarth Woods. The Snake Mountain Wildlife Management Area is administered by the Vermont Fish and Wildlife Department and is open to regulated hunting, trapping, hiking, and wildlife viewing. Motorized and wheeled vehicles, including mountain bikes, are prohibited in the WMA. Groups larger than ten individuals or associated with a commercial operation will need a special-use permit from the Fish and Wildlife Department, 1 National Life Drive, Montpelier, VT 05620; 802-828-1000; vtfishandwildlife.com.

NEARBY

Vermont Fish and Wildlife Department's Dead Creek Visitor Center is open from 8 A.M. to 4 P.M. on weekdays (and Tuesday through Sunday in September and October), 4.6 miles northwest on VT 17. Branbury State Park has lake swimming and the magnificent Falls of Lana (Trip 20), 25 miles southeast in Salisbury. Middlebury, 11.4 miles southeast, has restaurants, groceries, and a variety of shops.

24
SUNSET LEDGE

This rolling ridge hike on the Long Trail leads to western-facing ledges with magnificent views of Lake Champlain and the Adirondacks.

DIRECTIONS

From the intersection of VT 100 and Main Street in Warren, travel 0.7 mile south on VT 100. Turn right onto Lincoln Gap Road (labeled Lincoln Mountain Road in places) and follow it 4 miles to the Long Trail crossing at Lincoln Gap, where parking is along either side of the road. The height of land accommodates about 20 vehicles; a lower parking lot holds an additional 15. (Lincoln Gap Road is not maintained in winter; snowshoers should park at the gate and add 1.2 miles round-trip to the hike.) *GPS coordinates:* 44° 05.70′ N, 72° 55.70′ W.

LOCATION
Lincoln, VT

RATING
Easy

DISTANCE
2.2 miles

ELEVATION GAIN
387 feet

ESTIMATED TIME
1.5 hours

MAPS
USGS Lincoln

TRAIL DESCRIPTION

Sunset Ledge (2,811 feet) juts from the side of a gradually sloping ridge between Mount Grant (3,623 feet) and Lincoln Gap (2,424 feet). This section of the Long Trail undulates over rock slabs and through small hollows, making the walk almost as scenic and interesting as the broad views at the destination. Kids of most ages will enjoy scrambling along the ridgeline, after an initial steep pitch.

From Lincoln Gap, follow the Long Trail south into the Breadloaf Wilderness. The largest of Vermont's eight designated Wilderness Areas, Breadloaf encompasses almost 25,000 acres of the main ridge of the Green Mountains between Lincoln Gap Road and VT 125. As in other designated Wilderness Areas, trail work and signage are not always evident. Once heavily logged, the mountains of Breadloaf Wilderness are mostly reforested and now well populated by moose. A fair number of black bears roam here as well.

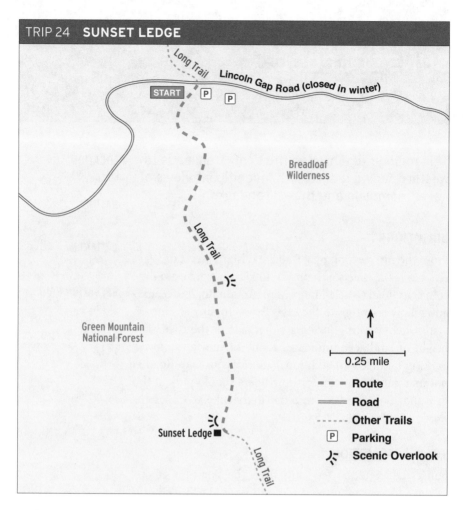

The Long Trail climbs steadily for a few tenths of a mile after entering the Wilderness Area. After a switchback at the top of a sidehill climb, the trail eases to a gradual pitch through beeches and sugar maples, with hobblebushes and ferns filling in the understory. A right turn in the trail leads to a ledgy, rooty scramble up an S-curve. Halfway up, an informal trail goes left to a rock with a view north and east over the spruce trees to the Northfield Range, paralleling the high ridge of the Green Mountains on the opposite side of the Mad River valley.

Continuing uphill around another couple of curves, the Long Trail tops the ridge. Sky appears through the branches on both sides of the path as the trail rolls along over low ledges. In spring, look for deep maroon blooms of purple trillium and showy white and pink petals of painted trillium in these low spots. In late summer, look for a bright red berry that replaces the trillium flower, perched at the top of its stalk and surrounded by three broad leaves.

At 1.1 miles, the forest opens on the right to reveal Sunset Ledge and wide views to the west. Leash dogs and keep children close in this cliffy area. The mountainside falls away beneath the ledge, swooping down into the forested and pastoral valley of the town of Lincoln and up into Bristol Cliffs Wilderness. A sharp notch in the ridgeline allows views of Lake Champlain spreading across broad lowlands. The Adirondacks rise above everything, the tallest of the distant peaks reaching elevations of more than 5,000 feet. If you're on Sunset Ledge in colder months, look for the Adirondacks' snow-covered landslide scars.

The cliffs continue raggedly northward, with dark green conifer spires on top and smooth deciduous canopy below. High above, the pointy peak of Mount Abraham pokes into the sky at just over 4,000 feet. Below it, the rounded peaks of the Hogback Mountains march northward. To the south, Robert Frost Mountain (2,411 feet) rises between the towns of Middlebury and Ripton.

Return to the trailhead the way you hiked up.

DID YOU KNOW?

Lincoln Gap and its namesake town were not named for our country's 16th president, as nearby Mount Abraham was. Instead, they honor Major General Benjamin Lincoln, a farmer from Massachusetts whose militia repelled the British in the Battle of Bennington during the Revolutionary War.

This hike offers views east to the Northfield Range and west across the Champlain Valley.

MORE INFORMATION

Breadloaf Wilderness is a place where human impact is kept to a minimum: Do not leave any personal property or use any wheeled device, such as a mountain bike or a wagon. Breadloaf Wilderness is managed by the U.S. Forest Service, Rochester Ranger District, 99 Ranger Road, Rochester, VT 05767; 802-767-4261; www.fs.usda.gov/gmfl. The Long Trail is maintained by the Green Mountain Club, 4711 Waterbury–Stowe Road, Waterbury Center, VT 05677; 802-244-7037; greenmountainclub.org.

NEARBY

Swim in the Mad River at various holes in Warren, 4 miles east, and along VT 100 north through Waitsfield, 10 miles northeast. The multiuse Mad River Path parallels the river, and whitewater paddling is popular downstream of Warren. Sugarbush, 8.2 miles northeast, has alpine skiing, mountain biking, disc golf, and other outdoor activities. Restaurants and grocery stores are on VT 100 in Waitsfield and along VT 17 in Bristol, 9.5 miles west.

25

MOUNT ABRAHAM

Hike a section of the celebrated Monroe Skyline to find rare arctic plants and 360-degree views on this rocky summit.

DIRECTIONS

From the intersection of VT 100 and Main Street in Warren, travel 0.7 mile south on VT 100. Turn right onto Lincoln Gap Road (labeled Lincoln Mountain Road in places) and follow it 4 miles to the Long Trail crossing at Lincoln Gap, where there is parking along both sides of the road (space for 20 cars). A lower parking lot holds an additional 15 vehicles. (Lincoln Gap Road is not maintained in winter; snowshoers should park at the gate and add 1.2 miles round-trip to the hike.) *GPS coordinates:* 44° 05.70′ N, 72° 55.70′ W.

TRAIL DESCRIPTION

Mount Abraham (3,999 feet, though many consider it one of Vermont's 4,000-footers) is Vermont's fifth-highest peak, barely reaching the 4,000-foot line that marks the approximate edge of alpine tundra in the Green Mountains (see "The Sparse Tundra of Vermont," page 200). The hike from Lincoln Gap is relatively short, but difficult footing in places makes it more challenging than the distance alone would imply.

The 272-mile Long Trail (see "Thru-Hiking," page 30) crosses the highest point of Lincoln Gap Road. From the parking area, head north on the Long Trail, following white blazes up a steep pitch into the woods. The path traverses the hill above the road for a short distance then turns away and climbs moderately through beech, maple, and fir. The trail is rocky and narrow, lined with club moss, trillium, and blue-bead lily.

After a short descent and a left curve over a sloping ledge, you will have a view of the ridgeline ahead through the trees. Mount Abraham marks the southern end of the spectacular

LOCATION
Lincoln, VT

RATING
Strenuous

DISTANCE
5.2 miles

ELEVATION GAIN
1,582 feet

ESTIMATED TIME
3.5 hours

MAPS
USGS Lincoln

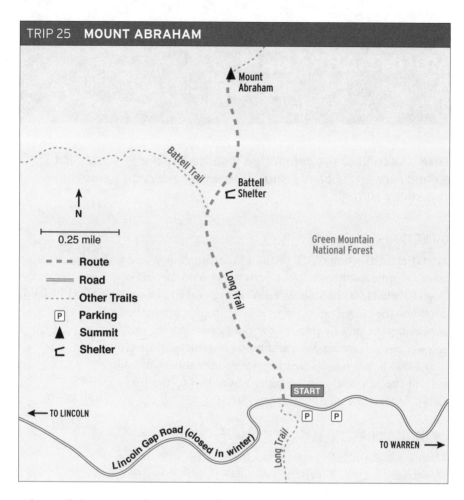

ridge walk known as the Monroe Skyline. Extending north to the Winooski River valley, the 30-mile route follows high ridges with numerous vistas and bald summits.

The shift to high-elevation forest falls early on the hike up Mount Abe, as it is locally nicknamed. This transition occurs around 2,700 feet, and your nose may alert you before your eyes do: Balsam firs are exceptionally fragrant. As you enter the spruce-fir forest, the climb steepens, but as you round the steep-sided mountain, the pitches are interrupted by brief level respites. Where the path is not on sloping ledges, it's across uneven slopes of half-buried rocks crisscrossed with tannic streams.

At 1.7 miles, the blue-blazed Battell Trail joins from the left. One-tenth of a mile farther, Battell Shelter provides a resting place in advance of the final 0.8-mile push to the summit. (A Green Mountain Club caretaker collects a $5 fee from hikers who spend the night in the shelter.) From the shelter, the Long Trail climbs up ledges and over bog bridges. The trees grow shorter until, a little more than 0.5 mile above the shelter, you climb out of the branches. The

Bright quartz rests near the trail on the final ascent to the summit. Breadloaf Wilderness stretches south from the high point of Mount Abraham.

views along the final ascent to the summit are magnificent. An enormous egg of quartz rests beside the trail, providing a good perch for viewing the ridge that stretches south into the Breadloaf Wilderness. You can follow the route of the Long Trail with your eyes, scanning the high ground to cross the side-by-side peaks of Grant (3,610 feet) and Cleveland (3,470 feet) and beyond, to the prow of Breadloaf Mountain (3,835 feet), which seems to plow westward.

At the summit, the ridgeline path of the Long Trail is evident as it continues northeast, first to Lincoln Peak (3,950 feet), 0.8 mile away, where a viewing platform perches over the ski trails of Sugarbush, and then on to the high crest of Mount Ellen (4,050 feet). To the west, 125-mile-long Lake Champlain sprawls beneath the Adirondack Plateau and its high peaks.

Mount Abraham's 1-acre summit is a patchwork of Bigelow's sedge; schist studded with quartz and covered with map lichen; and stunted, gnarled spruce and fir trees called krummholz (crooked wood). Hikers should leash their dogs here and walk only on rocks to avoid trampling the summit vegetation. Areas of particular concern may be designated by low rock walls or string perimeters.

Descend the way you came up.

DID YOU KNOW?

As you hike uphill, the temperature typically drops between 3.5 and 5.5 degrees Fahrenheit for every 1,000 feet you climb—and that's before accounting for windchill. Humidity traps heat, so on dry days the temperature drop is greater than if it's raining or snowing.

MORE INFORMATION

Mount Abraham is in the Green Mountain National Forest, Rochester Ranger District, 99 Ranger Road, Rochester, VT 05767; 802-767-4261; www.fs.usda.gov /gmfl. The Long Trail and Battell Shelter are maintained by the Green Mountain Club, 4711 Waterbury–Stowe Road, Waterbury Center, VT 05677; 802-244-7037; greenmountainclub.org.

NEARBY

Swim in the Mad River at various holes in Warren, 4 miles east, and along VT 100 north through Waitsfield, 10 miles northeast. The multiuse Mad River Path parallels the river, and whitewater paddling is popular downstream of Warren Village. Sugarbush, 8.2 miles northeast, has alpine skiing, mountain biking, disc golf, and other outdoor activities. Restaurants and grocery stores are on VT 100 in Waitsfield and along VT 17 in Bristol, 9.5 miles west.

26

BURNT ROCK MOUNTAIN

This bare summit provides a fun rock scramble and panoramic views along one of the most scenic sections of the Long Trail.

LOCATION
Fayston, VT

RATING
Strenuous

DISTANCE
5.2 miles

ELEVATION GAIN
2,090 feet

ESTIMATED TIME
3.5 hours

MAPS
USGS Waterbury,
USGS Huntington

DIRECTIONS

From Waitsfield Village, follow VT 100 north 3 miles and turn left onto North Fayston Road. After 4 miles, at the forked junction with Center Fayston Road and the unmarked Sharpshooter Road, go right onto Sharpshooter. Take an immediate left onto Big Basin Road and follow it 0.9 mile to the parking lot for Hedgehog Brook Trail. Parking is on either side of the gravel road (space for 8 cars). *GPS coordinates:* 44° 14.98′ N, 72° 52.43′ W.

TRAIL DESCRIPTION

This hike up Hedgehog Brook and along a section of the Long Trail starts gently then gradually gets steeper and more challenging—and more fun! The payoff matches your efforts: The ridgeline leads you through a beautiful stretch of boreal forest and interesting rock formations before culminating in long views on the bare crest of Burnt Rock Mountain (3,159 feet).

Hedgehog Brook Trail starts by descending to a rock hop across its namesake stream. Ascending rock steps on the far side, the narrow, blue-blazed route leads you into a deciduous forest, paralleling the brook as the trail climbs gradually uphill. Hedgehog Brook Trail undulates over hummocks and across small streams then descends to cross the wide brook. A short distance after this crossing, Hedgehog Brook Trail turns sharply left and becomes wider and sandier—the remnant of an old road. Look for the teeth marks and dangling strips of bark that indicate moose have visited the striped-maple saplings along this section of trail. As you walk up the right side of the brook, an enormous

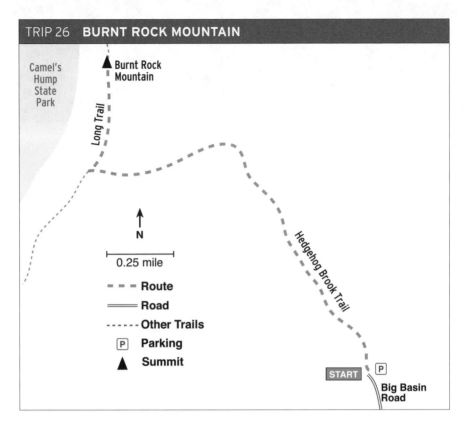

Camel's
Hump
State
Park

▲ Burnt Rock
Mountain

Long Trail

Hedgehog Brook Trail

↑
N

0.25 mile

‒ ‒ ‒ **Route**

══════ **Road**

‒‒‒‒‒ **Other Trails**

P **Parking**

▲ **Summit**

START   P

Big Basin
Road

mossy boulder with birch and spruce trunks sprouting from its scalp pushes the trail briefly off the straight track, which is lined with purple-flowering raspberry. Hedgehog Brook Trail gradually becomes narrower and a little rockier and begins to zigzag steeply uphill, leaving the stream far below. A double blaze marks a left turn, and the trail crosses the slope, rising moderately and occasionally following smooth rock spines.

After a rocky stream crossing, the trail again heads steeply uphill. When you enter the Long Trail Easement Lands, the trees are noticeably shorter. A steep scramble over rocks and up three log ladders brings you into a spruce-fir forest with the occasional mountain ash. The trail jogs back and forth, climbing several ledges before arriving on the ridgeline, marking the end of Hedgehog Brook Trail.

Turn right onto the white-blazed Long Trail and head north through a dim, mossy conifer forest. After scrambling through a narrow, rocky canyon and up a steep pitch, break out of the trees and onto the open face of Burnt Rock Mountain. The white blazes are now painted on the rocks, although if you hike early in the season, some may have been scoured off by winter's ice. Making your way through patches of short trees as you climb this rocky crest, you are walking on the spine of the highest range in Vermont. Along most of the Green Mountains' main range, the spine is fully forested, but in some unusual spots like this one, the bedrock is bare beneath the sky, and visitors get the benefit of a view over the treetops.

Hikers are treated to dramatic views—such as these trailside cliffs—along the hike up Burnt Rock Mountain, as well as spectacular vistas from its magnificent ridgeline.

To the east, ridgelines stack up one behind the other into the distance. To the south, the dramatic bulk and crests of the high Green Mountains rise, the ski trails of Sugarbush and Mad River Glen tracing lighter paths through the dark green forests from late spring to summer and fall.

This section of the Long Trail—from Mount Abraham (Trip 25) at the southern end through where you stand on Burnt Rock Mountain and north over Camel's Hump (Trip 27)—is called the Monroe Skyline. Its long stretches of high elevation and magnificent views make it one of the most scenic and interesting parts of the 272-mile Long Trail (see "Thru-Hiking," page 30). To the north, the humps of Mount Ira Allen (3,450 feet) and Mount Ethan Allen (3,670 feet) lead to the striking summit of Camel's Hump. To the west, the rounded bulges of foothills descend to the blue expanse of Lake Champlain; beyond the lake, New York's Adirondack Mountains rise steeply.

Return downhill the way you climbed up.

DID YOU KNOW?

From the summit of Burnt Rock, the nation's last surviving single-seat chairlift is visible on General Stark Mountain. Its continued use is one of many ways the Mad River Glen ski area resists modern alpine ski culture: Snowmaking is minimal; snowboarding is not allowed; and the mountain is owned by a member cooperative that strives for low skier density.

MORE INFORMATION

Hedgehog Brook Trail and this section of the Long Trail are located on private land. Hikers are allowed to use the trail thanks to the generosity of the landowners. Please stay on the trail and away from buildings. Inconsiderate hiker behavior could lead to trail closure. Camping and fires are not allowed anywhere along Hedgehog Brook Trail or this section of the Long Trail. Both trails are maintained by the Green Mountain Club, 4711 Waterbury–Stowe Road, Waterbury Center, VT 05677; 802-244-7037; greenmountainclub.org.

NEARBY

Many sections of the Mad River flowing through Waitsfield, 7 miles southeast, are suitable for swimming and paddling; the multiuse Mad River Path runs parallel. Sugarbush, 14.4 miles south, offers alpine skiing, mountain biking, disc golf, and other outdoor activities. Restaurants and grocery stores are along VT 100 in Waitsfield, 7 miles southeast.

27

CAMEL'S HUMP
(EAST AND WEST SIDES)

Visit the craggy, windswept summit of Vermont's most famous peak via one of these two challenging, rewarding loops.

DIRECTIONS

To Monroe Trailhead (access to Dean and Long trails)

From I-89, Exit 10, go south on VT 100. Exit the rotary to continue on VT 100 south for 0.2 mile. Turn right onto Winooski Street and follow it 0.4 mile to its end. Turn right onto River Road and drive 3.9 miles then turn left on Camel's Hump Road. Drive 3.5 miles up Camel's Hump Road to a parking lot on the right (space for 20 cars) or straight ahead to the upper lots (space for 20 cars). The upper lots are gated at dusk and reopened at dawn. (The final 0.4 mile of Camel's Hump Road is not maintained in winter. Winter hikers: Park in the lot at the end of the maintained road and add 0.8 mile round-trip to the hike. This lot also serves as summer overflow parking.) *GPS coordinates:* 44° 18.99′ N, 72° 50.87′ W.

To Burrows and Forest City trails (access to Long Trail)

From Huntington, follow Main Road south 2.5 miles and turn left on Camel's Hump Road. Go 3.4 miles (passing the turnoff for Forest City Trail) to the end of the road, at the Burrows Trail parking lot (space for 30 cars). *GPS coordinates:* 44° 18.30′ N, 72° 54.48′ W.

TRAIL DESCRIPTION

Camel's Hump (4,083 feet) cuts a large profile, literally and figuratively, in Vermont. The peak's isolated height and distinct shape are a National Natural Landmark, recognizable from great distances and featured as a symbol of the state in many places, including on the 2001 Vermont state quarter. One of the first stretches of the Long Trail

EAST SIDE VIA MONROE, DEAN, AND LONG TRAILS:
LOCATION
Duxbury, VT

RATING
Strenuous

DISTANCE
7 miles

ELEVATION GAIN
2,585 feet

ESTIMATED TIME
6 hours

WEST SIDE VIA BURROWS, LONG, AND FOREST CITY TRAILS:
LOCATION
Huntington, VT

RATING
Strenuous

DISTANCE
5.3 miles

ELEVATION GAIN
2,230 feet

ESTIMATED TIME
5.5 hours

MAPS
USGS Waterbury, USGS Huntington; vtstateparks .com/assets/pdf/camels_ hump_trails.pdf

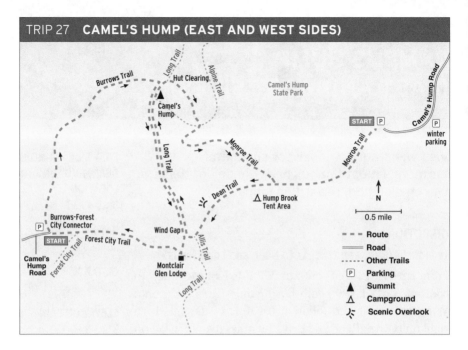

was built here, and the mountain remains the only undeveloped 4,000-footer in the state. The summit is busy with hikers on most fair-weather days, so go for immense views, rare plants, and fun rock scrambles but not necessarily for solitude or quiet. Be sure to bring a leash for your dog; it's required above treeline.

East Side via Monroe, Dean, and Long trails

This eastern-slope lollipop loop can be hiked in either direction. The more scenic and challenging route ascends Dean Trail and scales a steep, rocky ridge on the Long Trail, treating hikers to views early and frequently. Monroe Trail is a steady green tunnel better left for the descent.

The blue-blazed Monroe Trail rises gradually at first then turns alongside Hump Brook's deep ravine and climbs steadily and moderately to the junction with Dean Trail at 1.3 miles. Go left onto Dean Trail (also blue-blazed, as are all trails connecting to the Long Trail). Pass Hump Brook Tent Area at 0.2 mile then climb steadily for 0.5 mile and enter a spruce-fir forest. A spur trail leads right to a wetland, with a view of the sheer southern face of Camel's Hump above the trees. A closer cliff gives a dramatic preview of the next leg of your hike.

Dean Trail ends 0.2 mile farther, where it meets the Long Trail at Wind Gap. Turn right onto the white-blazed northbound Long Trail. A sign reports that the summit is 1.7 miles ahead, but you'll be heartened to know it's only 1.5 miles. A steep rock scramble brings you to a clifftop with a view northeast to the Worcester Range Skyline (Trip 39) and south to Mount Ethan Allen (3,670 feet).

Atop the ridge, clamber up several steep pitches and squeeze through a jumble of giant boulders before the Long Trail descends into the trees. Occasional glimpses of the towering summit lead you through the forest and up switchbacks to the base of the cliff. Alpine Trail heads right here, a bad-weather bypass to Monroe Trail. (Some remains of a 1944 B-24 bomber crash are flung across the mountainside along Alpine Trail, although most of the plane has been removed.) Stay left on the Long Trail, cutting beneath the rock face and climbing its western side. Take care to avoid trampling delicate mountain sandwort, Bigelow's sedge, and bilberry; leash your dog and step only on rocks.

A clear day on the summit of Camel's Hump is a visual feast, with New Hampshire's White Mountains and New York's Adirondacks backing rows of Green Mountains and the shining expanse of Lake Champlain. Whether it is sunny or not, be prepared for wind and cool temperatures.

Follow the Long Trail's white blazes north, descending 0.2 mile to junctions at the Hut Clearing. Now a grassy, flat spot and trail hub, the mid-nineteenth-century hotel formerly located here hosted adventurous guests for about 15 years until it burned down. Go right on Monroe Trail, descending about 0.3 mile of moderately steep, rocky trail before the pitch eases. After 0.6 mile from the Hut Clearing, Alpine Trail crosses Monroe Trail, and 0.3 mile below that, Monroe Trail swings left and proceeds beneath a cliff band about 0.3 mile before turning downhill again. Two miles below the summit, you will arrive at the junction with Dean Trail; continue straight down Monroe Trail the way you hiked up.

West Side via Burrows, Long, and Forest City trails

The west-side loop provides a short, steep, and ledgy ascent to the summit; a scenic and sometimes scrambly descent via the Long Trail; and the lovely, gentle pitches of Forest City Trail.

The blue-blazed Burrows Trail climbs gently for the first mile then begins power-stepping up ledges. The trees become shorter as you rise along a rocky ridgeline, and the trail climbs steeply before descending a short pitch to arrive at the Hut Clearing, at 2.1 miles. Follow the Long Trail's white blazes south and uphill from the Hut Clearing and leash your dog for this 0.2-mile leg into the alpine zone, where arctic plants cling tenuously to thin soils and are easily damaged by footsteps. Round the steep edge of the summit before climbing to the highest point.

The views stretch to eternity from rocky Camel's Hump, but if you focus in closer, you'll see many microenvironments: low pockets, crevasses, tunnels, pools of standing water, and dramatic cliff edges. Mats of krummholz and grasslike sedges anchor the small amount of soil that has developed in this harsh environment. Wherever you go, step only on rock to preserve these delicate patches of vegetation.

If the rock is slick with rain or ice, consider descending the way you climbed up, as this next stretch of trail is fun only when dry. Continue southbound on the Long Trail, following white blazes painted on the rock to find your way down steep ledges. Scramble over boulders and ledges beneath towering cliffs

Above treeline, the Long Trail is marked by white blazes painted on the open rock. Whichever routes you follow on majestic Camel's Hump, you're sure to have an adventure.

until you descend past the Alpine Trail junction and into the forest. The next 1.4 miles to Wind Gap are rugged, with rocky descents that occasionally require sitting and scooting.

At 3.8 miles, the trail levels at Wind Gap, and Dean Trail departs to the left. Go 0.1 mile farther on the Long Trail, to the junction of Forest City Trail on your right. Two hundred feet farther south on the Long Trail, on the other side of a small ravine, is Montclair Glen Lodge, an overnight shelter and several tent platforms maintained by the Green Mountain Club.

Turn down Forest City Trail and enjoy 1.3 miles of comparatively easy footing and gentle grades until you arrive at Forest City–Burrows Connector Trail, on your right. Turn onto it, cross a river gully on a wide bridge, and proceed 0.1 mile to finish where you began, at the base of Burrows Trail.

Did You Know?

Camel's Hump has had many names; its current appellation derives from Camel's Rump, the name given to it by Ira Allen, one of the founders of Vermont.

MORE INFORMATION

Trails are closed from snowmelt until Memorial Day weekend. Camel's Hump State Park is managed for multiple uses by Vermont Department of Forests, Parks and Recreation, 111 West Street, Essex Junction, VT 05452; 802-879-5682. Trails and hiker facilities are maintained by the Green Mountain Club, 4711 Waterbury–Stowe Road, Waterbury Center, VT 05677; 802-244-7037; greenmountainclub.org.

NEARBY

Backcountry camping is available at Montclair Glen Lodge and Hump Brook Tent Area; fees may be charged. Camel's Hump State Park does not have a developed campground; frontcountry camping is available at Little River State Park in Waterbury (12.7 miles from Monroe Trailhead; 23 miles from Burrows Trailhead). Paddle and swim at Waterbury Center State Park (11.4 miles from Monroe Trailhead) or at Lake Iroquois in Hinesburg (15 miles from Burrows Trailhead). Mountain biking is plentiful in Hinesburg, as well as the Waterbury–Stowe area (see appendix). Food is in Waterbury, Hinesburg, and Richmond.

28

BALD TOP MOUNTAIN

Experience a stretch of the 36-mile Cross Rivendell Trail as you climb from the shores of Lake Morey to an open summit on the borderland between the Green and White mountains.

DIRECTIONS

From I-91 Exit 15 (Fairlee), head west on Lake Morey Road for 1.3 miles, rounding the southern end of the lake and heading up the western shore. Trailhead parking is on the left (space for about 12 cars), across the street from the public boat launch. *GPS coordinates: 43° 55.27′ N, 72° 09.62′ W.*

TRAIL DESCRIPTION

Bald Top Mountain (1,776 feet) is a broad, grassy summit high above the Connecticut River valley—a great place to get perspective on the dense, steep-sided hills that make lakes Morey and Fairlee so scenic. There are multiple paths to this summit. This route, along Cross Rivendell Trail, is not the shortest among them, but its start and finish on the lakeshore and its optional, short detour to Glens Falls give it additional appeal. There's a fair bit of navigating through a web of old and current dirt roads in the first mile of this hike, but the route becomes simpler as you ascend the ridge. Given the distance and steady climbing, kids 10 and older would enjoy this hike.

From a trailhead kiosk with information about the two-state Cross Rivendell Trail, climb steeply into the woods. The path of Old Echo Mountain Road curves left, away from your route; you will cross this two-track several times, but think twice about taking its steep, eroded path instead of the more moderate, switchbacking footpath. The old road is not a fun walk in either direction. The

LOCATION
Fairlee, VT

RATING
Moderate to Strenuous

DISTANCE
6.8 miles

ELEVATION GAIN
1,320 feet

ESTIMATED TIME
4.5 hours

MAPS
USGS Fairlee;
rivendelltrail.org

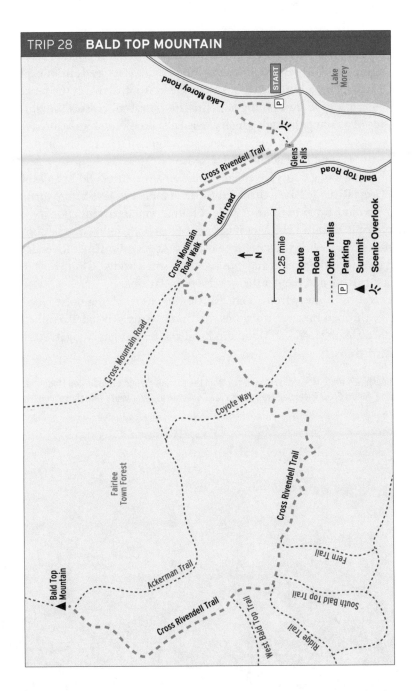

blue-blazed Cross Rivendell Trail zigzags up a steep slope through hemlocks and emerges at the top of the hill onto the old road. Follow the road a few steps before the blazes lead you left. If you want to skip the lookout and the side trail to Glens Falls, stay straight on the old road for 150 feet, to where it rejoins Cross Rivendell Trail.

Going left off the road, find a small lookout over Lake Morey at 0.4 mile. Notice the witch hazel, with its broad leaves and yellowish pods. This hardy shrub produces stringy, yellow-petaled flowers in fall and flings its seeds from exploding fruits. Curving back into the woods from the lookout, arrive at the junction of the Glens Falls spur trail on the left. This 200-foot trail crosses the hill to the steep side of a ravine through which Glens Falls Brook tumbles before reaching the lake. It's a worthwhile side trip, but use caution on the eroded, slippery edge of the gully as you find a good viewing spot.

Continuing along Cross Rivendell Trail, you again meet Old Echo Mountain Road; Cross Rivendell Trail turns left to join it for a few steps before turning left off it. Two more times in this first mile of hiking, you'll pass junctions where old roads go right toward Echo Mountain; stay left at both, following the contour of the hill and paralleling the stream below you. At 0.8 mile, Cross Rivendell Trail comes level with the stream and crosses it on a small bridge. Climb the far bank, cross a dirt road, and reenter the woods on the far side.

Now you climb away from Glens Falls Brook, its tumbling noise receding as you hike through mixed hardwoods. At 1 mile, Cross Rivendell Trail emerges onto the dirt-surface Cross Mountain Road and turns right along it. Stay left on

New Hampshire's White Mountains loom large from the summit meadow of Bald Top Mountain. Time permitting, follow Cross Rivendell Trail across the Connecticut River valley into those high peaks.

the dirt road at an unsigned junction; when the dirt road crosses a broad stream at 1.2 miles, you'll find the blue-blazed Cross Rivendell Trail on your left, leading you back into the woods for the rest of your journey to the summit.

Cross Rivendell Trail begins to climb in earnest now, entering a quieter, more open forest as it rises. At 1.8 miles, cross a stream and Coyote Way. Then, after a slight downhill the trail levels where logging opened the forest on the right. Meet a two-track here and follow Cross Rivendell Trail markers to turn right onto it. From this point, you'll follow a wide path the rest of the way to the summit, passing various other old tracks and adjoining trails, all well signed. The two-track has some steep hills as it rolls up the ridgeline, occasionally with a filtered view of the White Mountains across the Connecticut River. You'll know you're approaching the summit when you come upon some big, old, gnarly pines with thick, multiple stems.

Cross Rivendell Trail emerges onto a broad, shrubby meadow with views all around. The White Mountains to the east steal the show, with the higher peaks carrying the Appalachian Trail providing a backdrop to the lower foothills along the Connecticut River. Cross Rivendell Trail extends east into New Hampshire, crossing Sunday Mountain (1,823 feet), which appears east-southeast from this vantage point on Bald Top, and ending behind it on the tall point of Mount Cube (2,909 feet). From Bald Top west, Cross Rivendell Trail traipses over and around many small Piedmont hills before ending on Flagpole Hill (2,225 feet) in Vershire.

Descend the way you hiked up.

DID YOU KNOW?

Cross Rivendell Trail was proposed in 1998 as a physical way to connect four towns—Orford, New Hampshire, with Fairlee, West Fairlee, and Vershire, Vermont—when the towns banded together to create an interstate school district. The trail is still maintained as an educational resource for the schools.

MORE INFORMATION

Cross Rivendell Trail is maintained by the membership-based Rivendell Trails Association, P.O. Box 202, Fairlee, VT 05045; rivendelltrail.org. Consult the website before hiking for trail conditions and changes. All of the other trails you pass along the way to Bald Top are shown in detail on a map available on the town of Fairlee's website: fairleevt.org/recreation-council.

NEARBY

Paddle out onto the clear waters of Lake Morey from a public boat launch across the street from the trailhead. Lake Morey doesn't have a public beach; head to Treasure Island on the north end of Lake Fairlee for beach swimming and a picnic area, 7 miles south. A classic drive-in theater is 3.3 miles east on US 5.

29

WRIGHT'S MOUNTAIN

Spectacular views of pastoral Vermont and a vernal pool highlight this gentle mountainside loop hike.

DIRECTIONS

From the junction of US 5/VT 25, head west for 5.2 miles. Turn right onto Wright's Mountain Road and continue 2.3 miles to the parking area (space for 8 cars) on the right, at the height of land. *GPS coordinates:* 44° 03.22′ N, 72° 10.02′ W.

TRAIL DESCRIPTION

Wright's Mountain is not as well known as some Vermont day-hike destinations, but it's a nature lover's gem, with 800-plus acres of conserved woods. You'll reach the height of land, with its reward of long views, early in the hike; a shelter at the lookout rocks is 0.8 mile from the trailhead, making Wright's Mountain an ideal first backpacking trip for children.

Wright's Mountain Trail begins just beyond a gate on a wide woods road that's lined with tall red pines. The trail is not blazed, but all of the trail junctions—and there are many—are clearly signed. A short distance from the parking lot, a pit toilet perches off the left side of the trail, and not far beyond that the yellow-blazed Appreciation Way leaves to the right. Wright's Mountain Trail then climbs more noticeably into a deciduous forest.

At 0.4 mile, Sylvia's Trail departs to the left (part of your return route). Continue on Wright's Mountain Trail as it curves southwest and climbs to the ridge, where the top of Appreciation Way appears on the right, and a spur trail leads left to a wooden bench with a view of the Connecticut River valley and distant New Hampshire hills. The brushy understory of this ridgeline supports ruffed grouse. If you

LOCATION
Bradford, VT

RATING
Easy to Moderate

DISTANCE
2.7 miles

ELEVATION GAIN
326 feet

ESTIMATED TIME
1.5 hours

MAPS
USGS East Corinth; uvlt.org/docs/trails/ Wrights_2011_trailMap.pdf

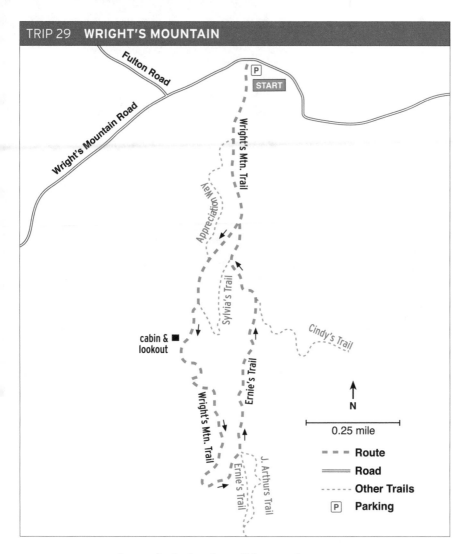

come across a mother with chicks, she will limp and moan to attract your attention, giving the young time to scurry to safety. The male ruffed grouse's wing drumming is frequently heard in Vermont's woods. Its deep, thumping tempo sounds like a heartbeat rapidly increasing.

The top of Sylvia's Trail joins on the left as you make your way around the forested summit. At 0.8 mile, Wright's Mountain Trail descends to a clearing with spectacular views west over the hilly farmland and forests of the Waits River valley. A large, airy shelter perches dramatically over the ledges. The outlook is a natural lunch spot, even though it's barely a third of the way into the hike.

Wright's Mountain Trail, now marked with yellow blazes, exits the clearing along a notable wall of rock that juts up from the forest floor. Heading south, pass two smaller viewpoints before swinging east and descending into oak and maple woods. When an abandoned leg of trail heads left, stay right on Wright's

Early on the loop around Wright's Mountain, an overlook with a large shelter makes a scenic picnic spot.

Mountain Trail and descend along a rope railing. The trail makes S-curves back and forth across the ridge, passing through dark, fragrant spruce-fir stands and clambering over mossy rock outcrops. Given the short ascent to the lookout, you lose more elevation on this side of the mountain than you'd expect.

As you approach the southernmost part of your loop, views appear through tall white pines, and the land drops away in front of you. Wright's Mountain Trail crosses onto the mountain's eastern slope and swings north, entering a damp deciduous forest. Before long, a depression that hosts a vernal pool in spring and early summer diverts the trail onto a low ridge. This shallow, seasonal pond not only provides a breeding habitat for wood frogs and spotted salamanders; it also serves as a watering hole for mammals and birds. Wright's Mountain Trail ends at a four-way junction, in a narrow gully just below the pool.

Go left onto Ernie's Trail and follow this old two-track north. The ground can be soggy, creating an impressionable surface for animal tracks and a good habitat for mosquitoes. The path gets drier as it ascends gradually through thick woods. After about 0.5 mile on Ernie's Trail, Cindy's Trail descends to the right. Stay straight on Ernie's Trail to the junction of Sylvia's Trail. Go right and follow the bottom leg of Sylvia's Trail to its junction with Wright's Mountain Trail. From here, go right, returning the way you came.

DID YOU KNOW?

The brightly colored red eft you may see moving at the speed of a sloth is the juvenile stage of the eastern, or red-spotted, newt. As larvae, they have gills and live in the ponds where they hatch; as adults, they return to aquatic life in the form of olive-green salamanders. In between, they spend up to seven years wandering on land.

MORE INFORMATION

Trails on Wright's Mountain are managed by the Bradford Conservation Commission, P.O. Box 339, Bradford, VT 05033; bradfordconservation.org. Conservation easements on the Wright's Mountain/Devil's Den Town Forest are held by the Upper Valley Land Trust, 19 Buck Road, Hanover, NH 03755; 603-643-6626; uvlt.org.

NEARBY

The Waits and Connecticut rivers are popular for paddling and bird-watching; a boat launch near their confluence, in Bradford, is part of the 240-mile Connecticut River Paddlers Trail (connecticutriverpaddlerstrail.org). Several riverside parks in Bradford provide picnic spots; food is available on US 5 (North Main Street), just north of its junction with VT 25. The Montshire Museum of Science in Norwich, 24 miles south, has indoor and outdoor exhibits geared toward kids but is entertaining for all ages.

IS IT A SWAMP OR A BOG?

You round a bend on the trail and see an opening in the forest. Shrubby plants grow on hummocks surrounded by still water. A few scraggly tree trunks poke up, and decaying logs lie in the muck. The ground becomes squishy under your boots, and you hear a faint splash as a small animal takes cover. This is clearly a wetland, but is it a swamp or a bog? How can you tell?

"Wetland" is a general term for the many types of soggy natural communities that exist somewhere between open water and terra firma. Vermont has 300,000 acres of wetlands, including marshes, swamps, bogs, and fens.

Freshwater marshes are wide-open, water-on-the-surface places: They are the grass-choked corridors you paddle through when a slow river spreads over a wide area. They are the reedy edges of ponds and lakes where frogs and dragonflies hang out. Marshes have many herbaceous plants, such as grasses, cattails, and pond lilies, but because water is usually present year-round, there are no trees.

Swamps are the slightly less wet version of marshes; in a swamp, trees survive seasonal flooding. At lower elevations, swamps have predominantly hardwood trees, such as maple and ash. Higher in the mountains, softwoods are the rule: cedar, tamarack, spruce, and fir.

While marshes and swamps have water flowing through them, bogs and fens develop where water collects and stagnates. Thick mats of vegetation may cover the entire surface of the water. Bogs and fens differ in the chemistry of their water. Bog water is acidic, with very few dissolved nutrients and very low levels of oxygen. This is a tough place for plants to live, and only a few thrive: sphagnum moss, heath shrubs, and the adaptable black spruce. Fen water is more accommodating to life, ranging from slightly acidic to slightly basic, with more dissolved nutrients, minerals, and oxygen than bog water. Fens may have some of the same plants as bogs, but they have much more diversity, including goldenrod, red osier dogwood, cattails, and sedges.

All of these soupy places are important parts of healthy ecosystems, although this may be difficult to appreciate as you slap mosquitoes and search for dry footing. Wetlands provide important habitats, and their absorbent soils help recharge water tables; slow floodwaters; stabilize shorelines; and filter out sediments, pollutants, and nutrients. (For more details, pick up a copy of *Wetland, Woodland, Wildland* by Elizabeth H. Thompson and Eric R. Sorenson, published by The Nature Conservancy and the Vermont Fish and Wildlife Department, 2000).

30

SPRUCE MOUNTAIN

A historical fire tower offers intimate views of Granite Hill peaks, as well as longer vistas of the highest Green and White mountains.

DIRECTIONS

From the blinking light at the junction of US 2 and Main Street in Plainfield, turn downhill onto Main Street. Follow it 0.5 mile and turn right onto East Hill Road. After 3.8 miles, turn left onto Spruce Mountain Road and drive 1 mile to the parking lot (space for 12 cars) at the road's end. *GPS coordinates: 44° 14.10′ N, 72° 22.68′ W.*

TRAIL DESCRIPTION

Spruce Mountain (3,010 feet) is on the western edge of a cluster of peaks known as the Granite Hills in the 26,183-acre Groton State Forest. Access to the summit, though, is through the abutting 642-acre L. R. Jones State Forest. Spruce Mountain Trail passes through a variety of landscapes before topping out on a treed summit with a sturdy fire tower. The pitches are generally not steep, although the last part of the hike is a sustained climb. The footing is uneven on the upper half of the mountain, making this trail best suited to hikers ages 10 and older.

Spruce Mountain Trail begins by heading downhill from the parking lot on the multiuse Tower Road, which accommodates both forestry vehicles and hikers. For the first few tenths of a mile, the terrain is flat.

At about 0.5 mile, the wide track passes near a spring and enters a small log landing, or clearing where loggers pile cut timber before transporting it out of the woods. When this land was purchased to become Vermont's first state forest in 1909, it was mostly open fields. Between 1910 and 1916, some 300,000 trees were planted, many of which since have matured and been harvested. You may see evidence of forestry practices on your hike.

LOCATION
Plainfield, VT

RATING
Moderate

DISTANCE
4.4 miles

ELEVATION GAIN
1,300 feet

ESTIMATED TIME
3.5 hours

MAPS
USGS Barre East,
USGS Knox Mountain

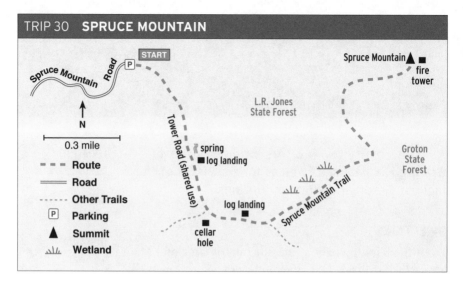

Proceed straight through the clearing, reenter the forest, and begin a moderate climb. Where the road turns east, a cellar hole (the remains of a farmhouse that predated the state forest) sits off the right side of the trail. Shortly after, about 1 mile from the trailhead, enter a larger log landing, where other former roads lead off through the overgrowth. This is the end of the multiuse section of the trail. Stay straight, following Spruce Mountain Trail into a forest with dense conifer walls and a hardwood canopy overhead.

Occasional faded blazes—some white, some blue—mark the route, although it is not difficult to follow Spruce Mountain Trail as it narrows and climbs gradually. A new trail heading south to Seyon Lodge State Park veers off to the right. Shortly afterward, rocks begin to stud the previously flat dirt trail as it curves northeast. This cobbled path leads past a wetland on the left, where spears of dead trees jab upward.

From here, the gradual and almost flat terrain leads toward a sharp left turn to the north, where the character of the hike changes significantly. Now Spruce Mountain Trail narrows as it weaves around jumbles of boulders and climbs over angled ledges lying across the slope. The woods shift to a higher-elevation spruce-fir forest, and needles cover the path.

The forest suddenly opens again after Spruce Mountain Trail climbs up and across many stretches of sloped ledge. The final leg of the hike ascends a ridge, with sky visible through the thick forest on either side of the trail.

The summit clearing is ringed with tall trees and dominated by the legs of the fire tower. In 1919, a wooden tower was constructed to watch for fires caused by the drying debris remaining from intense forest clearing. The legs of the tower formed the four corners of a caretaker cabin, which squatted beneath an open lookout platform. After a dozen years, a taller wooden tower was constructed, with an enclosed lookout room, called a cab.

Looking east over the trees from high in the tower, you will see a rumpled landscape of peaks and ponds that is largely within the borders of Groton State Forest. Signal Mountain (3,323 feet) is the tallest of the cluster of peaks to the south, with Burnt (3,100 feet), Butterfield (3,123 feet), and Knox (3,064 feet) mountains beyond it. To the west, the ridge of the highest Green Mountains marches across the horizon: from Killington Peak (4,235 feet) in the southwest; across the distinct, two-tiered summit of Camel's Hump (Trip 27) due west; to the long summit ridge of Mount Mansfield (Trips 45 and 46) in the northwest.

Return downhill the way you hiked up.

DID YOU KNOW?

Spruce Mountain's current steel tower began its career on Bellevue Hill, in Saint Albans. It was relocated here in 1943 and was staffed until the early 1970s.

MORE INFORMATION

L. R. Jones State Forest is managed by Vermont Department of Forests, Parks and Recreation, 5 Perry Street, Suite 20, Barre, VT 05641; 802-476-0170; vtfpr.org.

NEARBY

The seven state parks within Groton State Forest—New Discovery, Kettle Pond, Big Deer, Boulder Beach, Stillwater, Ricker Pond, and Seyon Lodge—offer many attractions, including campgrounds, backcountry camping, swimming, a rail trail, boat rentals, fishing, a nature center, and hiking trails, all within 25 miles of the Spruce Mountain trailhead via US 302 or US 2. Plainfield has restaurants and shops along Main Street and US 2. Grocery stores are 15 miles west on US 302 (Barre–Montpelier Road) in Berlin and in downtown Montpelier.

Hikers pass through the dense conifer forest of Spruce Mountain.

31
OWL'S HEAD

Pass through lovely fern meadows on your way to the open granite summit and unique stone octagon shelter at Owl's Head.

DIRECTIONS

From the junction of US 302 and VT 232 (State Forest Road) in Groton, go north on VT 232 for 9.3 miles (passing Owl's Head Road). Turn right into New Discovery State Park. Pay day-use fee at the gate and proceed to a fork; go right. Pass through a metal gate and immediately go left at another fork. Owl's Head trailhead parking is a shallow pullout (space for about 4 cars) a short distance down the road on the right. (Winter hikers: Park at Northern Parking lot on the west side of VT 232, 0.4 miles south of New Discovery, and walk in on the park's maintenance road on the east side of VT 232 to join Owl's Head Trail at the register box, adding 0.2 miles round-trip to the hike.) *GPS coordinates:* 44° 18.79′ N, 72° 17.26′ W.

TRAIL DESCRIPTION

Owl's Head (1,910 feet), a low but prominent and easily accessible peak with long views, is the knobby sentinel of Groton State Forest. A mile-long auto road (open during daylight hours when state parks are operating) ascends to within 0.25 mile of the summit and provides a good alternative for those who can't walk far. But the beautiful forests and gentle rise of the trail from New Discovery State Park make this one of the most enjoyable hikes in the area, suitable for kids ages 7 and older.

An old road leads north from the parking area into a shady forest of tall, thin conifers. Follow the road 0.3 mile to the trail register box at a junction just shy of a field with a campground maintenance building. Go left onto the blue-blazed Owl's Head Trail, turning almost 180 degrees

LOCATION
Peacham, VT

RATING
Easy to Moderate

DISTANCE
3.8 miles

ELEVATION GAIN
370 feet

ESTIMATED TIME
2 hours

MAPS
USGS Marshfield;
vtstateparks.com/assets/
pdf/groton_trails.pdf

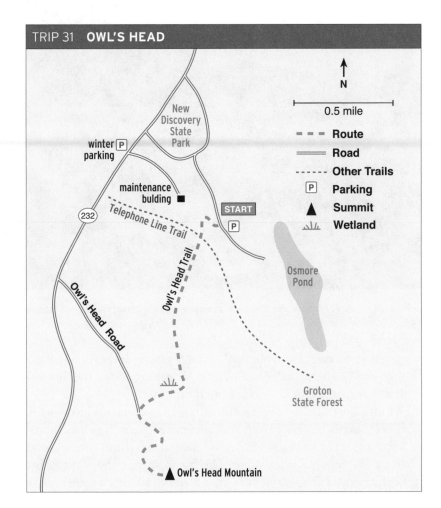

New
Discovery
State
Park

winter P
parking

maintenance
bulding ■

232

Telephone Line Trail

START

P

Owl's Head Trail

Osmore
Pond

Owl's Head Road

N

| | 0.5 mile |

- - - **Route**

==== **Road**

------ **Other Trails**

P **Parking**

▲ **Summit**

⟋⟋⟋ **Wetland**

Groton
State Forest

▲ Owl's Head Mountain

to head south, parallel to the old road. Canada mayflowers and bunchberries sprout amid club moss alongside the path. The flat, rooty trail leaves the conifer forest that dominates the campground, shifting to beech and maple.

Ascending gradually, you will arrive at the junction of the nonmotorized multiuse Telephone Line Trail, which heads out into Peacham Bog. An old split sign off to the left seems to point to Lake Groton, although it is so weathered it's barely legible. The area that is now Groton State Forest was one of Vermont's earliest colonial settlements. Farming—never easy in the mountains—was especially difficult here, where granite chunks are plentiful, so logging has long been a dominant activity in these woods. The state forest is managed for tree harvesting and recreation today. Cross Telephone Line Trail, staying on Owl's Head Trail, and begin a gentle climb.

As the trail rolls gradually uphill, you are likely to hear white-throated sparrows, ovenbirds, and the distinct fluty calls of wood thrushes, hermit thrushes, and veeries. In light gaps where trees have fallen, the understory grows rapidly,

Kettle Pond gets its name from the way it formed: a massive, partially buried chunk of ice from the retreating glacier created what's known as a kettlehole basin, which then filled with water.

narrowing the trail corridor in places. A series of gentle curves with easy climbing brings you to a remarkable sea of ferns stretching across the forest floor beneath widely spaced trunks, 1 mile from the trailhead.

At 1.4 miles, the trail descends slightly to a small wetland, studded with ferns growing on hummocks. Owl's Head Trail curves right, crossing a lichen-crusted ledge 5 feet above the wet ground. Beyond the swamp, climb over a low knoll and begin a long, gradual descent into a hollow. A string of bog bridges brings the trail through a low spot, followed by a short climb into another airy fern meadow and the final rise to Owl's Head Road.

Go left on the road, turning left again onto the summit trail for the final 100 feet of elevation gain. The other, unmarked trail leads from the road to a picnic pavilion. Passing toilets, you will begin the steep, rocky final 0.2 mile. Rock steps ascend into a boreal forest of paper birch, spruce, and fir. Blueberry bushes sprout between moss-covered rocks as you round the final curve to the stone octagon built on the summit by Civilian Conservation Corps crews in the 1930s (see "From the CCC to the VYCC: Conservation Corps in Vermont," page 257). Granite ledge rolls away below the octagon, giving views west and south, most notably of Kettle Pond, pointing west to the distant peak of Camel's Hump (4,083 feet).

Return downhill the way you climbed up.

DID YOU KNOW?

At more than 26,000 acres, Groton State Forest is the second-largest landholding of the state, with only the 43,049-acre Mount Mansfield State Forest eclipsing it in size.

MORE INFORMATION

Hiking trails in Groton State Forest (designated with blue blazes) are for foot travel only. Multiuse trails are for foot, horse, or bicycle travel; no motorized vehicles are allowed. State parks within Groton State Forest open for the season on Memorial Day. New Discovery, Kettle Pond, and Ricker Pond state parks are open through Columbus Day; Boulder Beach, Big Deer, and Stillwater state parks are open through Labor Day. Overnight camping and campfires are allowed only at designated remote sites and in the developed campgrounds. Day use of the parks is 10 A.M. to official sunset. Seyon Lodge State Park operates year-round with brief seasonal closures and is open for day use 6 A.M. to official sunset. New Discovery State Park, 4239 Route 232, Marshfield, VT 05658; 802-426-3042; vtstateparks.com/newdiscovery.html.

NEARBY

The seven state parks (New Discovery, Kettle Pond, Big Deer, Boulder Beach, Stillwater, Ricker Pond, and Seyon Lodge) in Groton State Forest provide abundant swimming, paddling, camping, and picnicking options, in addition to many more hiking trails. Bike or ski on the multiuse Montpelier Wells River Rail Trail, which hosts the Cross-Vermont Trail through Groton State Forest. Restaurants and shops are limited along US 2 in Marshfield, 6 miles northwest, and Plainfield, 12 miles west, with more variety in Barre, 22 miles west, or Montpelier, 23 miles west.

Probably the shortest fire tower in Vermont, this structure was built atop Owl's Head in 1935 by the CCC.

QUARRIES AND ROCKFIRE

Have you ever considered what's deep beneath your boots as you scamper up a rocky ledge in the Green Mountains? If you peeled back the dirt, sand, and trees of central Vermont, you would uncover granite that extends miles deep into the earth. A tall, visible example of this rock aboveground is found in the Granite Hills of Groton State Forest, particularly the knobby, granitic summit of Owl's Head (Trip 31).

Nearby in Barre, the miles-deep granite has been quarried for years, with massive blocks hauled up out of the ground and loaded onto trains bound for artists and builders all over the world. Thousands of workers—many of them immigrants from Scotland, Ireland, Italy, and Francophone Canada—flocked to central Vermont in the late-nineteenth century to excavate the Barre granite plutons. They stripped a thousand acres of trees, opened deep holes in the ground with the help of dynamite, and jumbled massive slabs of rock in tall piles around the quarries. Between 50 and 75 individual quarries were operating at the turn of the twentieth century, creating Vermont's largest industrial landscape: a barren, dusty zone of rock, bearing the enormous production of cables, booms, bull wheels, and other machinery used to haul the blocks from their depths.

Today most of those quarries sit abandoned, filling with water and surrounded by trees. Barre Town Forest and the Millstone Trails Association together maintain a network of multiuse trails around and alongside the now-silent quarries, which provide a unique and curious landscape for hikers, mountain bikers, snowmobilers, and disc golfers. The trail to Grand Lookout in Barre Town Forest is adorned with surprising, sometimes hidden rock carvings: faces, animals, symbols, and other mysterious elements carved into the chunks of granite left behind. Remnants of the extraction industry are visible elsewhere, in rusty cables descending from cliffsides into the watery depths of quarry pools and massive heaps of rock called grout piles that issue cool breezes on the hottest summer days. Warning signs and the growl of machinery alert visitors to active quarrying still occurring in some areas.

In Barre, the Vermont Granite Museum has converted a vast, old granite shed into a showcase of the art and industry of quarrying, giving artists and craftspeople studio space and initiating a new class of carvers through its Stone Arts School. One of the most unique annual events in central Vermont is RockFire, a nighttime celebration of granite heritage, including traditional music, bonfires, and art. Paths lit by luminarias lead attendees to multiple performance locations throughout the woods and to a new appreciation for the varied cultural treasures that quarries provide to central Vermont.

Once industrial moonscapes, central Vermont's granite quarries have mostly revegetated and now provide unusual, scenic landscapes to explore on foot or via mountain bike. Photo by Jerry Monkman.

NORTHWESTERN VERMONT

The immense, shining marvel of northern Lake Champlain dominates the landscape of northwestern Vermont. Sometimes referred to as the country's "sixth Great Lake," it supports a range of natural communities with its long shorelines, large tributary deltas, and varied depths and temperatures. After the last ice age, while the land was still compressed from the weight of the recently melted glacier, the Atlantic Ocean poured into this valley. For a time, until the land rebounded and the salt water drained, whales and seals swam here, and the Green Mountain slopes descended directly into the Champlain Sea. Remnants of the ocean are still in the area: Endangered Champlain beach grass grows along sandy beaches and dunes, which are themselves difficult to find. Most of the big lake's shoreline is rocky, and many of those rocks are vertical, creating a landscape that is strikingly beautiful, if recreationally challenging.

The many islands in the northern half of the lake are known as the flattest terrain in the Green Mountain State. Their jaw-dropping views of the surrounding water and mountain ranges, as well as their own inherent pastoral beauty, make the islands a popular destination for visitors. Many of the smaller islands, including Burton Island (Trip 37), have the added attraction of being a refuge from cars, accessible only by boat. Agricultural use of the land has declined in recent years, with abandoned farm buildings and homesteads on smaller islands not uncommon sights, but farming and orchards are still prevalent on the larger, more settled islands.

Three very large, very old rivers flow west through the Green Mountains and spill a constant stream of sediment and water into Lake Champlain: the Missisquoi in the north; the Lamoille, emptying near South Hero; and the Winooski, ending next to Burlington. Their deltas not only provide rich habitats for birds,

Sweet flag, a tall, fragrant grass found in the marshes around Burton Island, was once strewn on settlers' floors as air freshener.

amphibians, fish, and some mammals but also support some rare and uncommon species. Missisquoi National Wildlife Refuge (Trip 38) preserves acres of saturated ground around the bird-foot delta of that river, including some remarkable natural communities found in the sprawling Maquam Bog.

Burlington and surrounding Chittenden County are densely developed by Vermont standards, but farmlands and wooded areas are the norm just a few miles from the city. South of Burlington, the northernmost Taconic Mountains jut from the farmland in small, steep knobs—most notably, Mount Philo (Trip 32). For a small hiking effort, these cliffy little peaks give spectacular views of the dramatic northwestern Vermont landscape.

32

MOUNT PHILO

Trek beneath a dramatic cliff band to breath-taking views of the Champlain Valley and surrounding mountains.

DIRECTIONS

From the junction of US 7 with Ferry Road and Church Hill Road, travel 2.5 miles south on US 7. Turn left onto State Park Road and follow it 0.6 mile to its end, at Mount Philo Road and the park entrance, where you will pay a day-use fee in season and find parking (space for 70 cars). *GPS coordinates:* 44° 16.68′ N, 73° 13.32′ W.

TRAIL DESCRIPTION

Mount Philo (968 feet) is a small peak packed with pleasant surprises. The hill rises steeply from gently rolling farmland, visible for miles across the Champlain Valley. Although the climb is not long, the steepness and the occasionally rough terrain make it most suitable for kids ages 6 and up.

House Rock Trail begins where the paved road to the summit leaves the parking lot. The wide, needle-covered trail climbs steeply at first, following blue blazes through hop hornbeam, sugar maple, and tamarack. After a few minutes, the trail's massive namesake boulder looms above a flight of rock steps. House Rock is one of many erratics that traveled south in glaciers during the last ice age and dropped to the ground on Mount Philo when the ice melted, about 11,000 years ago. Climb beneath House Rock's shady overhang and skirt its left side. The trail climbs more gradually from here to the auto road.

Turn right on the road and follow it about 50 yards then turn left onto Summit Trail. Climb up around a curve to a junction where Devil's Chair Trail heads right and Summit Trail continues straight up. Go right onto Devil's Chair

LOCATION
Charlotte, VT

RATING
Moderate

DISTANCE
2.4 miles

ELEVATION GAIN
580 feet

ESTIMATED TIME
2 hours

MAPS
USGS Mount Philo; vtstateparks.com/assets/pdf/philo.pdf

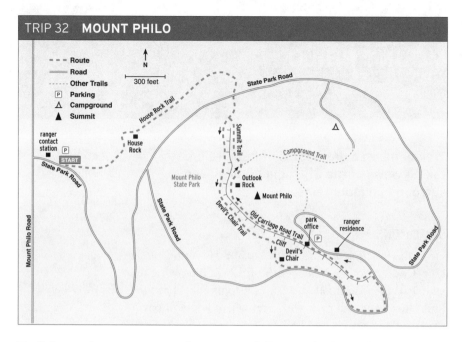

Trail for an alternate route to the summit, following the base of an impressive cliff band that runs around the south side of the mountain, zigzagging between boulders that have splintered away from the main ledges. Near the beginning of Devil's Chair Trail, look for grooves etched in trailside boulders. These ridges were formed by water eroding cracks in the rock, and they help identify these rocks as dolomite, different from the harder, more erosion-resistant quartzite that dominates Mount Philo.

The cliffs rise higher the farther you walk, with ferns and white cedars growing vertically out of cracks in the rocky face. After you pass the tallest of the cliffs, a gradual ascent leads to an intersection. A blue blaze on your left seems to indicate that Devil's Chair Trail turns left and climbs steeply between the cliffs, where metal poles remain from an old railing. Do not climb this abandoned trail; continue straight on the more developed footpath. As the cliffs recede, the trail enters thick woods and begins a short descent along a ridgeline. The chair-shaped rock that gives the trail its name perches on this hill.

Devil's Chair Trail ends at the auto road; go left (uphill) along the road's edge for 0.2 mile. Vehicle traffic is one-way; be aware of cars approaching from behind during the park's operating season. In winter, the closed road makes a fun ski trail. After a long left curve, turn left onto Old Carriage Road Trail, following the top of the cliffs. Pass close to the park office and summit parking lot before wending through grassy picnic areas.

Old Carriage Road Trail ends at a grassy lawn where Adirondack chairs offer a commanding view of Lake Champlain and the Adirondacks. Climb the rocky knob on the right side of the lawn (somewhat hidden by trees) for a higher vantage point of the Vermont peaks. Stretching south in line with Mount Philo, similar lone hills rise up from the valley floor: Shellhouse (705 feet), Buck (925 feet), and Snake (1,270 feet, see Trip 23) mountains. Along with Mount Philo, these small peaks are the northern extent of the Taconic Mountains.

Descend on Summit Trail, which you will find on the north side of the outlook rock amid clumps of honeysuckle, raspberry, and sumac. Follow switchbacks down a steep hillside to complete your loop at the junction of Devil's Chair Trail. Go right, following Summit Trail to House Rock Trail, the same way you walked up.

Climb the steps to House Rock, the first of many intriguing finds along this hike.

DID YOU KNOW?

Poison parsnip burns the skin similarly to poison ivy, but its toxin is photosensitive. If you encounter poison parsnip on a cloudy day, you may never know it, but if the sun comes out, you will likely develop a rash. Identify the clump growing behind the ranger's booth at Mount Philo's entrance so you know what to avoid.

MORE INFORMATION

Mount Philo State Park is open Memorial Day weekend through mid-October, 10 A.M. to official sunset, although hikers and skiers can use the trails year-round. A day-use fee is charged when the park is open; a campground with tentsites and lean-tos has a separate fee. Picnic areas, water, and restrooms are available on the summit in season. Dogs must be leashed at all times on state park trails. Mount Philo State Park, 5425 Mount Philo Road, Charlotte, VT 05445; 802-425-2390; vtstateparks.com/philo.html. For campsite reservations: Vermont State Parks Reservation Center; 888-409-7579; vtstateparks.com/reservations.html.

NEARBY

Swim and paddle at Kingsland Bay State Park, 10.4 miles southwest. Rokeby Museum, 4.6 miles south on US 7, is a National Historic Landmark with walking trails and one of the country's best-preserved stops on the Underground Railroad. Dining can be found along US 7 north into Shelburne and on VT 22A, 7 miles south in downtown Vergennes.

33

WILLIAMS WOODS

Wander through sucessional oaks and tall pines in this mature valley clayplain forest, a rare natural habitat in the Champlain Valley.

DIRECTIONS

From the junction of US 7 and Ferry Road in Charlotte, drive west on Ferry Road 0.3 mile. At the stop sign, turn left onto Greenbush Road (County Road 22K). After 1.9 miles, bear left to stay on Greenbush Road where Thompsons Point Road goes right. Follow Greenbush Road another mile to a small dirt pullout (space for 3 cars) alongside the road on the right (street address: 5754 Greenbush Road, Charlotte, VT). *GPS coordinates: 44° 16.21′ N, 73° 15.10′ W.*

TRAIL DESCRIPTION

Williams Woods Natural Area is a 63-acre island of mature forest surrounded by open, active farm fields. It harbors two of the largest swamp white oaks in Charlotte, each estimated to be more than 200 years old, and offers a rare opportunity to see how the Champlain Valley looked before agricultural clearing left few stands of the native clayplain forest. This type of forest grew in the thick sediment deposited by the receding glaciers that carved Lake Vermont and the Champlain Sea. The lollipop-loop trail rolls over undulating ground, making it a pleasant cross-country ski outing. This hike is suitable for all ages; dogs are not allowed, with the exception of service animals.

Hamilton Trail descends from the roadside onto a curving string of bog bridges. Fifty feet into the woods, The Nature Conservancy (TNC) maintains a registration box with maps and interpretive brochures. The tall, shady white-pine and hemlock canopy is interspersed with bright spots of sunlight where big trees fell. In this wet environment, trees keep their roots close to the surface to

LOCATION
Charlotte, VT

RATING
Easy

DISTANCE
1.2 miles

ELEVATION GAIN
Minimal

ESTIMATED TIME
1 hour

MAPS
USGS Charlotte; TNC map at trailside register box

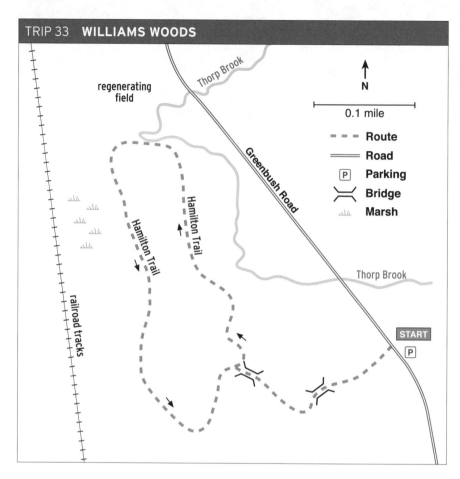

avoid drowning, making an unstable anchor in the wind. Logs in various states of decomposition are scattered thickly over the forest floor throughout Williams Woods. Look for saplings growing on top of downed trees called nurse logs. These logs' additional height above the water table provides better growing conditions than the saturated ground does.

Curving around conifers, cross a narrow gully on a bridge, using caution on the awkwardly spaced treads. A slight rise brings you near the edge of the woods, with an open farm field visible beyond. Following white blazes, curve sharply to the right along the small stream. In early spring, look for the small white, pink, or lavender flowers and fuzzy stems of hepatica. As spring warms to summer, tiny yellow blooms of barren strawberry appear. Bog bridges over low spots give way to root-covered humps as you approach the second bridge at 0.2 mile. On the far side of the bridge, the trail splits, forming a loop. Go right.

The path bumps over clusters of roots, passing from shady hemlocks into hardwoods interspersed with tall white pines. Thorp Brook appears in a gully on the right, winding its way slowly toward Lake Champlain. Decomposing trunks of blowdowns, or trees that have fallen in the wind, give plentiful opportunity to

The wet ground in Williams Woods causes tree roots to grow along the surface; hikers should be cautious.

examine insect activity, woodpecker holes, mosses, and fungi. Turkey tail mushrooms—with their fluted, striped edges—are particularly striking.

The trail dips slightly downward toward the regenerating field on the northern border of Williams Woods. When the path curves left, look downhill to the right to find a very large swamp white oak, about 3.5 feet across, on the edge of the field. Along the northern end of the trail loop, the pine canopy blocks so much light there's almost no undergrowth, just a blanket of orange needles on the forest floor. Among the thin, young spires, a massive white pine stretches its branches horizontally into the forest. This old tree is a "wolf tree"—probably left standing when the forest was harvested, giving the tree plenty of sun and space to grow wide, as well as tall.

Curving back to the south, the trail edges along a marsh. In sunny patches, watch for garter snakes sunning on the bog bridges. The trail can be difficult to discern as it passes through hemlock stands and weaves over mossy ground, although prevalent TNC trail markers clarify the route.

A mile into your walk, you will arrive back at the Hamilton Trail junction, completing the loop portion of the hike. Turn right, descending to cross the bridge, and return the way you walked in.

DID YOU KNOW?

The humpy-bumpy landscape of hemlock and pine stands is called pillows and cradles. Cradles are the pits left when trees fall over and pull up soil with their roots; pillows are the mounds of soil left after those upturned roots decay.

MORE INFORMATION

Williams Woods Natural Area is limited to passive recreational activities, such as hiking, snowshoeing, cross-country skiing, bird-watching, photography, and nature study. Motorized vehicles and bicycles are not allowed. Remove no plants, animals, artifacts, or rocks; do not build fires. Dogs and pack animals are not allowed; service animals are welcome. The Nature Conservancy, 575 Stone Cutters Way, Montpelier, VT 05602; 802-229-4425; nature.org/vermont.

NEARBY

Go to Kingsland Bay State Park, 10 miles southwest, for swimming and paddling, and to Mount Philo State Park, 2.5 miles east, for camping. The Lake Champlain Maritime Museum, 15 miles southwest, provides tours to historical shipwrecks. A couple of restaurants and markets are on Ferry Road in Charlotte, 3 miles north, with more variety in Shelburne Village, 9 miles north.

34

ALLEN HILL

This hike along Lake Champlain passes through a rare cedar-pine forest on a cliffy hilltop and offers plenty of opportunities for swimming.

DIRECTIONS

From the traffic light at US 7 in Shelburne Village, go west on Harbor Road 1.6 miles and turn right onto Bay Road. Drive 0.5 mile to Shelburne Bay Park on the left. The parking lot closest to the road provides access to the Shelburne Recreation Path, an alternate route. Continue toward the lake and park where the road ends (space for about 50 cars). *GPS coordinates:* 44° 24.00′ N, 73° 14.23′ W.

TRAIL DESCRIPTION

Allen Hill (270 feet) is a steep, rocky knob on the edge of Lake Champlain that supports a cedar-pine forest located on a limestone bluff—a rarity in Vermont. Three parallel trails in Shelburne Bay Park lead to the hill, making hiking loops possible. Shelburne Recreation Path begins from the parking lot closest to Bay Road and meanders through woods and fields for 1.4 miles to end at Harbor Road. It has a wide, hardened surface, and except for some bumpy culvert crossings and two short, steep hills (one near the beginning, one at the end), the rec trail is mostly flat and suitable for outdoor wheelchairs. (An extension of the rec path called Ti-Haul Trail is across Bay Road and extends south toward the village). An unnamed middle trail explores the woods in the center of the park. The most scenic route, described below, follows Clarke Trail along the shore to the Allen Hill Trail loop and returns via Clarke Trail. Cross-country skiers and hikers of all ages will enjoy the combination of woods and shore along the 0.5-mile Clarke Trail; kids ages 4 and older will be able to complete the 0.9-mile loop over Allen Hill. In winter, the loop is

LOCATION
Shelburne, VT

RATING
Easy

DISTANCE
1.9 miles

ELEVATION GAIN
120 feet

ESTIMATED TIME
1.5 hours

MAPS
USGS Burlington, shelburnevt.org/Facilities/Facility/Details/Shelburne-Bay-Park-14

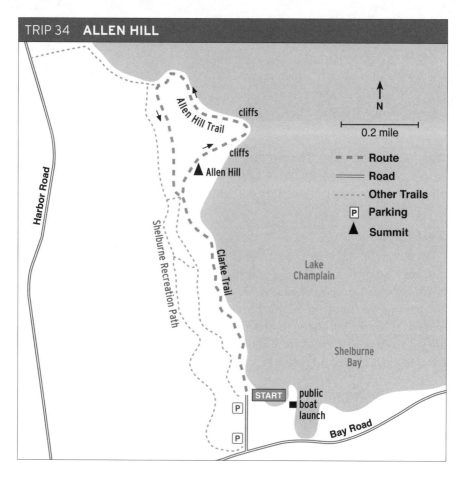

Allen Hill Trail

cliffs

N

0.2 mile

cliffs

▲ Allen Hill

- - - **Route**
——— **Road**
- - - - - - **Other Trails**
P **Parking**
▲ **Summit**

Harbor Road

Shelburne Recreation Path

Clarke Trail

Lake
Champlain

Shelburne
Bay

START public
P   boat
       launch

P

Bay Road

better suited to snowshoes than it is to skis. Lookout ledges are near the summit perch on tall cliffs; use caution. Dogs must be leashed in the park.

Clarke Trail begins where the parking area and grassy lawn border the woods. It initially follows a wide gravel path through a dark stand of cedar, hemlock, and white pine. Numerous short side trails lead to smooth rock ledges that slide gently into Shelburne Bay. After the third side trail to the lake, Clarke Trail becomes narrower and more rugged. Bog bridges over a damp area lead to a short climb up slanted bedrock, followed by more bog bridges. Following the shoreline north, you wander through open grassy areas, dark conifer stands, and muddy spots where water trickles from the ledgy hillside. Almost 2 miles of water stretch across Shelburne Bay on your right, and the tall ridge of Mount Mansfield (4,393 feet) and tiered top of Camel's Hump (4,083 feet) rise above the Champlain lowlands.

Descend from the bluff onto a shaded gravelly beach where a stream enters the lake then climb through red oaks and trout lilies to arrive at a five-way junction on the hillside. The left trail leads through the woods back to the parking lot. Straight ahead, a connector trail leads to the wide, graded Shelburne Recreation

Path. The two right legs are the beginning and end of Allen Hill Trail. Take the first right turn—which is actually a couple of steps back downhill toward the lake—and follow the east leg of Allen Hill Trail 0.2 mile up a steep slope to the summit. Trillium and hepatica grow between oaks on the dry, rocky sides and flat top of Allen Hill. Look for chestnut oaks, with their deeply grooved bark and toothed—rather than lobed—leaves.

Leaving the high point, Allen Hill Trail descends gradually, skirting the cliffy edge of the limestone bluffs; use caution here. Northern white cedars line the top of these headlands, giving way to white pines and hemlocks as you drop to lake level. Rounding the northern tip of this peninsula, you'll see a sandy beach on your right. Allen Hill Trail turns left where a short connector trail leads straight ahead to the recreation path. Turn left, leaving the lakeshore for a shady pine forest full of big old trees, some hollow and some pocked with the rectangular holes of pileated woodpeckers. A short climb over the shoulder of Allen Hill brings you beneath steep mossy cliffs. Look up to see the summit you were just on. In early spring, bloodroot blooms in these woods, opening its white petals in the sunlight and closing them up at night.

A gradual descent brings you back to the five-way junction. Go left, returning to the parking lot via Clarke Trail.

Hikers will encounter bogs and shoreline in Shelburne Bay Park. Photo by Julia Roberts.

DID YOU KNOW?

Northern white cedars, also called arborvitae, or "tree of life," dominate in environments with difficult living conditions: coniferous swamps and dry, rocky cliffs. Although challenging habitats keep them from growing large, they can live a long time. The oldest-known individual is more than 1,100 years old.

MORE INFORMATION

Shelburne Bay Park is managed by the town of Shelburne's Parks and Recreation Department, P.O. Box 88, 5420 Shelburne Road, Shelburne, VT 05482; 802-985-9551; shelburnevt.org.

NEARBY

An interpretive paddle trail exploring Shelburne Bay begins at the boat launch next to Shelburne Bay Park; a brochure guide is available through the Lake Champlain Basin Program, lcbp.org/wp-content/uploads/2013/03/ShelburneBayBrochure.pdf. Shelburne Farms is an education center, a 1,400-acre working farm, and a National Historic Landmark open to the public, 0.5 mile west. Restaurants and shops are in Shelburne Village, 2 miles southeast.

35

COLCHESTER POND

Walk through open farm fields and shady woods as you circle the quiet waters of this mile-long pond.

DIRECTIONS

From the junction of US 2 (also US 7) and VT 2A in Colchester, go east on VT 2A for 0.8 mile to the center of Colchester Village. Turn left onto East Road and proceed 1 mile then turn right onto Depot Road. Drive 2.3 miles to a fork and bear left onto Colchester Pond Road. In 2.2 miles, bear right into the Colchester Pond parking area (space for 18 cars). *GPS coordinates:* 44° 33.05′ N, 73° 07.50′ W.

TRAIL DESCRIPTION

Colchester Pond Natural Area is a quiet refuge in a busy part of Vermont. With Indian Brook Reservoir Park on its eastern border and Milton Town Forest to the north, the pond lies within a tract of more than 1,600 acres of contiguous forest. Walking the circumferential trail brings you through different stages of land use and forest succession, from shoreline hayfields to abandoned orchards to young forests growing over old pastures, a good exploratory hike for kids 6 and older.

Colchester Pond's unnamed loop trail begins next to a kiosk. Leash your dog before heading down the grassy slope, past the boat launch for paddle craft on the water's edge. The trail turns left and follows the shoreline northward. Pass through small stands of shagbark hickory, basswood, and sumac between hayfields that rise to a scenic barn on your left. Sections of bog bridges keep your feet out of the soggy soil.

The trail enters woods halfway up the length of the pond. At first it stays close to the shore, curving through white pines and passing clearings with access to the water.

LLOCATION
Colchester, VT

RATING
Easy to Moderate

DISTANCE
3.2 miles

ELEVATION GAIN
150 feet

ESTIMATED TIME
2 hours

MAPS
USGS Essex Center;
USGS Colchester;
wvpd.org/colchester-pond

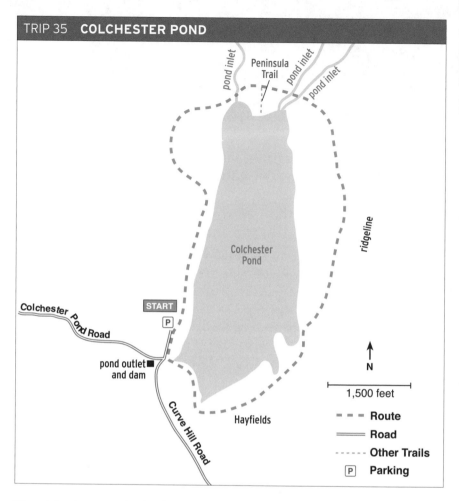

Colchester Pond

Peninsula Trail

pond inlet

pond inlet

pond inlet

ridgeline

Colchester Pond Road

START

P

pond outlet■ and dam

Curve Hill Road

Hayfields

N

1,500 feet

- - - **Route**
=== **Road**
····· **Other Trails**
P **Parking**

Then it begins a gentle climb into a mixed hardwood forest, staying high on the hillside for a short time before descending again to water level. As you approach the top of the pond, a rocky opening in the trees reveals a picturesque view southward across the water, providing an opportunity to spot ducks swimming or, if you're lucky, a bald eagle soaring. Colchester Pond attracts many species of birds and has been designated an Important Bird Area by Vermont Audubon. Canada geese, mallards, great blue herons, and common and hooded mergansers are some of the more frequent visitors. If you visit at dusk, you may be treated to barred owls calling *who-cooks-for-you?*

The trail rounds the damp north end of the pond on a series of step stones and bog bridges; it then climbs a small hill to the junction of Peninsula Trail. This path leads south 425 feet down a gentle slope to a clearing and water access: a promontory providing the last good swimming opportunity until you return to the trailhead. Continue straight on the main trail, descending to cross several threads of inlet streams.

After this soggy area, follow the trail as it clambers up rocky ledges and switch-backs on the steep hillside. By the time you've mounted the ridge that follows the eastern side of the pond, thick woods prevent any views of the water below. Walk south along the relatively flat height of land on the remains of a narrow road. This area was once cleared of woods and used agriculturally, probably as pasture, but it's difficult to imagine a farmer driving anything with wheels across this rough, rocky road. Watch for red efts (the juvenile stage of the eastern, or red-spotted, newt), which gravitate to these muddy, mossy areas.

The trail becomes smoother and the woods drier as you descend to walk a long string of bog bridges and emerge in a meadow with views of the pond. Cross several hayfields on your way to the marshy south end of the pond, where the trail returns to the shoreline. As the trail curves northward over bog bridges, tall cattails sprout up amid thick shoreline vegetation on one side, and a fence, grown over with honeysuckle and raspberries, lines the other. At the end of this verdant corridor, the trail hits dirt again and climbs to a road next to the pond's outlet. Turn right on the road and walk onto a bridge. Look down from its left side to see the 25-foot-tall dam controlling the pond's water level. Continue across the bridge to the trailhead parking area.

Colchester Pond is a quiet haven, attracting anglers, paddlers, bird-watchers, swimmers, and hikers.

DID YOU KNOW?

Invasive plant species, such as common buckthorn, aren't eaten by Colchester Pond Natural Area's wildlife, so they have an advantage over species that are a source of food. As invasive species overtake habitats, animals in search of food are displaced, and whole food chains are disrupted. Winooski Valley Park District actively removes invasive species to encourage native ones to thrive here.

MORE INFORMATION

Colchester Pond Natural Area is open dawn to dusk. Dogs must be leashed. Motorized boats, motorized vehicles, bicycles, and campfires are not permitted. Winooski Valley Park District, Ethan Allen Homestead, Burlington, VT 05408; 802-863-5744; wvpd.org.

NEARBY

Some dining options are available on Main Street and Blakely Road (VT 127) in Colchester, with more south in Winooski. Niquette Bay State Park has a sandy swimming beach 7 miles west on US 2. Camping is available near Mallets Bay in Colchester and at North Beach in Burlington, 9 miles south.

36

EAGLE MOUNTAIN

A peaceful hike through woods rich with wildflowers leads to the highest point on the Vermont side of Lake Champlain's shoreline and a broad view of islands and mountains.

DIRECTIONS

From I-89 Exit 17, go west on US 2 for 2.4 miles. Turn right onto Bear Trap Road and travel 1.8 miles to a fork. Bear left toward a barn and then turn left at the T intersection onto Cadreact Road. Follow Cadreact Road 2 miles to a stop sign. Go straight onto Beebe Hill Road and drive 0.9 mile. Turn left onto Henry Road and drive a little more than 0.1 mile to the parking lot, at the road's end. (The Henry Road parking lot was built in 2012 to replace the Cold Spring Road parking lot.) *GPS coordinates*: 44° 40.28′ N, 73° 12.08′ W.

TRAIL DESCRIPTION

Eagle Mountain (578 feet) was a pasture and a sugar bush, or maple syrup operation, 70 years ago, but today it is a forest of rich variety. The limestone bluff/cedar-pine forest found here is increasingly rare in Vermont, and the 226-acre natural area encompasses a remarkable diversity of wildflowers, including trillium, hepatica, false Solomon's seal, jack-in-the-pulpit, bloodroot, white baneberry, and blue cohosh. Eagle Mountain's trails are appropriate for hikers of all ages. Hoyt Lookout is a good destination for cross-country skiers, while the summit's slightly steeper, rockier slope may be more easily climbed with snowshoes.

From the parking area, Hoyt Lookout Trail (blue trail) follows diamond-shaped markers across a field, bears left between two rows of trees, and climbs gradually to arrive at the edge of the woods, at 0.25 mile. Enter a forest of cedar, maple, and hop hornbeam, with large, blocky,

LOCATION
Milton, VT

RATING
Easy

DISTANCE
2.1 miles

ELEVATION GAIN
200 feet

ESTIMATED TIME
1 hour

MAPS
USGS Georgia Plains

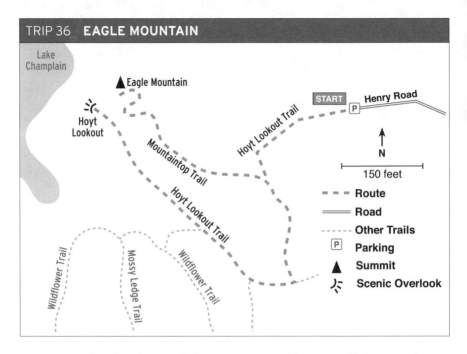

TRIP 36 **EAGLE MOUNTAIN**

Lake Champlain

▲ Eagle Mountain

Hoyt Lookout

START

Henry Road

P

Hoyt Lookout Trail

Mountaintop Trail

Hoyt Lookout Trail

Wildflower Trail

Mossy Ledge Trail

Wildflower Trail

N

|—————————————|
150 feet

▬ ▬ ▬ **Route**

════ **Road**

┄┄┄ **Other Trails**

P **Parking**

▲ **Summit**

ᐥᐣ **Scenic Overlook**

moss-covered rocks. Curving left, cross over an old stone wall. At 0.3 mile, you will arrive at a T junction where Hoyt Lookout Trail descends left toward Hoyt Lookout, and the 0.2-mile Mountaintop Trail (yellow trail) goes right to the summit. Turn right onto Mountaintop Trail and ascend a moderate pitch. Look for the red-and-black segmented bodies and tiny red legs of millipedes crawling across rotting birch trunks and decaying leaves.

In a short distance, follow Mountaintop Trail when it turns sharply right where a discontinued trail heads straight. Cross a rocky hillside and curve left up the hill. In spring this slope supports a patch of large-flowered trilliums, which blossom white and then turn pink as they age and wither. When Eagle Mountain was farmed, this wooded hillside sheltered animals, such as the horses that helped with the maple sugaring. Today white-tailed deer, porcupines, mink, fishers, foxes, and bobcats have replaced the horses. At 0.5 mile, you will arrive on the thickly wooded summit, which is marked by four rock cairns and is the highest point along Vermont's Lake Champlain shoreline. The views are not at Eagle Mountain's summit, despite its elevation, but a little farther down the trail at Hoyt Lookout.

Return down Mountaintop Trail to the junction with Hoyt Lookout Trail and continue straight, descending on Hoyt Lookout Trail to another T junction in a clearing. The discontinued trail to Cold Spring Road is on the left. Turn right, staying on Hoyt Lookout Trail, and notice a large rock outcrop on your right. This dolomite bedrock leaches calcium into the soil, part of the reason these woods are so hospitable to a wide variety of wildflowers and plants. Walk through a large, flat field of goldenrod, milkweed, and Queen Anne's lace to reenter the

Large-flowered trilliums thrive on Eagle Mountain. Petals start white and grow rosy-pink with age.

woods. Climb gradually for about 0.3 mile to Hoyt Lookout and its tree-framed view west.

Lake Champlain's Inland Sea—its eastern arm—opens in front of you. The small islands of Lower and Upper Fishbladder are centered in your view, while Savage Island stretches to the north, and Cedar Island is just visible to the south. What looks like mainland beyond these small islands is actually the broad expanse of Grand Isle; slivers of Main Lake are visible beyond it. The Adirondack Mountains rise in the distance, and turkey vultures frequently soar overhead in wide, slow circles, searching for food.

Return to the parking lot the way you hiked in.

DID YOU KNOW?

The dolomite bedrock underlying Eagle Mountain was once the floor of an ocean. The calcium it provides to the soil comes from seashells slowly dissolving.

MORE INFORMATION

Lake Champlain Land Trust donated Eagle Mountain Natural Area to the town of Milton and retains a conservation easement: 1 Main Street, Suite 205, Burlington, VT 05401; 802-862-4150; lclt.org.

NEARBY

The town of Milton maintains several trail systems, including the Lamoille River Walk and a circuit in the woods and wetlands around Milton Pond (maps at miltonvt.org). Swim and picnic on the shore of Lake Champlain at Sand Bar State Park, 7 miles southwest. Camp at Grand Isle State Park, 15 miles west. Food is along US 7 in Milton, 7 miles southeast, with more options around Colchester, 12 miles south, or along US 2 in South Hero, 11 miles west.

37

BURTON ISLAND

This island hike passes through woods and fields teeming with wildflowers and along rocky shorelines with astounding views and plenty of swimming.

DIRECTIONS

From US 7 (South Main Street) in downtown Saint Albans, turn west onto Lake Street (VT 36). Go 2.9 miles (Lake Street becomes Lake Road) to Saint Albans Bay and stay on Lake Road as it swings right, along the bay. After crossing the bay's inlet, turn left on Hathaway Point Road. After 2.8 miles, Hathaway Point Road runs directly into Kamp Kill Kare State Park (space for about 100 cars). Ferry service runs in season from Kamp Kill Kare to Burton Island ($8 per person round-trip), or you can boat the approximately 0.8 mile in your own craft. Off-season, park on the side of Hathaway Point Road, being careful not to block the gate, and carry your boat in about 0.2 mile. Winter explorers will need a dependable craft before freeze or reliable ice thickness after it to get to Burton Island. *GPS coordinates:* 44° 46.74′ N, 73° 10.89′ W.

TRAIL DESCRIPTION

Burton Island comprises 253 acres of nearly flat woods, fields, and marshes ringed by rocky Lake Champlain shoreline. A campground, swimming beach, and marina are at the north end, but most of the rest of the island is undeveloped. Several trails link to make a beautiful 2.8-mile hike around the perimeter of the island. Kids 4 and older will have fun exploring the varied shoreline and spotting wild strawberries, raspberries, and thimbleberries as they hike.

From the marina, follow the campground road along the north shore, keeping right at all junctions to stay near the water. Where the road ends, North Shore Self-Guided

LOCATION
Saint Albans, VT

RATING
Easy

DISTANCE
2.8 miles

ELEVATION GAIN
Minimal

ESTIMATED TIME
2 hours

MAPS
USGS Saint Albans Bay; vtstateparks.com/ burton.html

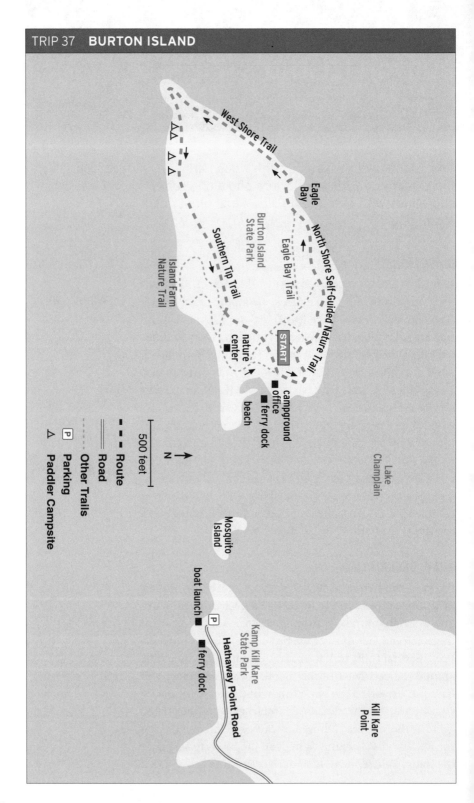

West Shore Trail

Eagle
Bay

Burton Island
State Park

Eagle Bay Trail

North Shore Self-Guided Nature Trail

Southern Tip Trail

Island Farm
Nature Trail

nature
center

START

campground
office

ferry dock

beach

Lake
Champlain

Mosquito
Island

boat launch

ferry dock

Kamp Kill Kare
State Park

Hathaway Point Road

Kill Kare
Point

N →

500 feet

▪ ▪ ▪ **Route**

——— **Road**

········ **Other Trails**

P   **Parking**

△   **Paddler Campsite**

Nature Trail departs into a tunnel of staghorn sumac. Numbered posts along this 0.4-mile stretch to Eagle Bay correspond to an interpretive brochure available at the campground office. The trail winds generally along the water's edge, the forest shifting between dark, dry cedar and hemlock stands (common on rocky, thin-soiled shores) to lighter, greener stands of poplar, paper birch, and ash (where farm fields stood not long ago). Canada anemone, goldenrod, milkweed, dame's rocket, daisy fleabane, and bedstraw are just a few of the wildflowers that sprout in sunny, open spots around the island.

At 0.3 mile, Eagle Bay Trail leaves to the left. Continue on North Shore Trail through the trees to a curved cove. The rare sandy beach here is a treat for bare feet, making this one of the best swimming spots on the island. Startling spikes of wild red columbine sprout from pebbly ground high on the beach. A narrow peninsula defines the southern edge of the cove, giving wide views across the lake's Inland Sea. Grand Isle and North Hero lie to the west, and the low profiles of Woods and Knight islands are visible to the north.

Passing Eagle Bay, continue southwest along the shore and find the fainter, unsigned West Shore Trail climbing into the woods. West Shore Trail stays mostly within the trees for the next 0.5 mile, passing a wetland before emerging on the rocky shore near the island's southern tip. Walk along the water and,

Burton Island's shoreline leads from one fabulous view to the next with plenty of swimming options.

where the rocky beach gives way to a bluff, climb to a grassy lawn with picnic tables, benches, and spectacular views south to the distant Adirondack Mountains beyond nearby Ball Island.

On the eastern side of the promontory, find the mowed two-track of Southern Tip Trail, which leads 0.7 mile back to the island's developed east side. An outhouse perches in the woods on your left, and a boardwalk leads past access trails to four paddler campsites on the right. After passing the campsite trails, the wide, grassy Southern Tip Trail meanders through sumac until it reaches its end in a field. Continue in the same, northeast direction to join a campground road. As you approach the marina, the path to the nature center diverges to the right across a grassy lawn. From the nature center, Island Farm Nature Trail leads through a pretty marsh of sweet flag; a brochure guide is available at the campground office if you decide to explore this short loop.

Return to the marina to catch a ferry back to the parking area at Kamp Kill Kare.

DID YOU KNOW?

During much of the 8,000 years since Abenaki moved into this area, the lake was lower, and Burton Island was part of the peninsula stretching from the mainland. By the time Europeans arrived, the lake level had risen enough to isolate this spot as an island.

MORE INFORMATION

Burton Island State Park operates Memorial Day to Labor Day; the island is open to the public year-round, but no facilities are available in the off-season. Burton Island State Park, P.O. Box 123, Saint Albans, VT 05481; 802-524-6353; vtstateparks.com/burton.html. The ferry and boat launch are operated by Kamp Kill Kare State Park, 2714 Hathaway Point Road, Saint Albans, VT 05481; 802-524-6021; vtstateparks.com/killkare.html. A day-use fee is charged unless you're camping on Burton Island. Kamp Kill Kare is open for day use only, 10 A.M. to official sunset, Memorial Day to Labor Day. Pets are not allowed in Kamp Kill Kare except en route to Burton Island.

NEARBY

Camp and swim on Burton Island or at state parks on the more remote Woods and Knight islands nearby. A small store and a grill provide food near the marina; more food options are in Saint Albans, 6 miles east. Paddling on the lake can be difficult due to wind and waves, but the Missisquoi National Wildlife Refuge (Trip 38), 13 miles north, has a slow river and excellent wildlife watching.

38

MISSISQUOI NATIONAL WILDLIFE REFUGE

Birds swoop, call, feed, and float around you as you pass through fields, woods, and wetlands on this flat hike to the shore of Lake Champlain.

DIRECTIONS

Follow VT 78 west from its intersection with US 7 in downtown Swanton. After 0.3 mile, cross the Missisquoi River and turn right at the stop sign, staying on VT 78. Go 5.4 miles, entering the Missisquoi National Wildlife Refuge and passing several trailheads. Turn left onto Tabor Road and travel 1 mile, passing the refuge headquarters and visitor center, and turn left into the trailhead parking lot (space for 10 cars). *GPS coordinates:* 44° 57.24′ N, 73°12.32′ W.

TRAIL DESCRIPTION

Missisquoi National Wildlife Refuge is an important migratory stopover for birds on the Atlantic flyway between Canada and South America. Encompassing 6,729 acres of the Missisquoi River's bird-foot delta, so called for its webbed-foot appearance from above, the refuge hosts a diversity of natural communities. In addition to migratory birds, it supports many resident species, including the state-threatened spiny softshell turtle and Vermont's largest great blue heron rookery, on Shad Island. Old Railroad Passage Trail takes advantage of the height of an abandoned railroad bed to visit four natural communities in the refuge: field, wetland, pitch-pine bog, and lakeshore. Kids of any age can handle the flat terrain of this hike; the distance makes it most suitable to kids 4 and older.

From the trailhead kiosk, follow the mowed path across an open field. In summer, bobolinks and Savannah sparrows may be hopping about, eating insects and seeds, and tending nests hidden in the grass. A thin line of trees on

LOCATION
Swanton, VT

RATING
Easy

DISTANCE
3 miles

ELEVATION GAIN
Minimal

ESTIMATED TIME
1.5 hours

MAPS
USGS East Alburg

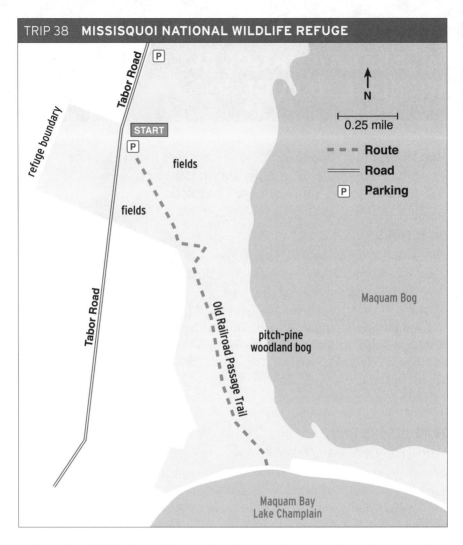

either side of Old Railroad Passage Trail marks the beginning of its path along the old rail bed. In 1883, the Lamoille Valley Extension Railroad was built from what is now Swanton Town Beach to Rouses Point, New York, but the 11-mile line was not commercially viable and closed six months after opening.

The field vegetation beyond the narrow band of trees shows its increasing sogginess with the appearance of cattails, red osier dogwood, alders, winterberry holly, and a variety of willow species. After 0.5 mile, Old Railroad Passage Trail diverges from the rail bed on an S-curved path through a slightly elevated woodland. In the middle of this copse, a couple of ancient maples raise thick, gnarled limbs amid oak and beech saplings.

The path passes through a stand of paper birch as it returns to the railroad bed. Ahead, the corridor stretches straight for as far as you can see; you are entering an 890-acre open peatland called Maquam Bog, the only pitch-pine woodland bog in Vermont. In addition to many bird species, several mammal species—including the white-tailed deer, meadow vole, and red squirrel—call the bog home. The ebb and flow of annual flooding is critical to maintaining the flora and fauna. Fires, whether naturally caused or human created, allow the shrub understory to thrive, producing large quantities of fruits and berries—especially blueberries, which feed both wildlife and humans.

The surface of the bog is peat, ranging in depth from 2 to 8 feet. Peatland water is acidic, so only a few trees can live here beside the pitch pine: gray birch, black spruce, and red maple. Most of the peat is covered with low shrubs, the dominant being rhodora, which adorns the bog in late May with pink flowers. Other common shrubs are bog laurel, Labrador tea, leatherleaf, and sheep laurel.

Approaching Lake Champlain, Old Railroad Passage Trail curves southeast and enters a lakeside floodplain forest, with silver maple, green ash, red maple, and cottonwood creating a towering canopy. Beyond the trees, Maquam Bay opens south to the Inland Sea, the northeastern arm of Lake Champlain. Look for herons wading and spearing fish along the shore and ospreys and the occasional bald eagle soaring overhead.

Retrace your steps to return to the trailhead.

The hike through Maquam Bog provides an abundance of berries, such as highbush blueberry (pictured), mountain holly, wild raisin, black chokeberry, and large and small cranberry.

DID YOU KNOW?

Before the explorer Champlain named this lake after himself, it was called Bitawbagok, or the "Lake Between." The lake is the western edge of the Wabanaki's homeland, which extends across northern New England and the Canadian Maritime provinces. The town of Swanton remains a center of Wabanaki population and culture.

MORE INFORMATION

Portions of the Missisquoi National Wildlife Refuge are closed to hikers and boaters to protect sensitive habitats. Fishing, berry picking, and hunting are permitted in specific areas; get details at the visitor center. Camping, open fires, removal of plants or animals, snowmobiles, off-road vehicles, and overnight parking are not allowed. Dogs must be leashed. Missisquoi National Wildlife Refuge, 29 Tabor Road, Swanton, VT 05488; 802-868-4781; fws.gov/refuge/missisquoi.

NEARBY

The Missisquoi, Lamoille Valley, and Alburg rail trails are multiuse recreational paths exploring this region. Via water, the 740-mile Northern Forest Canoe Trail's route includes Lake Champlain and the Missisquoi River. Alburg Dunes State Park, 13.4 miles southwest, has interesting geologic history and vegetation, as well as a picnic area and beach for swimming. The Abenaki Tribal Museum—on US 7 in Swanton, 4.5 miles southeast—has a small exhibit. Food is available along VT 78 in Swanton.

Old Railroad Passage Trail passes a lakeside floodplain forest, verdant with ferns and broadly spaced trees.

NORTH-CENTRAL VERMONT

North-central Vermont is almost exclusively mountainous, and a certain toughness is associated with
the northern Green Mountains. They are rugged
and tall, standing more in individual peaks than
in long ridges, and Long Trail thru-hikers count
on having to work harder here. Vermont's highest
peak, Mount Mansfield (Trips 45 and 46), is recognized for its long, rocky, windswept crest, which
spills over the steep walls of Smugglers' Notch in
avalanches and landslides. Jay Peak (Trip 51) is
known for being bare, windy, so far north it's almost
in Canada, and, above all, the snowiest place in Vermont. But despite these true-enough reputations,
the northern Green Mountains have some very
pleasant day hikes that are—perhaps surprisingly—
not necessarily the most strenuous in the state.

A concentration of big peaks occurs between the western-flowing Winooski
and Lamoille rivers. The tall main range of the Green Mountains forms a dramatic landscape here, leading the Long Trail and Catamount Trail (cross-country ski trail) across some of their most challenging terrain. A short distance to
the east, the parallel Worcester Range has steep sides and rocky summit domes,
shown characteristically on its most well-known peak, Mount Hunger (Trip 41).
Most of these two ranges are conserved by state forests and state parks.

From the Lamoille River north to the Missisquoi River along the Canadian
border, the mountains are a little lower and more spread out, with ranges less
frequently explored by hikers. That relative isolation gives places like Devil's
Gulch and Big Muddy Pond (Trip 49) a feeling of remoteness, despite their locations along the popular route of the Long Trail.

In the far-northeastern corner of this section, the 25-mile-long Lake Mem-
phremagog spreads across the international border, surrounded by the Sutton
Mountains on the north side and the Green Mountains on the south side, where
Long Trail thru-hikers begin or end their journeys.

39

WORCESTER RANGE SKYLINE

This rugged ridgeline hike traverses four peaks and winds through remote, moss-covered woods for a full day on one of Vermont's most beautiful and challenging trails.

DIRECTIONS

From VT 12 in the village of Worcester, head west on Minister Brook Road 1.5 miles to Hampshire Hill Road. Turn right on Hampshire Hill Road, travel 2.3 miles, and turn left on Mountain Road where Hampshire Hill bends sharply to the right. Follow Mountain Road 0.1 mile to its end at the trailhead parking for Mount Worcester (space for 12 cars). *GPS coordinates:* 44° 25.31′ N, 72° 34.44′ W.

For directions to this hike's endpoint in Middlesex, see Trip 40 directions to White Rock Mountain's trailhead.

TRAIL DESCRIPTION

The Worcester Range is home to the well-loved Mount Hunger (Trip 41), Stowe Pinnacle (Trip 44), and Elmore Mountain (Trip 42), as well as the less frequently visited gems of White Rock Mountain (Trip 40) and Mount Worcester (3,225 feet). All of these rocky high points give perspective over the big mountains and picturesque valleys of northern and central Vermont, so their appeal to hikers is understandable. But the range also harbors a more remote and meditative hiking experience along Skyline Trail, which traverses two tall, forested peaks between the bookends of Mount Worcester in the north and Mount Hunger in the south. Looking at a satellite map, you could be lured into thinking the ridgeline has less elevation drop and gain than it does; in fact, this is a rigorous 10.5 miles. The 3,350 feet of elevation gain is the sum of ascending four peaks along Skyline Trail, starting in the north and heading south as described below, which has most of the elevation gain in the beginning and less as

LOCATION
Worcester and Middlesex, VT

RATING
Strenuous

DISTANCE
10.5 miles end-to-end

ELEVATION GAIN
3,350 feet (cumulative over four peaks)

ESTIMATED TIME
8 hours

MAPS
USGS Worcester, USGS Stowe

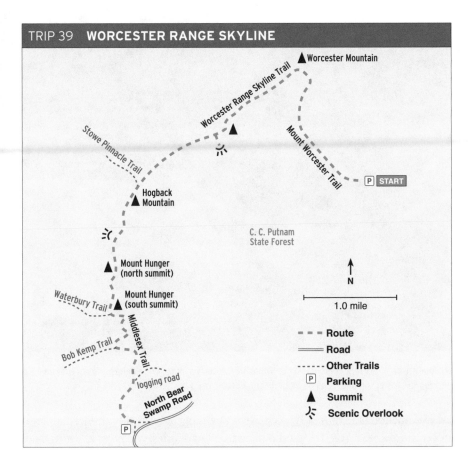

Worcester Mountain

Worcester Range Skyline Trail

Stowe Pinnacle Trail

Mount Worcester Trail

P START

Hogback Mountain

C. C. Putnam State Forest

Mount Hunger (north summit)

Waterbury Trail

Mount Hunger (south summit)

Middlesex Trail

Bob Kemp Trail

logging road

North Bear Swamp Road

P

N

1.0 mile

- - - Route
=== Road
----- Other Trails
P Parking
▲ Summit
⅄ Scenic Overlook

you get farther along and more tired. A shorter alternative is the more popular southern segment of Skyline, accessed from the western side by connecting Stowe Pinnacle to Mount Hunger for a 6.8-mile hike with a healthy 2,780 feet of climbing when hiked north to south, end-to-end. No matter which way you approach Skyline, you'll need to either spot a second car at the other end of your point-to-point hike or plan to turn around and hike back to your starting point.

Mount Worcester Trail begins on the west side of the parking area as a blue-blazed two-track, ascending at a measured pace for the first mile and then becoming increasingly steep. At 1.8 miles, climb a rocky, narrow, conifer-lined gully and arrive at the open pitches leading to Worcester's summit. Thick bands of quartz contrast brightly with the gray summit ledges, and their slick white surfaces make precarious footing. There isn't much flat ground on the pointed summit of Worcester, but you will find a view of the route ahead: distinct peaks stacked up to the south. Skyline Trail begins with a steep drop off the summit into dark green woods, zigzagging down the ridge through moss-covered humps and bumps, brushing past thickly needled boughs of balsam fir and red spruce. Cross a saddle and begin climbing. Infrequent use can cause the trail to be easily disguised by a windblown pile of birch leaves, so you'll need to keep

A broad stripe of brilliant white quartz in Mount Worcester's summit ledges alerts hikers they're nearing the top of the first peak on magnificent Worcester Range Skyline Trail.

an eye out for blue blazes in some less obvious spots, although Skyline Trail never wanders far from the crest of the range. At 4 miles, you cross an unnamed, wooded summit (3,470 feet). At 4.2 miles, a spur trail leads left a short distance (there are no long spur trails when you're walking such a narrow spine) to a small window in the trees, which gives a view southeast.

For the next mile, Skyline Trail continues gently downhill and across a saddle then begins climbing the next peak, the tallest one in the Worcester Range at 3,600 feet. It is known sometimes as Hogback Mountain, sometimes as Putnam Mountain, and sometimes, oddly, as an unnamed mountain. Log ladders assist your ascent over ledges with sheets of moss blanketing the rock and hanging off the edges. The ladders and a wider, more obvious trail are the first signs you're approaching the more frequently visited southern half of Skyline. Sure enough, at 5.8 miles, you arrive at a T junction, with the trail downhill to Stowe Pinnacle (also blue blazed) on your right and the continuation of Skyline Trail heading left. Go left and uphill, reaching the forested height of land at 5.9 miles. From here, the ridgeline rolls along its highest stretch, passing an opening on the western rim with views of Mount Mansfield's skyward-facing profile and the bumpy line of peaks to its south: Dewey Mountain (3,323 feet), Mount Clark (2,970 feet), Mount Mayo (3,110 feet), and Bolton Mountain (3,690 feet), the latter recognizable by a wind tower rising from a divot in its summit ridge. Waterbury Reservoir reflects the sky in the southwest, with the two-tiered top of Camel's Hump beyond it.

Skyline Trail descends to the 7-mile mark, at which point it begins to climb Mount Hunger. Reach Hunger's north summit (3,570 feet) at 7.3 miles and continue another 0.6 mile in and out of woods, undulating over big rocks and down slabby ledges to the south summit (3,539 feet). In addition to views of Mount Mansfield and the Stowe Valley, Mount Hunger's broad, bald top gives a magnificent vantage point east to the Granite Hills of Groton State Forest; south to the Northfield Range and the tall peaks of Monroe Skyline stretching south from Camel's Hump; and west, where the Winooski River cuts a deep cleft in the main chain of the Green Mountains, opening a view to Lake Champlain and the distant Adirondacks.

There are two trails off the south dome of Mount Hunger: Waterbury Trail heads west (see Trip 41: Mount Hunger), and Middlesex Trail—our route—goes east. Middlesex Trail's descent is very steep and exposed for the first 0.3 mile. Footing on the open slabs can be tricky in dry conditions and dangerous when wet or icy. If conditions make Middlesex Trail a poor option, or if you simply want to hit one more excellent Worcester Range peak, you can descend instead via White Rock Mountain (3,150 feet) on a slightly less steep, somewhat less exposed route that rejoins Middlesex Trail after 1.6 miles, adding 0.6 mile to your total hike. (To do so, head west on Waterbury Trail 0.1 mile, dropping to the junction of White Rock Mountain Trail on your left. Follow that 0.8 mile to the open shoulder of White Rock Mountain [Trip 40] and Bob Kemp Trail, which descends east to meet Middlesex Trail.)

From the summit of Hunger, go east on Middlesex Trail and follow blue blazes painted on the open rock, clambering downhill on wide slabs with little to grab for handholds. I sit and scoot a lot of it, preferring a hole in my pants to tumbling. The steepest final pitch usually has ropes you can grab to slow your descent into the forest. When you put your boots back on dirt at the base of the ledges, the going is still rugged and rocky for another 0.7 mile until you reach the junction of Bob Kemp Trail on your right at 8.9 miles. Turn left, continuing down Middlesex Trail on an old two-track with easy footing and a gentle pitch. After crossing a wide stream, the trail reverts to single-track and passes a register box just before descending onto a wide logging road at 9.7 miles. Turn right and follow the logging road 0.7 mile, watching for a spur trail on the right shortly after passing a metal gate (which may be open or closed). The spur trail ducks through dense woods for 0.1 mile to the trailhead parking lot.

DID YOU KNOW?

Moose sometimes use Skyline Trail in their rambles. Although it seems like an improbable and difficult place for these big creatures to climb, they winter in higher-elevation forests, preferring stands of balsam fir and paper birch, which are prevalent here. If you encounter a moose, do not approach it, as it may be threatened by your presence. Give it space and time to move on its way before you proceed.

MORE INFORMATION

Most of the Worcester Range is within the C. C. Putnam State Forest, managed by Vermont Department of Forests, Parks and Recreation; fpr.vermont.gov. Primitive camping is permitted only below 2,500 feet. To minimize erosion along fragile, high-elevation terrain, the state closes Worcester Range trails between mid-April and Memorial Day. The Green Mountain Club helps maintain trails in the Worcester Range. Green Mountain Club, 4711 Waterbury–Stowe Road, Waterbury Center, VT 05677; 802-244-7037; greenmountainclub.org.

NEARBY

Swimming holes along Shady Rill Road are well marked by a dirt road pull-off with picnic shelters, 4 miles southeast of the Middlesex trailhead. A little farther down the road, Wrightsville Reservoir has a public beach and boat launch. Hancock Brook swimming hole is a beautiful spot 1.4 miles from the Worcester trailhead. There's a general store in Worcester, with more shops and restaurants in Montpelier, 9 miles south.

Mountain ash berries and sunset color the eastern view from Mount Hunger, the final summit along the challenging and spectacular Worcester Range Skyline Trail.

40
WHITE ROCK MOUNTAIN

The rugged spire of White Rock provides an adventurous hike and exhilarating views.

DIRECTIONS

From downtown Montpelier, follow VT 12 north 5.3 miles and turn left onto Shady Rill Road. Go 2.1 miles and turn right onto Story Road. At 0.5 mile, stay straight onto Nellie Chase Road; 0.1 mile farther, bear left onto North Bear Swamp Road. Drive 1.9 miles to the parking lot (space for 15 cars) on the right. *GPS coordinates: 44° 22.31′ N, 72° 38.41′ W.*

TRAIL DESCRIPTION

White Rock Mountain (3,150 feet) is a ledgy peak off the south shoulder of Mount Hunger. Open, flat terraces with panoramic views circle its summit, and the hand-over-hand scrambling required to get to the tip-top makes this one of Vermont's more exciting peaks to attain. The top third of the trail up White Rock is particularly rugged, steep, and often wet, but the payoff is worth muddy feet.

From the parking lot, Middlesex Trail follows a 500-foot, blue-blazed connector trail to a dirt road; turn left and follow the road north past a metal gate. Martin's Brook gurgles mostly unseen on the left as the road climbs gradually through a mixed hardwood forest. At 0.8 mile, just after a cascade tumbles out of the woods, turn left off the road onto a footpath marked by a small sign reading simply, "Trail." The footpath climbs moderately, curving through birches and maples and traversing occasional rock steps. After crossing a wide brook on rocks, Middlesex Trail becomes wider, reminiscent of its early days as a carriage road. After a gradual climb, the

LOCATION
Middlesex, VT

RATING
Moderate to Strenuous

DISTANCE
4.6 miles

ELEVATION GAIN
1,558 feet

ESTIMATED TIME
3.5 hours

MAPS
USGS Middlesex, USGS Stowe

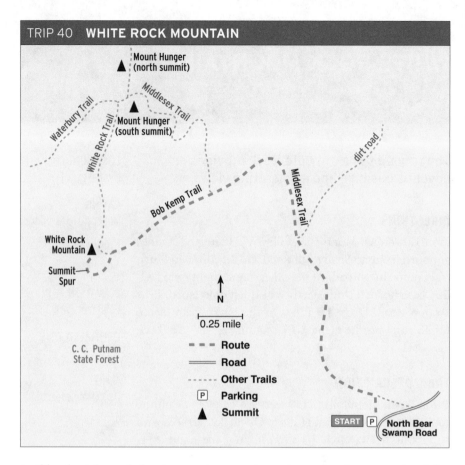

Mount Hunger
(north summit)

Waterbury Trail

White Rock Trail

Middlesex Trail

Mount Hunger
(south summit)

dirt road

Bob Kemp Trail

Middlesex Trail

White Rock
Mountain

Summit—
Spur

N

0.25 mile

C. C. Putnam
State Forest

- - - **Route**

═══ **Road**

----- **Other Trails**

P **Parking**

▲ **Summit**

START P North Bear
Swamp Road

trail levels. A logged clearing can be seen through a strip of trees on the right, and the trail curves west and enters a tunnel of young beech trees.

The trail alternately crosses and climbs a damp, ledgy hillside. At 1.6 miles, a small clearing marks a junction. Middlesex Trail turns right here, toward Mount Hunger. Don't follow it; instead go straight onto the blue-blazed Bob Kemp Trail. The next 0.5 mile is steeper and more rugged than Middlesex Trail, with numerous ledges and rock steps to mount and muddy saddles to cross. After two stream crossings, a long rock escarpment slices down through the forest. Follow the trail up into a cleft in the cliff then climb through an airy stand of paper birch with long, slightly obstructed views as the mountainside drops away on the right. The trail then climbs steeply into balsam firs, where thick mosses blanket the forest floor.

After a short scramble that requires hands as well as feet, two log bridges lead across a foamy, copper-colored pool. Tannic acid from decomposing conifers gives the water its dark color. A short distance above the pool, Bob Kemp Trail climbs a bare rock slope into a gully and emerges onto flat, open rock with views eastward. The bald summit of Mount Hunger rises behind you to the north. Although these views are magnificent, they get better as you circle and ascend the peak. Weave through small clumps of trees, across broad terraces of rock, and climb to a trail junction. Bob Kemp Trail, also called White Rock Trail on the Waterbury side, heads right here to meet Waterbury Trail just below the summit of Mount Hunger. Go left on the 0.1-mile spur to White Rock's summit.

Cross an open, rocky area with a view of Camel's Hump (4,083 feet) then climb a tricky rock pitch, where a long crack makes the best toeholds. Ascending this kind of slab using a combination of friction and balance is characteristic of hikes in the Worcester Range. Around the next curve, dramatic western views appear. The dark waters of Waterbury Reservoir snake through the hills, and the notch of the Winooski River valley points west to distant Adirondack peaks. As you continue around the curve, the profile ridge of Mount Mansfield (4,393 feet) and the pointed summit of Whiteface Mountain (3,714 feet) come into view. Hoist yourself through a crack in the boulders to clamber onto the little bare summit of White Rock.

Return the way you came up.

Climbing to the tip-top of White Rock Mountain is a fun scramble over rugged outcrops. For easier destinations with the same great views, opt for the rock terraces surrounding the summit.

DID YOU KNOW?

When settlers cleared farmland in Middlesex in the 1760s, White Rock and Mount Hunger were covered with trees. Forest fires left the peaks in their current bald state.

MORE INFORMATION

White Rock is within the C. C. Putnam State Forest, managed by Vermont Department of Forests, Parks and Recreation; vtfpr.org. Primitive camping is permitted only below 2,500 feet. To minimize erosion along fragile, high-elevation terrain, the state closes Worcester Range trails between mid-April and Memorial Day. Green Mountain Club helps maintain trails in the Worcester Range. Green Mountain Club, 4711 Waterbury–Stowe Road, Waterbury Center, VT 05677; 802-244-7037; greenmountainclub.org.

NEARBY

Swimming holes along Shady Rill Road are well marked by a dirt road pull-off with picnic shelters, 4 miles southeast. Wrightsville Reservoir also has a public beach and boat launch, 5.2 miles southeast. Groceries, shops, and restaurants are in Montpelier, 10 miles southeast.

VERMONT'S ANCIENT, ILLOGICAL RIVERS

Logic says that water takes the path of least resistance: Rain and snowmelt flow downhill off mountains and continue to the sea. The ridge of highest mountains divides the watersheds. As in the Continental Divide in the Rocky Mountains, the Green Mountains' high peaks shed water from their east side easterly and from their west side westerly. Why, then, do some rivers start on one side of a mountain range and, instead of continuing downhill to the ocean, cut through those high hills to drain on the other side?

Look at three of Vermont's big rivers: the Missisquoi, the Lamoille, and the Winooski. Each rises on the eastern side of the Green Mountains and slices through the highest ridgeline to empty into Lake Champlain on the western side. How did the water come to take such an illogical path?

The simple answer is that these three rivers have been flowing since before the Green Mountains were born. Their ancient routes were established and continued as continental plates crashed into one another and thrust mountains up around them. The Acadian orogeny—the mountain-building period in which the Greens arose—was immensely disturbing to the landscape, but also took 40 million years. During this time, the rivers continued down their paths and cut into the new mountains as the peaks heaved upward.

Ancient rivers that predate and cut through mountain ranges are known as antecedent drainages, and there are many across North America, as well as in other mountainous parts of the world. In the Appalachian Mountains, the Potomac and Delaware rivers are prime examples. Both rivers have water gaps, or places where the rivers slice through a ridge. The Columbia River similarly cuts a deep canyon through the Cascade Mountains on the Washington–Oregon border as it flows westward to the Pacific.

Because they provide passage through steep terrain, antecedent rivers are natural routes for people finding their way through the mountains. Abenaki used the relatively slow flows of the Missisquoi River for upstream canoe travel into the Green Mountains and the more rollicking descent of the Lamoille River to return through the mountains to Lake Champlain. Today four parallel roads and a railroad take advantage of the Winooski River's mighty erosive power as it plows its illogical route through the Green Mountains' highest peaks.

41

MOUNT HUNGER

"The mountaintop is one of the pleasantest places of earth, and will be visited so long as people inhabit the country." Mount Hunger's rocky, domed top was a favorite with hikers, even before Middlesex resident William Chapin penned this thought in 1880, and has remained so ever since.

LOCATION
Waterbury Center, VT

RATING
Moderate to Strenuous

DISTANCE
4 miles

ELEVATION GAIN
2,290 feet

DIRECTIONS

ESTIMATED TIME
3.5 hours

From I-89 Exit 10, follow VT 100 (Waterbury–Stowe Road) north 1.2 miles and turn right onto Guptil Road. Travel 2 miles to the town green in Waterbury Center and bear right onto Maple Street. Go 0.2 mile and turn right onto Loomis Hill Road. Drive up Loomis Hill Road 1.9 miles; here it curves left and becomes Sweet Farm Road. Go 1.5 miles north on Sweet Farm Road to the trailhead parking lot on the right (space for about 20 cars). Overflow parking is along the far side of Sweet Farm Road, leaving space for emergency vehicles to pass. *GPS coordinates:* 44° 24.14′ N, 72° 40.52′ W.

MAPS
USGS Stowe

TRAIL DESCRIPTION

Mount Hunger (3,570 feet at its treed north summit, although the south summit, where most hikes end, is 3,539 feet) is a rounded bald spot at the southern end of the Worcester Range. Its rocky top is a fun place to explore, in addition to providing immense views. Waterbury Trail is moderate, but the final 0.5 mile becomes progressively steeper, with ledges to scramble up. Most kids 8 and older will enjoy scrambling up if they're prepared for the distance and steepness. Dogs and winter hikers may struggle to climb the steep slab.

The rocky, rooty Waterbury Trail leads east from the parking lot into a hardwood forest sprinkled with a few

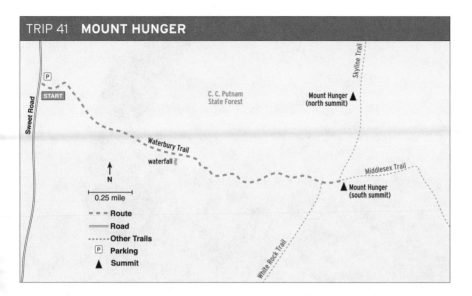

hemlocks. The climb begins gently, although as the trail curves southeast, it becomes more moderate. Pass between mossy boulders and climb rock steps. Listen for hermit thrush, Vermont's state bird, trilling short, ethereal phrases that almost sound like they have their own echo. Named for their shy behavior, these little brown-and-white songbirds are difficult to spot in a thick forest, but their haunting song is the soundtrack of many summer hikes.

Waterbury Trail climbs steadily but easily for about half a mile then descends gradually to cross two small streams. After the second stream, the trail becomes steep and climbs to the edge of a boulder-filled stream. A scenic waterfall tumbles from above during wet weather. Continue up the eroded slope on the left side and cross the stream above the waterfall. The trail continues moderately or steeply up a rocky slope that is loose and eroded in places. Following a streambed, you will enter the boreal forest of the upper mountain. Canada mayflowers, bunchberries, and blue-bead lilies cover the forest floor beneath spindly sprigs of hobblebushes, and the first steep ledge appears. Zigzag up it and continue uphill another couple tenths of a mile to the next set of ledges. Climb cautiously on this steep rock, which may be especially slick on wet or humid days.

At 1.9 miles, between two vertical scrambles, the White Rock Mountain Trail heads right. Continue straight uphill on Waterbury Trail, skirting small stands of wind-stunted trees, to arrive on Hunger's rock summit. Skyline Trail (see Trip 39: Worcester Range Skyline) leads north into the trees, passing over Hunger's forested north peak. The south peak of Mount Hunger was also treed before a fire left the rock bare. Middlesex Trail leads straight ahead, down the eastern side of the mountain, joining the trail from White Rock Mountain.

Views from Mount Hunger are vast and unencumbered, justifying this small peak's popularity. To the south, along Hunger's descending ridgeline, are the rocky terraces and pointy summit of White Rock Mountain. To the west, the

The views from Mount Hunger's bare summit reward hikers willing to scale its ledges.

long ridge of the Green Mountains' highest peaks stretches as far as you can see south and north. The Winooski River cuts a deep gouge between Camel's Hump (Trip 27) and Bolton Mountain (3,690 feet). Waterbury Reservoir shines in the foreground, and the craggy profile of Mount Mansfield (Trips 45 and 46) dominates the ridgeline heading north. The eastern side of the Worcester Range is mostly low foothills, with the exception of the Granite Hills in the southeast. This cluster of tall peaks is related geologically to the White Mountains in New Hampshire, which are also visible on a clear day.

Return the way you came.

DID YOU KNOW?

In 1878, a road ascended the eastern side of Mount Hunger. It was broad and smooth enough to accommodate six horses pulling a carriage of 20 people to within half a mile of the summit.

MORE INFORMATION

Mount Hunger is within the C. C. Putnam State Forest. To minimize erosion along fragile, high-elevation terrain, the state closes the upper mountain trails in the Worcester Range between mid-April and Memorial Day; lower Waterbury Trail is open as far as the waterfall during mud season (see Introduction, page xvi). Vermont Department of Forests, Parks and Recreation, 5 Perry Street, Suite 20, Barre, VT 05641; 802-476-0184; vtfpr.org. The Green Mountain Club helps maintain trails in the Worcester Range. Green Mountain Club, 4711 Waterbury–Stowe Road, Waterbury Center, VT 05677; 802-244-7037; greenmountainclub.org.

NEARBY

Waterbury Center State Park, 4 miles west, has swimming and boating on Waterbury Reservoir; the Winooski River also has good paddling. Camp on the reservoir at Little River State Park, 12 miles west, or at Smugglers' Notch State Park, 12.5 miles northwest. The Green Mountain Club's Hiker Center is along VT 100 in Waterbury Center, 4.5 miles west. Food is found on VT 100 in Waterbury, 7 miles south, or in Stowe, 7 miles northwest.

42

ELMORE MOUNTAIN

Elmore's loop hike explores many facets of the mountain: multiple outlook points, a historical fire tower, a ridgeline walk, and an unusual balanced boulder.

DIRECTIONS

From the junction of VT 12 and Beach Road in Elmore, head north on VT 12 for 0.2 mile. Turn left into Elmore State Park, where a day-use fee is charged in season. Follow the road through the campground to a parking area (space for about 15 cars) by a metal gate. (Winter hikers: Follow Beach Road 0.1 from VT 12 to the park's day-use parking lot on the right. Walk through the campground to the trailhead, adding 0.7 mile round-trip to the hike distance.) *GPS coordinates:* 44° 32.38′ N, 72° 32.17′ W.

TRAIL DESCRIPTION

Elmore Mountain (2,590 feet) is a low peak at the north end of—and slightly detached from—the higher peaks of the rugged Worcester Range. Elmore's solitary location and many ledgy outlooks afford spectacular views in all directions, a plus for hikers who prefer to keep their boot soles on the ground rather than ascend to the windy, swaying cab of a fire tower. Formerly an out-and-back hike, Ridge Trail now connects Balancing Rock with the beginning of the mountain trail, creating a loop. At the foot of the mountain's treed slopes, the 219-acre Elmore Lake's sparkling waters top off the list of reasons why this mountain is a favorite. The hike is appropriate for kids ages 7 and older.

From the parking area, walk past the metal gate to head uphill on Fire Tower Trail, a multiuse dirt road. The road climbs gradually as it heads first west then south, paralleling the ridge of the mountain high above. The

LOCATION
Lake Elmore, VT

RATING
Moderate

DISTANCE
4.5 miles

ELEVATION GAIN
1,145 feet

ESTIMATED TIME
3 hours

MAPS
USGS Morrisville; vtstateparks.com/ elmore.html

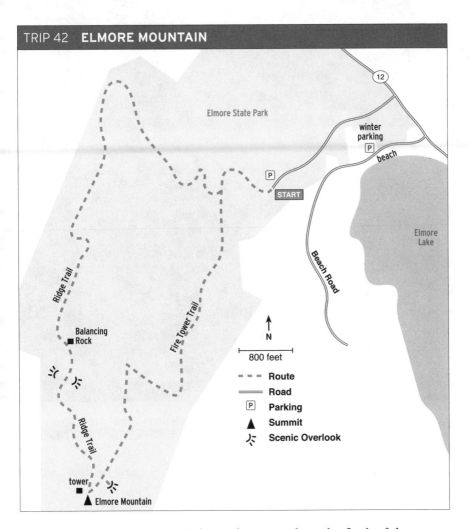

long-distance Catamount Trail shares this route along the flank of the mountain. At 0.3 mile, Ridge Trail departs right; this is the bottom of your return route. Stay straight and continue climbing the wide track of Fire Tower Trail.

At 0.6 mile, follow Fire Tower Trail when it turns right off the road and climbs rock steps into the forest. Blue blazes mark the route through hobblebushes and ferns as it continues southward along a stream. Climbing moderately, the trail crosses patches of bare bedrock and occasional step stones. A switchback to the right leads onto a rugged, rocky path through a tall maple forest. After several more switchbacks, Fire Tower Trail flattens, and the forest becomes noticeably shorter due to the elevation and exposure. At 1.6 miles, where the trail bends right, an opening straight ahead beckons. Follow this short side trail onto a rocky outcrop with an old ranger cabin foundation and a view east. Look up to the ridgeline to spot the 60-foot-tall fire tower above the trees. From 1938, when the present tower was erected to replace one destroyed by that year's infamous

Canine hikers are welcome on Elmore Mountain. The long ridge features several rock outcrops, providing plentiful views east over Elmore Lake and west to Vermont's tallest peak, Mount Mansfield.

hurricane, through 1974, a fire lookout lived in a cabin here on the ledge and hiked to the summit each day to work.

Return to Fire Tower Trail and go left, continuing uphill. This final 0.2 mile to the summit is steep, with scrambles over rooty sections and steps blasted into the bedrock. A T intersection marks the top of the climb; go left to the fire tower (1.8 miles), which provides extensive views over the treetops. The spine of the Worcester Range snakes south, and the tallest Green Mountains lie to the west, including Mount Mansfield's 4,393-foot Chin, the highest point in Vermont. Lamoille River valley farmlands spread across the landscape north of Elmore, and boats are visible on Elmore Lake beneath the eastern slope.

Return to the T intersection and follow the blue-blazed Ridge Trail north. Rocky outcrops provide views east and west from this high spine. At 2.4 miles, a whale-sized boulder raises its mighty bulk from a precarious-looking perch on a bed of ferns. Known as a glacial erratic, Balancing Rock was left here when the glacier transporting it melted about 11,000 years ago.

Many informal, exploratory trails around Balancing Rock make finding the continuation of Ridge Trail a little challenging; it is on the hillside just above the boulder, heading west across a level area before continuing north another mile along the ridge. At 3.4 miles, a long U-turn steers you off the ridge and south through a hollow between the main ridgeline and a lower, parallel ridge. Ridge Trail continues generally southeast for its final 0.5 mile, descending through mixed hardwoods and alongside tall walls of mossy rock before crossing a depression and climbing back onto Fire Tower Trail. Turn left and return downhill 0.3 mile to the trailhead parking lot.

DID YOU KNOW?

A turn-of-the-twentieth-century hotel hosted guests on the eastern slope of Mount Elmore. It was removed when the Civilian Conservation Corps developed the recreation area that became Elmore State Park in 1936.

MORE INFORMATION

Elmore State Park is open for day use from 10 A.M. to official sunset, Memorial Day through Columbus Day. Dogs are allowed except on the beach; bring proof of rabies vaccination. Elmore State Park, 856 VT Route 12, P.O. Box 93, Lake Elmore, VT 05657; 802-888-2982; vtstateparks.com/elmore.html.

NEARBY

Swimming, paddling, and camping are at the base of the mountain in Elmore State Park. The Lamoille River has good paddling as well, and mountain-bike trails can be found in Morrisville, 4.5 miles west, and Stowe, 13 miles southwest. A small general store is on VT 12 next to Elmore Lake; head to Morrisville or Stowe for more food options.

43

WIESSNER WOODS

Tall hemlocks and bubbly brooks characterize this leisurely loop walk to a lookout point with a quintessential Vermont view.

DIRECTIONS

From the junction of VT 100 and VT 108 in Stowe Village, take VT 108 (Mountain Road) 3.3 miles and turn right onto Edson Hill Road. Drive 0.5 mile and, just past the Stowehof (an inn), turn right into a drive. Parking is in a lot on the left (space for 8 cars). *GPS coordinates: 44° 29.81′ N, 72° 43.62′ W.*

TRAIL DESCRIPTION

Wiessner Woods is a lovely, shady forest sprawling over 79 acres near Stowe Village. Its network of wide trails is inviting for hikers of all ages as it ambles over rolling ground, passing through stands of mature trees and crossing small brooks.

From the parking area, cross a private driveway and a grassy meadow to a kiosk at the trailhead. Enter Wiessner Woods on a broad dirt path and immediately cross a wide bridge over a stream. Blue paw-print trail markers let you know you're on a section of Catamount Trail, a 300-mile cross-country ski and snowshoe trail that extends the length of Vermont. Follow the flat path through birch, maple, and broad patches of jewelweed, a native plant that sends up soft, leggy stems in spring and dangles a small orange or yellow open-mouthed flower between June and September.

Around a bend, white pines surround the Four Corners junction at 0.1 mile. Meadow Trail, your return route, rises gently to the left; Main Street continues straight ahead. Go right, following Catamount Trail, also called Hardwood Ridge Trail here. The path narrows and crosses a long line

LOCATION
Stowe, VT

RATING
Easy

DISTANCE
1.5 miles

ELEVATION GAIN
100 feet

ESTIMATED TIME
1 hour

MAPS
USGS Stowe,
USGS Sterling Mountain;
stowelandtrust.org/
fileadmin/slt/maps/
WiessnerWoodsMap.pdf

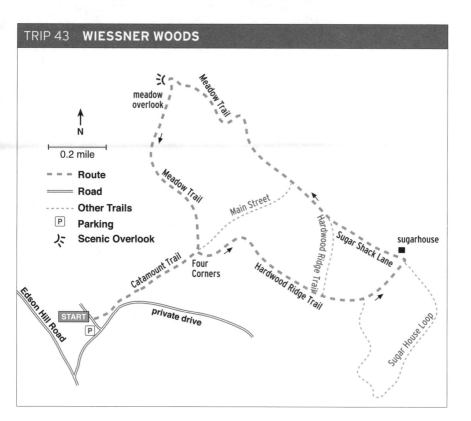

meadow
overlook

Meadow Trail

N

0.2 mile

- - - Route
═══ Road
· · · · Other Trails
P   Parking
✦   Scenic Overlook

Meadow Trail

Main Street

Hardwood Ridge Trail

Sugar Shack Lane

sugarhouse

Catamount Trail

Four
Corners

Hardwood Ridge Trail

Hardwood Ridge Trail

Sugar House Loop

Edson Hill Road

START

P

private drive

of bog bridges before entering a lovely, mature hemlock forest. The thick canopy of these large trees blocks so much sun that few plants grow in the understory; the ground is covered with copper needles and the soft, mossy remains of rotting logs. Dip through a stream valley before climbing out of the conifers. At 0.4 mile, Hardwood Ridge Trail goes left; stay straight on Catamount Trail. Pass the junction for Sugar House Loop on your right and reach the boundary of Wiessner Woods. The large metal-roofed sugarhouse (actually a privately owned warming hut) stands in a clearing. Check the mailbox for a surprise; if the flag is up, a bag of dog treats is probably stuffed inside.

Reenter Wiessner Woods and turn right, following Sugar Shack Lane over bog bridges along a wide, rolling trail. As you pass through this moist area, watch for patches of wood sorrel, which looks like clover growing low to the ground. Its heart-shaped leaves have a thirst-quenching, lemony flavor, but don't overdo it; the sourness comes from oxalic acid, which is toxic in large amounts. Delicate white flowers veined with dark pink bloom above the leaves between June and August.

After crossing the Bridge of Si's, Sugar Shack Lane gives way to Hardwood Ridge Trail, continuing in the same, northwesterly direction. You will pass several junctions, where private trails lead to the right and Main Street departs left (returning to Four Corners). After the junction with Main Street, the trail

Catamount Trail, a long-distance cross-country ski trail stretching the length of Vermont, uses the gentle paths of Wiessner Woods on its route through Stowe. Photo courtesy of Stowe Land Trust.

is called Meadow Trail, and it passes into a stand of relatively young conifers. Unlike more mature forests, these smaller trees let some sunlight through to the forest floor, encouraging thick undergrowth. Meadow Trail dips through a stream valley and climbs out the other side to a wooden bench alongside a stone wall. A large field rolls away on the far side of the wall, below the gently rounded Dewey Mountain (3,323 feet).

From the viewpoint, follow Meadow Trail downhill through a mixed hardwood forest. After crossing a stream, enter the widely spaced pine forest once again and soon arrive at Four Corners. Turn right to follow Catamount Trail out to the trailhead.

DID YOU KNOW?

Jewelweed is also commonly called spotted touch-me-not for its tendency to burst and fling seeds when disturbed late in the season. It can be used to soothe irritation from poison ivy, poison oak, and stinging nettle. Break open the stem and rub it on the affected area; the juice inside the stem can help stop the itch.

MORE INFORMATION

Wiessner Woods is for day-use hiking, skiing, and snowshoeing only; no camping, fires, mountain bikes, horses, or hunting. Please respect surrounding private property by parking in the designated lot and observing No Trespassing signs. Keep dogs under control and clean up after them. Please stay on the marked trail to protect plants, nesting sites, and fragile habitats. Wiessner Woods is owned and managed by the Stowe Land Trust, P.O. Box 284, Stowe, VT; 802-253-7221; stowelandtrust.org.

NEARBY

Swim and paddle at Waterbury Center State Park, 11 miles south. The Winooski and Lamoille rivers both have whitewater and flatwater paddling. Camp near a scenic waterfall and swimming hole at Smugglers' Notch State Park, 4 miles northwest. Food and shops are along VT 100 and VT 108 in Stowe, 4 miles southeast.

WHERE ARE THE CATAMOUNTS?

Catamounts seem to be everywhere in Vermont. The big, tawny-colored mountain lion is the unofficial state animal (the official one is the Morgan horse), appearing as the mascot of the state university and in the names of local companies and organizations. But look in vain for a live catamount, also called eastern mountain lion, cougar, puma, and panther. The last confirmed one in Vermont was killed in 1881.

Nowadays hikers (and, more often, drivers) see other animals—white-tailed deer, moose, beaver, turkeys, loons, and ospreys—that were scarce or missing from Vermont in the last century. So where is the catamount?

When colonists arrived in Vermont in the seventeenth century, they cleared forests for farms. According to Vermont's Fish and Wildlife Department, the state was at its barest in the 1840s, with 60 percent of the state cleared. This loss of habitat led to dwindling numbers—or to the complete disappearance—of many native animals. A cultural zeal to exterminate predators completed the job, driving catamounts out of the northeastern United States altogether. Over the past century, changing economies led to regrowth of the region's vast woods—today Vermont is 78 percent forested. Changing attitudes toward wildlife and the value of complete ecosystems are supporting the return of many native species to Vermont.

But the road back has been more challenging for the big cat that, at more than 100 pounds and 7 feet long from nose to tip of tail, towers over its 35-pound, 3.5-foot-long kin, the bobcat and the lynx. Female catamounts don't move far from where they are born, so it takes a long time for populations to spread.

Many people believe, however, that the catamount is back. Dozens of sightings are reported each year to the Fish and Wildlife Department. Biologists who investigate catamount sightings agree that some may be big cats but believe these to be escaped or intentionally released exotic pets. No one has yet found field evidence of a breeding population, such as tracks, scat, kill remains, scent mounds, or a body.

In March 2011, the U.S. Fish and Wildlife Service declared the catamount extinct. Even so, catamounts retain endangered status in Vermont, and the department maintains an online "Rare Furbearer Reporting Form," so you can let them know about any sightings. It seems members of the department, like many other Vermonters, hope to find the elusive cat back in the wild—rather than just on a sports jersey.

44

STOWE PINNACLE

The Pinnacle's rocky knob provides dramatic, close-up views of the Worcester Range, Mount Mansfield, and the pastoral Stowe Valley.

DIRECTIONS

From the junction of VT 100 (Main Street) and VT 108 (Mountain Road) in Stowe, head north on VT 100 and take the third right onto School Street. After 0.2 mile, when Taber Hill forks left, bear right onto Stowe Hollow Road. After 0.8 mile, at the junction with Covered Bridge Road, go left to stay on Stowe Hollow Road. After another 0.7 mile, when Stowe Hollow Road turns right, stay straight onto Upper Hollow Road. Follow this 0.6 mile to the parking lot (space for about 9 cars) on the left, just past Pinnacle Road (also on the left). *GPS coordinates:* 44° 26.19′ N, 72° 40.04′ W.

TRAIL DESCRIPTION

Stowe Pinnacle (2,610 feet) is a rocky bald spot poking out of the side of the Worcester Range, giving hikers unrivaled views of the high peaks of north-central Vermont. The steepness of the climb makes the short hike vigorous, and the open summit is a good picnic spot. This is a popular hike in a popular resort town, so don't expect solitude, but you can look forward to the wide-open skies and long views usually reserved for higher summits.

From the parking area, Stowe Pinnacle Trail proceeds through an overgrown field before entering woods. Blue blazes mark the route as it ascends gradually over bog bridges and large step stones through maples, white pines, and paper birches. An overgrown rock cairn, continuously built by hikers over the years, sprawls in the middle of the trail at the point where the climb becomes more sustained.

LOCATION
Stowe, VT

RATING
Moderate

DISTANCE
2.8 miles

ELEVATION GAIN
1,520 feet

ESTIMATED TIME
2.5 hours

MAPS
USGS Stowe

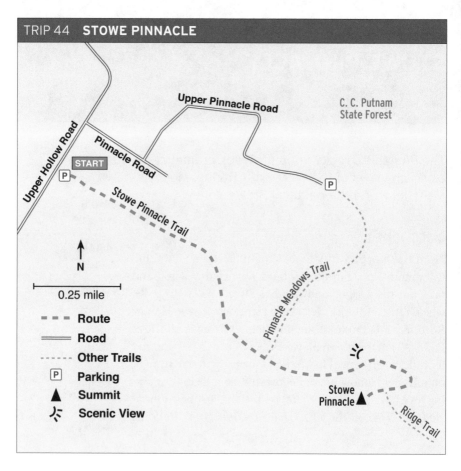

Stowe Pinnacle Trail takes the most direct route up a steep wooded ridge between two stream valleys. Rock staircases provide a relatively flat treadway on this highly angled route; they prevent erosion and gullying of the trail. At 1 mile, catch your breath in a clearing where Pinnacle Meadows Trail leaves to the left. Climb rock steps out of the clearing and follow the blazes for Stowe Pinnacle Trail to the right, where an old footpath veers left.

More climbing, more ledges, and flight after flight of rock steps lead, finally, to a small saddle between two steep slopes. A spur trail heads up the left slope to a view of the ridgeline between Camel's Hump (4,083 feet) and Mount Mansfield (4,393 feet) and of the farm fields and rolling hills of Stowe. Stowe Pinnacle Trail continues straight ahead, curving through beech, hobblebush, and striped maple as it circles behind Stowe Pinnacle. Rock steps lead down briefly before the trail levels across the contour of the hill and then begins to climb again. A hard-right turn brings you into woods full of fragrant balsam fir. Wide wooden ladders help with the scramble up vertical ledges. Just before the summit, Ridge Trail (also called Hogback Trail) departs left. Stay on Stowe Pinnacle Trail as the trees open, and the views take over.

From Stowe Pinnacle, hikers can see dramatic views of Mt. Mansfield.

The long ridge of summits before you includes, from south to north, Monroe Skyline, Camel's Hump, Bolton Mountain (3,690 feet), Mount Mansfield, Whiteface Mountain (3,714 feet), Belvidere Mountain (3,330 feet), and north to Jay Peak (3,830 feet) on the Canadian border.

Looming overhead to the east, the steep ridge of the Worcester Range stretches 18 miles between the Lamoille River in the north and the Winooski River to its south. Elmore Mountain (2,590 feet) is the somewhat isolated peak on its northern end. Rising steeply from there, the rocky tip of Mount Worcester (3,225 feet) is one end of the high, densely forested Skyline Trail, which traverses the spine over an unnamed peak before climbing Hogback Mountain (3,600 feet) and the wooded north summit of Mount Hunger (3,570 feet) to Hunger's bald south summit (3,539 feet), not visible from Stowe Pinnacle. A short distance south of Mount Hunger, a thrust of rocky ledges makes up White Rock Mountain (3,150 feet, see Trip 40). The Worcester Range's large tracts of red-spruce and balsam-fir subalpine forest support the inconspicuous spruce grouse, the elusive Bicknell's thrush, and one of the boreal forest's savviest hunters, the fisher. On lower slopes, red-oak forests feed black bears, and the dense cover of mixed hardwoods provides protection and food for breeding neotropical songbirds, such as wood thrushes.

Return downhill the way you hiked up.

DID YOU KNOW?

Gold Brook Covered Bridge, just down the slope from Stowe Pinnacle's trailhead, is reportedly haunted by the ghost of a lovelorn nineteenth-century girl. Read Tim Simard's *Haunted Hikes of Vermont* (PublishingWorks, 2010) for the spooky details.

MORE INFORMATION

The C. C. Putnam State Forest is managed by Vermont Department of Forests, Parks and Recreation; vtfpr.org. To minimize erosion along fragile, high-elevation terrain, the state closes trails in the Worcester Range between mid-April and Memorial Day. The Green Mountain Club helps maintain trails in the Worcester Range. Green Mountain Club, 4711 Waterbury–Stowe Road, Waterbury Center, VT 05677; 802-244-7037; greenmountainclub.org.

NEARBY

Swim and paddle at Waterbury Center State Park, 8 miles south. The Winooski and Lamoille rivers have popular whitewater and flatwater paddling. Camp near a scenic waterfall and swimming hole at Smugglers' Notch State Park, 9.5 miles northwest. Food and shops are along VT 100 and VT 108 in Stowe, 4 miles northwest.

45
MOUNT MANSFIELD'S CHIN

The exceptional Sunset Ridge hike to Vermont's highest summit quickly rises above treeline for spectacular vistas and includes a visit to the remarkable Cantilever Rock.

DIRECTIONS

From VT 15 east in Underhill Flats, bear right onto River Road, following the sign for Underhill State Park. After 2.7 miles, go straight at the stop sign in Underhill Center onto Pleasant Valley Road. In 0.9 mile, turn right onto Mountain Road and ascend 2.5 miles to the entrance of Underhill State Park, which can accommodate 60 day-hiker vehicles in addition to overnight campers. (Winter hikers: Park at a plowed area partway up Mountain Road and add 3 miles round-trip to the hike.) *GPS coordinates:* 44° 31.78′ N, 72° 50.52′ W.

LOCATION
Underhill, VT

RATING
Strenuous

DISTANCE
6.2 miles

ELEVATION GAIN
2,543 feet

ESTIMATED TIME
4.5 hours

MAPS
USGS Mount Mansfield; vtstateparks.com/assets/pdf/underhilltrails.pdf

TRAIL DESCRIPTION

Mount Mansfield's easily recognizable summit ridge appears like a profile in repose. From the Forehead (3,940 feet) at the south end, over the craggy Nose (4,060 feet) dotted with transmitter towers, to its highest point at the Chin (4,393 feet), and down to the Adam's Apple (4,060 feet) at the north end, the ridge stretches 2.5 miles. The high-elevation ridgeline supports the biggest patch of rare alpine tundra (see "The Sparse Tundra of Vermont," page 200) in Vermont, but to the peril of those delicate plants, more than 40,000 visitors explore Mansfield each year.

Sunset Ridge, which ascends from the valley to Mount Mansfield's Chin, is a favorite of day-hikers for good reasons: It is one of the easier ascents (its strenuous rating comes more from overall distance and time than from hiking difficulty), and its relatively quick arrival on open rock means the awe-inspiring views are part of the hike,

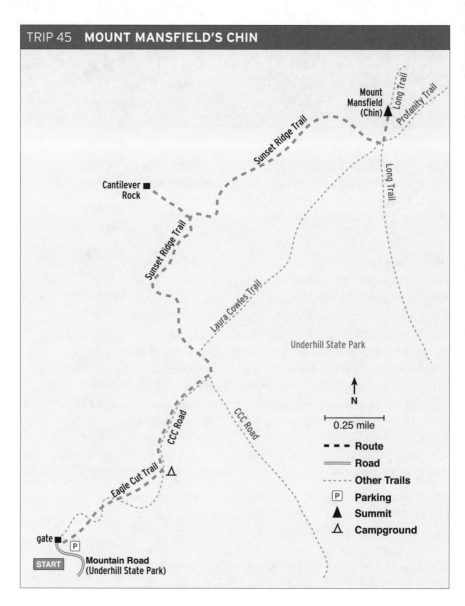

not just the reward at the summit. While this hike may be too ambitious for kids younger than 10, the shorter trips to Cantilever Rock or onto the open rock of lower Sunset Ridge are excellent destinations on their own merits.

After paying a day-use fee and getting the day's high-elevation forecast at the ranger station, follow the blue-blazed Eagle Cut Trail up a gentle pitch 0.3 mile, crossing the CCC Road three times before turning left onto it at your fourth encounter. Follow the CCC Road 0.4 mile to a clearing with a kiosk; turn left and cross a bridge to begin up Sunset Ridge Trail. After 0.1 mile, Laura Cowles Trail departs to the right; stay left on Sunset Ridge Trail. The wide, rocky trail heads north across the flank of the mountain, climbing moderately. After a small clearing, the trail gets steeper, passing cascades and a whale-sized glacial erratic.

At 0.7 mile, the spur trail to Cantilever Rock heads left. Follow it into a damp, dense conifer forest, scrambling between moss-covered boulders. In 0.2 mile, a cliff towers over a narrow canyon. Stuck in a high crack, the namesake rock juts 30 feet into open air over your head. This schist column likely ended up here due to ice and water eroding fractures in the cliff, causing occasional and sometimes drastic movement. Climb the huge boulder beneath the rock to get a view of Camel's Hump.

Return to Sunset Ridge Trail and continue climbing; you will encounter a more challenging section weaving through boulders and rocky gullies. The fragrance of balsam fir marks your arrival in the primarily coniferous forest above 2,700 feet.

Climb from a narrow gully onto open rock. The view is incredible, especially the long ridge of Mansfield looming steeply above. Minuscule hikers pick their way across the rocks between the Nose and the Chin. A large bulb of rock ahead appears to be the top of Sunset Ridge. This is the West Chin, which is closed to hiking for alpine revegetation; the summit proper is behind it. Crossing bands of rock and stunted, bent trees, you may notice lengths of thin white string at ankle height. These subtle guides help define the route and keep boot soles off fragile vegetation; please respect the tenuous existence of rare alpine plants by stepping only on rock.

After traversing beneath the West Chin, Sunset Ridge Trail passes the top of Laura Cowles Trail and continues to the ridgeline, ending at the Long Trail. Turn left, following the Long Trail north. Pass Profanity Trail—a steep, 0.5-mile bad-weather bypass of the Chin—on your right and climb up a rock gully to the summit. The views from here are in all directions, as you might expect when standing on the highest point in Vermont. The Adirondacks cut a jagged line across the western horizon, high above Lake Champlain. Camel's Hump (4,083 feet) is the tallest point in a sea of high peaks to the south. The Worcester Range stretches across the valley to the east, while just north of the Chin, across the rugged gap of Smugglers' Notch, Spruce Peak (3,320 feet) leads your gaze northward over Madonna Peak (3,668 feet) to Whiteface Mountain (3,714 feet).

Return the way you came up.

DID YOU KNOW?

You may hear occasional loud booms while hiking here. Some say that's Wampa-hoofus, the legendary creature who lives on Mount Mansfield and whose legs evolved to be shorter on one side of its body than the other due to always walking across the steep hillside. (Others say that the booming is from the Ethan Allen Firing Range in nearby Jericho.)

Hikers crossing Mount Mansfield's long, rugged, above-treeline ridge help protect delicate, rare tundra plants by walking only on rocks and plank bridges.

MORE INFORMATION

In the alpine zone, walk only on rock and keep dogs on a leash. The Underhill State Park office is open Memorial Day to mid-October, 9 A.M. to 9 P.M. daily; use self-pay envelopes prior to 9 A.M. Underhill State Park, 352 Mountain Road, Underhill, VT 05490; 802-899-3022; vtstateparks.com/underhill.html. The Long Trail is maintained by the Green Mountain Club, 4711 Waterbury–Stowe Road, Waterbury Center, VT 05677; 802-244-7037; greenmountainclub.org.

NEARBY

Underhill Center has a small store; more dining options are on VT 15 in Jericho, 10 miles west. The Bentley Museum in Jericho exhibits some of the 5,000 snowflake photographs made by Wilson "Snowflake" Bentley after 1885, when he discovered how to photograph a single snow crystal.

46

MOUNT MANSFIELD'S FOREHEAD

Mount Mansfield's craggy forehead requires hikers to slither through cracks and scramble along the edges of cliffs, rewarding bravery and agility with access to this special, rocky dome.

LOCATION
Underhill and Stowe, VT

RATING
Strenuous

DISTANCE
5.2 miles

ELEVATION GAIN
2,520 feet

ESTIMATED TIME
4.5 hours

MAPS
USGS Mount Mansfield;
vtstateparks.com/assets/
pdf/stevensville-trail.pdf

DIRECTIONS

From VT 15 east in Underhill Flats, bear right onto River Road. After 2.7 miles, go straight at the stop sign in Underhill Center onto Pleasant Valley Road. In 0.3 mile, turn right onto Stevensville Road and drive 2.6 miles to its end in the trailhead parking lot (space for 20 cars). *GPS coordinates: 44° 30.34′ N, 72° 50.83′ W.*

TRAIL DESCRIPTION

Mount Mansfield's Forehead (3,940 feet) is at the southern end of the 2.5-mile-long ridge of Vermont's tallest mountain. This mound of ledges and krummholz provides technically challenging hiking and, in some spots, requires steel nerves. Although leashed dogs are allowed on the Forehead, think twice before inviting four-legged friends along, as the trail includes ladders, steep slabs, and sheer dropoffs. This is not a route for children. A bad-weather bypass trail avoids the hairiest parts of the Forehead via a more typical woods route without exposure, but it passes 0.3 mile beyond the Forehead and the downhill route used in this description. That bypass on the east side of the ridge and Wampahoofus Trail on the west side are the best choices in wet or icy weather, as well as smarter routes for hikers with young kids, dogs, big backpacks, a fear of heights, or a lack of interest in crawling and scooting as part of their outing. The rewards of making it up the Forehead on a nice day are an exhilarating view and the fun of a thrilling climb. Check the summit weather forecast before you go; the air will be cooler, winds stronger, and

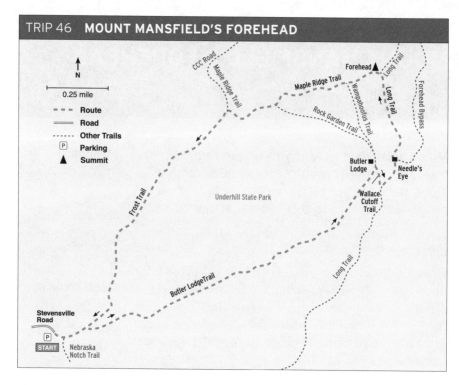

chance of precipitation greater on the ridgeline than in the valley. This lollipop route can be done in either direction and has steep ascents and descents on open slabs, whichever way you choose.

From the parking area, pass a kiosk and the beginning of Nebraska Notch Trail, which heads off to the right, and follow signs for Butler Lodge Trail. Walk on a two-track alongside Stevensville Brook, going around a metal gate and over a bridge before following markers left off the old road and arriving at the junction of Frost Trail and Butler Lodge Trail at 0.3 mile. Go right to stay on the blue-blazed Butler Lodge Trail, climbing away from the stream through hardwoods, ferns, and hobblebushes. The trail climbs steadily up a gentle ridgeline, occasionally providing glimpses of the looming ridgeline through gaps in the canopy. At 1.1 miles, the woods shift to higher-elevation spruce and fir, and the trail becomes rocky and ascends several ledges. At 1.9 miles, you will arrive at Butler Lodge, a Green Mountain Club cabin in a dramatic setting beneath the cliffs of the Forehead. This is the last water source until almost the end of the hike.

Wampahoofus Trail cuts west behind the cabin, providing a 0.6-mile alternate route to Maple Ridge Trail by crossing beneath the Forehead, but it's no walk in the park, with its scrambling route around boulders. To continue uphill to the Forehead, backtrack 75 feet on Butler Lodge Trail and find Wallace Cutoff on your left (on the right, coming uphill into the lodge clearing). Follow Wallace

Cutoff 0.1 mile through open, pretty balsam-fir woods up to the ridgeline, meeting the white-blazed Long Trail and turning north (left) onto it.

At 2.2 miles, squeeze through a low tunnel between two boulders—a tight spot called the Needle's Eye—and arrive at the Forehead Bypass junction on your right; this is the east-side bad-weather route that ends on the Long Trail 0.3 mile north of the Forehead. Go left, continuing on the Long Trail northbound and climbing the first of numerous ledges you will encounter in the next 0.5 mile to the top of the Forehead.

Just 0.1 mile past the Needle's Eye, the Long Trail traverses boulders along the edge of a steep drop directly above Butler Lodge, requiring some scrambling, squeezing, and bravery. This is the most exposure on the hike, and once you're past it, climbing ladders and steep slabs feels almost tame. Views extend east and west, as well as south behind you, as you climb northward. The open rock faces and low vegetation on the Forehead's south side feel as remote and wild as it's possible to get on this popular and developed mountain. Enjoy a break here before reaching the highest point of the Forehead at 2.8 miles, which is anticlimactic, with views of cell towers, a cluster of summit signs, and lack of a 360-degree view.

The hike to Mount Mansfield's Forehead is not for everyone: Ladders and precipices require steel nerves, agility, and a backpack small enough that it won't throw you off-balance.

Mount Mansfield's Chin anchors the north end of a windswept ridge, as seen from Maple Ridge Trail.

Turn left down Maple Ridge Trail from the summit, and quickly descend from the ridgeline on steep, open slab. Take in the stunning views of Mansfield's ridge, extending north to the massive Chin, and the expansive west shore of Vermont along the shining waters of Lake Champlain in front of you. Maple Ridge Trail drops precipitously at times and would be as tricky as the Forehead in bad weather. (Wampahoofus Trail heads left to Butler Lodge just 0.2 mile below the Forehead, or 3 miles into the hike, providing a less exposed alternate route downhill. Rock Garden Trail does the same 0.4 mile below that, but by this time, you've covered the steepest downhill terrain.) Continue on Maple Ridge Trail over alternately open and forested stretches, sometimes zigzagging across the ridge, sometimes climbing into and out of gullies. At 3.6 miles, turn left onto Frost Trail, continuing over open terrain and low trees until finally dropping into the forest. You will come alongside the wide Stevensville Brook; cross it and return to the junction of Butler Lodge Trail at 4.9 miles. Descend from the woods on the two-track Butler Lodge Trail and return to the trailhead the way you came.

DID YOU KNOW?

New England's famously changeable weather is due to many storm tracks that cross the continent, west to east and south to north, and converge over the Northeast, creating turbulent and quickly changing conditions. Mountains amplify the effect, obstructing the airflow and increasing its speed, the same way rivers become rapid when constricted. Mount Mansfield's ridgeline shows the impact of these high winds in its flag trees, with branches that grow only on the leeward side.

MORE INFORMATION

In the alpine zone, walk only on rock and keep dogs on a leash. These trails are maintained by the Vermont Department of Forests, Parks and Recreation (fpr.vermont.gov) and by Green Mountain Club, 4711 Waterbury–Stowe Road, Waterbury Center, VT 05677; 802-244-7037; greenmountainclub.org.

NEARBY

Underhill Center has a small store; more dining options are on VT 15 in Jericho, 8 miles west, and in Essex Junction, 15 miles west. VT 108, 12 miles north, is a twisty, wildly scenic, seasonal drive through Smugglers' Notch on the north side of Mount Mansfield (not for RVs or vehicles pulling trailers due to its very tight switchbacks around boulders). On the east side of the mountain, Stowe, 31 miles east via VT 108, or 38.4 miles in the winter via VT 15, has many shops and restaurants, including Vermont-style fine dining in the summit building under Mount Mansfield's Chin, accessed via gondola ride or by hiking. There are great mountain-bike trails in Essex and Stowe. Swim in Jeff Falls or Bingham Falls, both along VT 108 on either side of Smugglers' Notch. Camp at Underhill State Park, 4.4 miles away.

THE SPARSE TUNDRA OF VERMONT

Most hikers know that climbing a mountain is similar to traveling north: The air gets cooler, the winds get stronger, and the trees get shorter and then disappear altogether as the tundra begins. The word "tundra" conjures images of arctic places—Alaska, perhaps, or Canada. But peaks that rise higher than 4,000 feet in New England exhibit the same extreme conditions. Vermont has three of these special arctic alpine zones: one each on Mount Mansfield, Camel's Hump, and Mount Abraham.

The plants you most often see on Vermont's highest windswept peaks are grassy-looking sedges, lichens spreading over the rocks, and dwarf wildflowers adding splashes of color in spring. The word krummholz, meaning crooked wood, refers to the dense mats of stunted, bent spruce and fir trees that look more like creeping shrubs than proper trees.

Some of the plants that live above treeline in New England are arctic plants that don't occur anywhere else in the contiguous United States. They are therefore designated rare and, in some cases, threatened or endangered. These plants are adapted to the harsh life above treeline: They grow low to the ground in clusters that are designed to retain warmth and moisture; they absorb water from fog, as well as from precipitation; and they photosynthesize in low light to make the most of the brief season when they aren't under a cap of snow and ice.

That these plants are hardy is obvious; what isn't so easily observed is how fragile they are. While tundra plants have adapted to withstand harsh conditions, they are not equipped to being trod on by 150-pound people wearing hiking boots. Imagine a lawn of Bigelow's sedge, a grassy alpine plant that forms appealing meadows across open summits. When a patch of sedge is killed, its roots no longer stabilize the thin soil, and strong summit winds blow the soil away. This hole in the vegetation is now susceptible to further erosion at its exposed edges, and what started as a small patch of damage can spread quickly.

Be sensitive to the challenges of life on these harsh summits and keep your footsteps on the rocks or the trail. If you're hiking on Mount Abraham (Trip 25), Camel's Hump (Trip 27), or Mount Mansfield (Trips 45 and 46), take time to speak with the Green Mountain Club's summit caretakers to learn more about the fragile natural communities on the summits.

47

STERLING POND

This scenic hike leads around a high mountain lake perched above the steep cliffs of Smugglers' Notch.

DIRECTIONS

From the junction of VT 100 and VT 108 (Mountain Road) in Stowe, turn onto VT 108. Go 9.5 miles to the visitor center parking area (space for 20 cars) on the left, just beyond the height of land in Smugglers' Notch. (The final mile is a narrow roadway with switchbacks around enormous boulders and is not passable by recreational vehicles or buses. VT 108 is closed beyond the ski area in winter; add 4 miles round-trip for a winter hike.) *GPS coordinates:* 44° 33.39′ N, 72° 47.63′ W.

TRAIL DESCRIPTION

Sterling Pond rests in a thickly forested alpine basin between Spruce Peak (3,330 feet) and Madonna Peak (3,610 feet), both of which host ski areas. The spring-fed pond is a small refuge of beauty between these high-mountain developments. The hike to Sterling Pond Shelter is relatively short and quite popular, but looping around the far side of the pond, you are likely to find solitude on the craggy slopes before descending. Although the watery destination is appealing to children of all ages, the climb is steep in places and most enjoyable for kids ages 8 and older.

Sterling Pond Trail begins opposite the visitor center and ascends the east wall of Smugglers' Notch. A steep flight of rock steps climbs directly up then turns north to cross a gully. Blue blazes lead to a break in the trees and a view of 1,000-foot cliffs across the narrow valley. These awe-inspiring crags were exposed by mile-thick glaciers that plowed through the notch for thousands of years, gouging and scraping their massive way southward until

LOCATION
Cambridge, VT

RATING
Moderate

DISTANCE
3.3 miles

ELEVATION GAIN
1,320 feet

ESTIMATED TIME
3 hours

MAPS
USGS Mount Mansfield

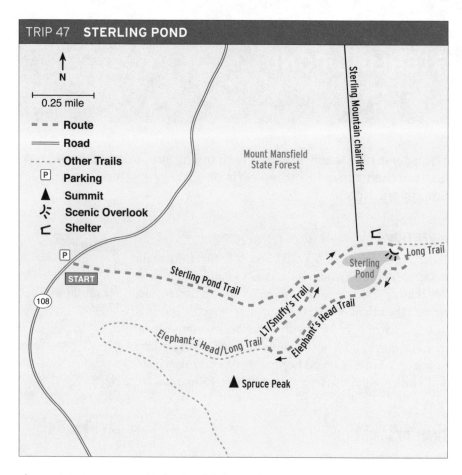

N

0.25 mile

- - - Route
===== Road
----- Other Trails
P   Parking
▲   Summit
𝄂   Scenic Overlook
⊏   Shelter

Mount Mansfield
State Forest

Sterling Mountain chairlift

P

START

108

Sterling Pond Trail

LT/Snuffy's Trail

Sterling
Pond

Long Trail

Elephant's Head/Long Trail

Elephant's Head Trail

▲ Spruce Peak

about 18,000 years ago. Today landslides and toppling rocks are part of the normal geomorphic activities shaping the notch.

For a short distance, Sterling Pond Trail traverses the steep hillside above the notch then turns up a drainage. Moderate pitches of rooty dirt trail are interspersed with sections of steep rock steps and stream crossings. In the dense spruce-fir forest on the upper section of Sterling Pond Trail, look and listen for high-mountain inhabitants. Red squirrels erupt in sudden annoyed chatter and leave piles of plucked spruce-cone scales, while white-throated sparrows call *old Sam Peabody-Peabody-Peabody*. In winter snowshoe hares leave oblong tracks in the snow, and fisher prints show five distinct toes.

At 1 mile, Sterling Pond Trail tops out at a wide swath of cleared forest. This is Snuffy's, a service road and ski trail, as well as part of the Long Trail (LT). Turn left, following the Long Trail's white blazes north 0.1 mile to Sterling Pond. Rock-studded soil rims the western shore, giving an open view across the water to the ridge of Madonna Mountain. Leash dogs in this sensitive area.

Continue north on the Long Trail, crossing a log bridge at the pond's outlet and climbing onto a ridge above the water. The trail weaves through thick shoreline woods then climbs away from the pond to cross a wide, grassy opening. Stay straight, reentering the woods and climbing to the top of the Sterling Mountain chairlift. Find white blazes on the opposite side of the lift and continue through the woods to Sterling Pond Shelter at 1.3 miles. From the shelter's southeast corner, pick up the blue-blazed Elephant's Head Trail and follow it downhill to a fork. Go right for a view across the pond to Mount Mansfield's steep ridge; return and take the left fork to continue your hike. This would be a good turnaround point for hikers who are losing steam, as there is a fair bit of climbing in the next 0.7 mile to rejoin the Long Trail.

Elephant's Head Trail circles the eastern end of the pond and follows the southern shore over rough, rooty terrain before climbing away from the pond, weaving through huge mossy boulders and crossing over slabs with footholds chipped into the rock. After scrambling beneath an overhang and through a narrow notch of rock, the ascent finishes steeply. This is the highest point of your hike. Pass through a hollow before meeting the Long Trail again. Elephant's Head Trail continues straight and descends steeply into Smugglers' Notch. Go right, following the Long Trail north and downhill for 0.3 mile of easy walking to the top of Sterling Pond Trail. Turn left here, descending the way you came up.

White birch is one of the first trees to repopulate a disturbed area such as a landslide or burned slope, but unlike other pioneers, it can persist for decades. Photo by Kip Roberts.

High above Smugglers' Notch, Sterling Pond reflects the northern shoulder of Mount Mansfield. Vermont's highest-elevation trout pond, it supports both fish and fish-eating wildlife.

DID YOU KNOW?

Stands of paper birch often indicate old debris slides, as these trees colonize disturbed soil. Sterling Pond Trail passes through an evenly aged white-birch stand that is believed to have taken root after the destructive 1938 hurricane.

MORE INFORMATION

Sterling Pond's trails and shelter are maintained by the Green Mountain Club, 4711 Waterbury–Stowe Road, Waterbury Center, VT 05677; 802-244-7037; greenmountainclub.org.

NEARBY

Camp at Smugglers' Notch State Park, 3.1 miles south, across the road from the scenic Bingham Falls, which is a good spot for a picnic and a swim. The Lamoille River, 8 miles north, has whitewater and flatwater paddling options. Shops and restaurants are along VT 108 south and on VT 100 in Stowe, 9.5 miles south.

48

PROSPECT ROCK

This small cliff provides panoramic views of the Lamoille River's braided channels and the high peaks rising steeply beyond them.

DIRECTIONS

From downtown Johnson, follow VT 15 west 2.7 miles to the Long Trail parking lot on the right (space for about 15 cars). *GPS coordinates: 44° 38.70′ N, 72° 43.70′ W.*

TRAIL DESCRIPTION

Prospect Rock is an open ledge jutting out of the trees above the pastoral Lamoille River valley. The hike passes through a lovely, diverse forest, and the rock is broad enough to accommodate numerous picnic blankets. The ascent is vigorous but short enough for kids ages 8 and older to accomplish. Because you will need to cross a side channel of the Lamoille River 0.4 mile into your hike, where high water could stop you in your tracks, check the river level before hiking by driving to the Long Trail crossing on Hog Back Road (which meets VT 15 about 1 mile east of the parking area). There used to be trailhead parking here, at the Hog Back Road/Long Trail crossing, but parking is no longer allowed on the shoulders.

From the parking area alongside VT 15, head north on the Long Trail across a field and into the woods. Walk 0.4 mile of gently rolling terrain to the bank of the Lamoille River. If the water is low enough to cross safely, descend to the first channel and cross to an island where an impressive suspension bridge gives you dry footing to cross the main channel. Climb to Hog Back Road and find the continuation of the Long Trail on the opposite side, heading uphill, away from the river. Ascend a steep pitch on a wide trail through mixed hard- and softwoods, followed by a couple of switchbacks across the hill and

LOCATION
Johnson, VT

RATING
Easy to Moderate

DISTANCE
3 miles

ELEVATION GAIN
540 feet

ESTIMATED TIME
2 hours

MAPS
USGS Johnson

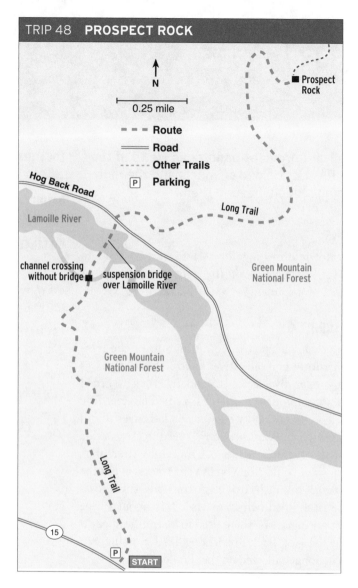

TRIP 48 PROSPECT ROCK

N

0.25 mile

- – – Route
═══ Road
- - - - Other Trails
P Parking

Prospect Rock

Hog Back Road

Lamoille River

Long Trail

channel crossing without bridge

suspension bridge over Lamoille River

Green Mountain National Forest

Green Mountain National Forest

Long Trail

15

P

START

another climb. The Long Trail continues in this pattern of climbing steeply, crossing a hill, and climbing again for most of the rest of the 1.5-mile distance between Hog Back Road and Prospect Rock.

The craggy, southwestern-facing hillside supports a diverse forest at this elevation. As you climb, you will pass hemlock, red oak, spruce, fir, birch, black cherry, red pine, red maple, and striped maple. Some striped maples have grown large here—to about 8 inches in diameter and 30 feet tall—for a species that grows very slowly. Striped maples are shade tolerant, so they often form the understory in mixed-hardwood forests of the Northeast. Because they grow mostly in the shade, their leaves are large, 5 to 7 inches long and wide, allowing them to catch as much sunlight as possible. The leaves have a rounded, web-footed appearance that lends this tree the nickname "goosefoot maple." Look for striped-maple trunks with sections of their pretty green-and-white bark missing. Moose eat the bark (giving rise to the nicknames "moosewood" and "moose maple"), as do rabbits, porcupines, and deer.

Climbing into a broad saddle, follow the faint remnants of an old road along the side of Prospect Rock before the Long Trail turns right to switchback up the slope onto drier ground. A flat, wooded area leads onto the open terraces, where a view opens broadly to the southwest and through small trees to the south. Use caution near the edges of the rock, which is steep enough and high enough to attract rock climbers. Below, the Lamoille River meanders west through its floodplain, which is largely cultivated. The river extends 85 miles from its headwaters in Glover to its delta in Milton, on Lake Champlain. The long ridge of the Sterling Range rises steeply from the river and points southeast to Whiteface Mountain (3,714 feet).

If you were standing on Prospect Rock about 13,000 years ago, you would have looked out over a lake formed by melting glaciers. At one point, Glacial

Prospect Rock overlooks the valley floodplains of Lamoille River and the mountains of Sterling Range.

Lake Winooski would have lapped at the edges of Prospect Rock. The massive lake was dammed by retreating glaciers; as the ice continued to melt, the lake drained partially, creating a series of subsequently lower-elevation glacial lakes. One of these, Glacial Lake Vermont, stretched across the Champlain Valley with a surface 500 feet higher than Lake Champlain's is today. Long, watery arms extended high into the Green and Adirondack mountains until a sudden catastrophic failure of the ice dam released the water, and the lake dropped 300 feet in just a few hours or days. The Lamoille River valley would have been revealed at that time, covered with muddy lake-bottom sediment.

Return to the trailhead the way you hiked up.

DID YOU KNOW?

Just beyond the Sterling Range, Smugglers' Notch is a narrow, cliffy gap through Vermont's highest mountains. In the early nineteenth century, embargoed cattle were sneaked through the notch to markets in Montreal, which were closer than legal American markets to the south. Later, fugitive slaves headed north through the gap en route to Canada, and Prohibition liquor headed south.

MORE INFORMATION

The Long Trail is maintained by the Green Mountain Club, 4711 Waterbury–Stowe Road, Waterbury Center, VT 05677; 802-244-7037; greenmountainclub.org.

NEARBY

The Lamoille River is popular for paddling, and the multiple waterfalls along the Gihon River in Johnson, 2.5 miles east, give steep-creek kayakers a wild run. Jeff Falls on the Brewster River along VT 108 in Jeffersonville, 9 miles west, is a clear, pretty swimming hole (public access on private property). Smugglers' Notch State Park has camping 16.7 miles southwest. Smugglers' Notch Resort has outdoor activities year-round, 13.5 miles southwest. Food and other shops are along VT 15 in Johnson, 1.5 miles east.

49

DEVIL'S GULCH AND BIG MUDDY POND

Two beautiful ponds, a boulder-strewn ravine, and a camp on a high perch keep this hike varied and interesting from beginning to end.

DIRECTIONS

From the junction of VT 100 and VT 118, go north on VT 118 for 4.6 miles. Just after a left curve, turn right into the Long Trail State Forest parking area (space for about 12 cars). *GPS coordinates:* 44° 45.84' N, 72° 35.27' W.

TRAIL DESCRIPTION

The Green Mountain landscape on the southwest side of Belvidere Mountain (Trip 50) is rumpled and gullied, with pockets of water between steep-sided hills and heaps of boulders beneath the cliffs that calved them. The Long Trail and Babcock Trail make a lollipop loop through this enchanting area, navigating boulders in Devil's Gulch, climbing to a lovely camp and overlook on Spruce Ledge, and traversing the shoreline of the more-scenic-than-it-sounds Big Muddy Pond. There is a lot to see in a relatively short distance, making this a fun hike for kids ages 8 and older. You will ascend and descend multiple times on this rolling route, and your overall elevation gain will be about 1,000 feet, but it comes in small chunks. Although many Long Trail thru-hikers have scrambled through Devil's Gulch with their canine companions, the slippery rock pile at the head of the ravine is challenging for most dogs.

From the parking lot, climb a short trail to VT 118 and cross carefully on this blind curve, heading slightly left to find the white-blazed continuation of the southbound Long Trail. The path rises for 0.4 mile then meanders along a pleasant wooded ridge for 0.5 mile, eventually descending along the right side of a stream ravine. As the path begins a more noticeable descent, Ritterbush Lookout appears at 1.3 miles,

LOCATION
Eden, VT

RATING
Moderate

DISTANCE
5.2 miles

ELEVATION GAIN
1,000 feet

ESTIMATED TIME
4 hours

MAPS
USGS Hazens Notch,
USGS Eden

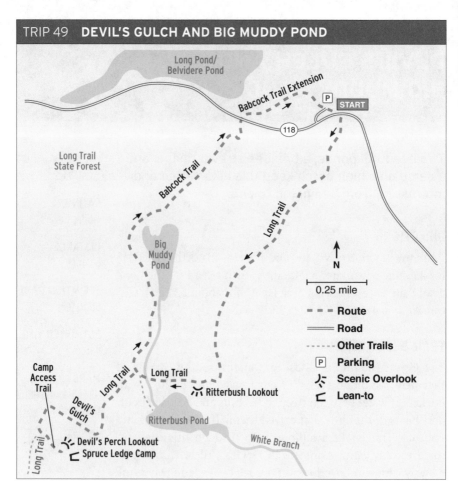

Long Pond/
Belvidere Pond

Babcock Trail Extension

P START

118

Long Trail
State Forest

Babcock Trail

Long Trail

Big
Muddy
Pond

N

0.25 mile

- - - **Route**
=== **Road**
----- **Other Trails**
P **Parking**
Scenic Overlook
Lean-to

Camp
Access
Trail

Long Trail

Long Trail

Ritterbush Lookout

Devil's
Gulch

Ritterbush Pond

White Branch

Devil's Perch Lookout
Spruce Ledge Camp

Long Trail

with a view of Ritterbush Pond beneath a steep, wooded hillside. From here, the trail descends steeply over multiple sets of rock steps, dropping to the hike's lowest point (1,100 feet) at the junction of Babcock Trail at 1.7 miles. The Long Trail continues straight across this intersection, with Babcock Trail rising to the right, and an unidentified extension of Babcock Trail dropping down a gully to the left.

Continue on the Long Trail across the hillside, where the landscape gets really interesting. Approaching a stream plummeting from a mossy gully, the trail bends right and ascends a log ladder. The path snakes between boulders and ledges to the entrance of Devil's Gulch at 2.1 miles, where enormous slabs of rock lean against one another like a massive house of cards. Pass under this rock A-frame and enter a mossy, drippy canyon. Sheer rock walls soar up to 70 feet high, undercut in large arcs where chunks of rock fell to the damp floor of the ravine. A line of bog bridges leads to the head of the short gully, which is choked by rockfall. Navigate the boulders, taking care on their slick surfaces. Suddenly,

A backpacker traverses the top of the rock pile at the head of Devil's Gulch, a narrow, craggy canyon that is one of several highlights on this hike through varied terrain. Photo by Jerry Monkman.

about 0.1 mile after entering it, you are out of the gulch and climbing gradually along the left side of a gentle valley.

Curving left, the pitch steepens and follows a stream up to a junction. Turn left onto the spur trail to Spruce Ledge Camp, climbing over a ridgeline before dropping to an attractive little cabin at 2.6 miles. Just beyond, a log bench perches atop a steep drop—watch children and dogs here—giving a broad view of Belvidere Mountain and a slice of Ritterbush Pond.

From Spruce Ledge Camp, retrace your steps 0.9 mile back through Devil's Gulch to the Babcock Trail/Long Trail junction. Go left on Babcock Trail, climbing steadily northward out of the valley along a rocky, blue-blazed path. The outlet of Big Muddy Pond appears through the trees 0.4 mile from the junction. As you skirt the western shore, look for signs of beaver. At the far end of the pond, Babcock Trail climbs out of the basin and crosses a narrow height of land. From here, 0.7 mile of mostly moderate descent leads to VT 118. Cross the road and continue northeast on the 0.4-mile Babcock Trail Extension, which passes a cellar hole and briefly follows a dirt road before returning to a footpath. The trail rises to parallel the dirt drive then climbs to the parking lot.

DID YOU KNOW?

In the hollows deep under the boulders of Devil's Gulch, winter ice is sheltered and melts slowly through the spring and early summer, keeping the ravine pleasantly ventilated. You may even feel cool breezes.

MORE INFORMATION

The Long Trail and Spruce Ledge Camp are maintained by the Green Mountain Club, 4711 Waterbury–Stowe Road, Waterbury Center, VT 05677; 802-244-7037; greenmountainclub.org. Babcock Trail is within Babcock Nature Preserve, owned by Johnson State College, College Hill Road, Johnson, VT; 800-635-2356; jsc.edu/student-life/arts-recreation/outdoor-recreation-opportunities/babcock-nature-preserve.

NEARBY

Paddle on Long Pond (also called Belvidere Pond), 0.5 mile west. Camp, paddle, and swim at Green River Reservoir State Park, 20 miles southeast. A general store is on VT 100 in Eden, 4.6 miles southeast, and more food and shops are in Johnson, 14 miles south.

50
BELVIDERE MOUNTAIN

Belvidere Mountain raises its bulky shoulders high above the surrounding farmlands, and its rocky top affords spectacular views across northern Vermont—even without climbing the summit fire tower.

DIRECTIONS

From the junction of VT 100 and VT 118, go north on VT 118 for 4.6 miles. Just after a left curve, turn right into the Long Trail State Forest parking area (space for about 12 cars). *GPS coordinates:* 44° 45.84′ N, 72° 35.27′ W.

TRAIL DESCRIPTION

You can't miss Mount Belvidere (3,330 feet) when you're driving or hiking across the northern tier of Vermont. Its distinct point, massive girth, and tailings pile from a defunct asbestos mine make it a landmark of the northern Green Mountains. A rugged section of the Long Trail ascends Belvidere's ledgy western ridge before heading north through remote terrain. This hike has some challenging sections over steep ledges, but the broad summit rocks and their fabulous vistas make it worth the vigorous climb.

From the trailhead parking lot, follow the Long Trail's white blazes northbound and slightly downhill. Cross a flat, wooded area before starting to climb. The trail descends briefly to cross a wide, rocky stream then heads up onto the hillside and follows parallel to the stream for about a mile. This section of trail climbs moderately and is rocky, rooty, and often muddy.

A big curve to the right brings you onto the ridgeline you'll follow the rest of the way up. At about 2 miles, you will begin a section of steep ledges that require big power steps and handholds to steady yourself. This kind of climbing continues most of the rest of the way

LOCATION
Eden and Lowell, VT

RATING
Moderate to Strenuous

DISTANCE
6 miles

ELEVATION GAIN
2,050 feet

ESTIMATED TIME
4.5 hours

MAPS
USGS Hazens Notch

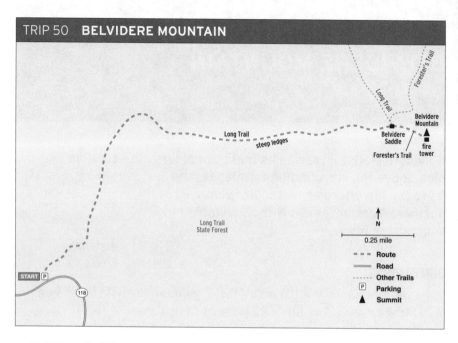

to Belvidere Saddle at 2.8 miles, although in places the trail rolls along pleasantly through upper-elevation spruce-fir woods. Along the way there are some interesting striated and wavy patterns in the ledge, and wildflowers—such as the rose twisted-stalk, the Canada mayflower, and the delicately pink-striped mountain wood sorrel—sprout from the mossy edges of the trail. The state of Vermont maintains a web page about the geology of Belvidere Mountain, which attracts interest not only from geologists but also from naturalists for the plant communities supported by the relatively high levels of magnesium, iron, and calcium leaching into the soil from the rocks. For more information, see dec.vermont.gov/geological-survey/Vermont-geology/Belvidere.

After a final stretch of ledge scrambling, arrive at Belvidere Saddle at 2.8 miles. This open area is grassy and shrubby, a low spot between Belvidere's summit on the right and a lower knob on the left. The Long Trail continues straight across the saddle, but you will head right, onto the final stretch of Forester's Trail, which is unmarked and looks like an old road climbing steeply from the clearing. Forester's Trail rises to Belvidere Saddle from the northeastern side of the mountain, joining the Long Trail just a few feet north of this junction. Head right onto Forester's Trail and begin the final 0.2-mile climb to the peak.

The summit of Belvidere is open, flat, and rocky. A fire tower is anchored in the center, but climbing it isn't necessary to get a wide view of the landscape to the east, north, and south. A shuttered asbestos mine is directly below to the southeast, its large tailing piles, ponds, and buildings left behind when health concerns led to environmental legislation and a massive reduction in use of the mineral. This mine closed in 1993, according to the state of Vermont. Beyond

Belvidere Mountain's fire tower provides an exciting climb to 360-degree views. Hikers who prefer to keep their boots on solid ground can also enjoy broad vistas from the summit rocks.

the mine, wind towers are visible on Lowell Mountain, and the big, pointed monadnock of Burke Mountain (Trip 52) sticks up above the ridges in the distance. On a clear day, New Hampshire's White Mountains are visible to the southeast. To the north, high ridges transport the Long Trail toward Jay Peak (Trip 51) and the Canadian border. Due south, the Worcester Range (Trip 39) is a distinctly tall ridgeline, and in the southwest, Mount Mansfield's Chin (Trip 45) juts above everything else.

Return downhill the way you came up.

DID YOU KNOW?

According to *Vermont Place-Names* by Esther M. Swift (Stephen Greene Press, 1977), the town and mountain of Belvidere were named by John Kelly, a New York City lawyer of Irish heritage who was granted this parcel of land before Vermont joined the colonies. He apparently named the region for Ireland's Lake Belvedere. Either way it's spelled, the name translates from Italian as "beautiful view."

MORE INFORMATION

Belvidere Mountain is within the Long Trail State Forest, administered by Vermont Department of Forests, Parks and Recreation, 5 Perry Street, Suite 20, Barre, VT 05641; 802-476-0174; fpr.vermont.gov. The Long Trail and Belvidere's fire tower are maintained by the Green Mountain Club, 4711 Waterbury–Stowe Road, Waterbury Center, VT 05677; 802-244-7037; greenmountainclub.org.

NEARBY

Paddle on Long Pond (also called Belvidere Pond), 0.5 mile west. Camp, paddle, and swim at Green River Reservoir State Park, 20 miles southeast. Food and shops are in Johnson, 14 miles south.

51
JAY PEAK

This boreal forest hike to the summit of Vermont's northernmost ski area features sweeping views of northern Vermont, New Hampshire, and New York, as well as southern Quebec.

DIRECTIONS

From its junction with VT 101 in Jay, take VT 242 west 6.5 miles, passing through the village and past the entrance to the ski area. At the height of land, the Long Trail crosses VT 242. Park on the southern shoulder of the road (space for about 15 cars). *GPS coordinates: 44° 54.77′ N, 72° 30.24′ W.*

TRAIL DESCRIPTION

Jay Peak (3,830 feet) is a quintessential peak: high and solo, with a distinct profile and incredible summit views. Its ardent fans are numerous, from skiers and snowboarders who cherish its rugged terrain and famously deep snowfalls, to Long Trail hikers for whom the singular summit is a milestone at the beginning or end of their journeys. The hike from Jay Pass is short and steep, rocky and beautiful. Snowshoers can expect to share some of their hike with skiers on the upper mountain.

Find the trailhead on the north side of VT 242, where the white-blazed Long Trail enters the trees and immediately encounters Atlas Valley Shelter. (This roofed resting area was built in 1967 by a plywood company and is not intended for overnight use. For campers, Jay Loop spur trail departs on the left here, leading to the bunks at Jay Camp, and rejoins the Long Trail 0.2 mile uphill.) The climb begins gradually through a deciduous forest. By the upper junction with Jay Loop, the trail has narrowed and steepened; within minutes, the forest becomes distinctly more boreal.

LOCATION
Westfield, VT

RATING
Moderate

DISTANCE
3.4 miles

ELEVATION GAIN
1,638 feet

ESTIMATED TIME
3 hours

MAPS
USGS Jay Peak

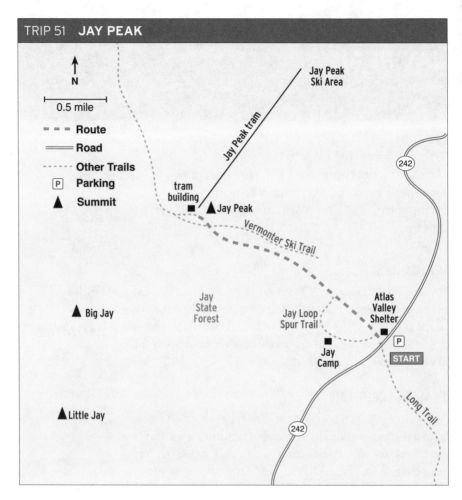

N

0.5 mile

- - - Route
=== Road
----- Other Trails
P   Parking
▲   Summit

Jay Peak
Ski Area

Jay Peak tram

tram
building
■ ▲ Jay Peak

Vermonter Ski Trail

242

Jay
State
Forest

▲ Big Jay

Jay Loop
Spur Trail

Atlas
Valley
Shelter
■

P

START

■
Jay
Camp

Long Trail

▲ Little Jay

242

The trail ascends steadily along the southwestern-facing slope of the ridge. (Where the Long Trail crests the ridge and traverses the top of it, an informal path leads right a short distance onto a ski slope.) The Long Trail curves to the west and continues climbing through a dense conifer forest. Moderate pitches are interspersed with scrambles up rocky ledges, and moss grows thickly on the forest floor. At 1.5 miles, the Long Trail crosses steel snowmaking pipes and emerges from the woods onto the Vermonter ski trail. To the left, the ski tram's summit building is visible a short distance up the open slope. The Long Trail continues directly across the ski slope, climbing steep ledges onto the ridgeline for the final 0.2-mile ascent. Walk on the rocks, weaving between spruce and fir krummholz: crooked wood, stunted and deformed by wind and snowpack. Passing a stone bench, arrive at the summit, next to the tram station.

The views from here are unparalleled in north-central Vermont. Big Jay (3,770 feet) hulks close by to the southwest, rising opposite a glacial cirque that connects it with Jay Peak. Little Jay (3,170 feet) is a short distance down Big

Jay's southern shoulder. The high ridge of the Green Mountains leads your eyes southwest over the distinct point of Mount Mansfield's Chin (Trip 45) to Camel's Hump (Trip 27), 46 miles away. To the west, beyond the low, rolling landscape of Franklin County's dairy farms, narrow slivers of Lake Champlain reflect the sky. Look southwest for the famed Adirondack High Peaks. You know you're about as far north as you can go in Vermont when the big peaks of the Adirondacks (and, to the southeast, the White Mountains) are south of you.

To the north, Quebec's Sutton Mountains continue where the Green Mountains leave off at the international border. Bear Mountain (2,192 feet) and Owl's Head (2,480 feet)—both with ski trails—perch on the western edge of the trans-border Lake Memphremagog. Much of the Sutton Mountain massif due north has been conserved by groups, such as Ruiter Valley Land Trust, which maintains hiking trails through its property, and Appalachian Corridor, which works with Vermont's Green Mountain Club and other American organizations to ensure that conservation strategies are developed on both sides of the border, linking important ecological areas to each other.

Descend the way you came up. To give your knees a brief respite, head down the wooden stairway to the top of Vermonter ski trail and follow its gentle grade downhill to rejoin the Long Trail.

Jay Peak's snowless season is short. Bag it while you can! Photo by Judy Lamphere.

DID YOU KNOW?

The 25-mile-long Lake Memphremagog hides curiosities beneath its surface. At least one car loaded with Prohibition-era whiskey rests in the murky depths, and divers have surfaced with still-corked jugs of hooch. A sea serpent called Memphre has been spotted numerous times in the lake since 1816.

MORE INFORMATION

Jay Peak is within Jay State Forest, managed by Vermont Department of Forests, Parks and Recreation, Saint Johnsbury Regional Office, 1229 Portland Street, Suite 201, Saint Johnsbury, VT 05763; 802-751-0116; vtfpr.org. The Long Trail is maintained by the Green Mountain Club, 4711 Waterbury–Stowe Road, Waterbury Center, VT 05677; 802-244-7037; greenmountainclub.org.

NEARBY

The Missisquoi River and Lake Memphremagog are part of the 740-mile Northern Forest Canoe Trail. The multiuse Missisquoi Valley Rail Trail extends 26 miles between Richford and Saint Albans. Big Falls State Park in Troy, with the state's largest undammed cascade and gorge, is a scenic picnic spot 10 miles northeast. Jay Peak Resort is a center of recreational activities, including skiing and a popular water park, 2.4 miles northeast. For food, head to Jay Peak Resort, or to the village of Jay, 5.5 miles east, or to Newport, 21 miles east. The Newport State Office Building on the lakefront houses an interesting exhibit about Memphremagog history.

NORTHEASTERN VERMONT

Commonly known as the Northeast Kingdom, or just the Kingdom, northeastern Vermont is a land slightly apart. It has been called Vermont's loneliest and loveliest corner, and it is a place where—even more so than in other parts of the state—the landscape and wildlife overshadow any human creations, such as towns or farms. As in other regions of Vermont, the landscape is mountainous and heavily forested, but unlike elsewhere, the Kingdom is dotted with lakes and ponds, such as Caspian Lake beside Barr Hill (Trip 53), Island Pond below Bluff Mountain (Trip 59), and Little Averill Pond beneath the cliffs of Brousseau Mountain (Trip 60) on the Canadian border.

Temperatures across the high ground of the Kingdom are generally a little lower than elsewhere in Vermont, and therefore the forests are more commonly coniferous. Accordingly, moose, spruce grouse, and other denizens of the boreal forest live here in greater numbers than in other parts of the state. Although timber harvesting has long been a primary economic activity in the Kingdom, large tracts of forest have been conserved in recent years; the state's 1999 purchase of 132,000 acres called the Champion Lands was Vermont's largest conservation project, stretching across 14 Northeast Kingdom towns. The extensive basin of the Nulhegan River watershed is protected by the Conte Refuge (Trip 57).

In a region of dramatic landscapes, perhaps the most spectacular in the Kingdom are the cliffy slopes of Mount Pisgah (Trip 54) and Mount Hor (Trip 55), rising more than 1,000 feet above the narrow, dark waters of Lake Willoughby. The mountains and lake together form Lake Willoughby Natural Area, which has been designated a National Natural Landmark. Just south of the Willoughby area, Burke Mountain (Trip 52) stands taller than anything else in the vicinity and is a hub of recreational activity, including Vermont's premier mountain-bike trail system, Kingdom Trails.

On the eastern border of the state, another solo peak, Monadnock Mountain (Trip 58), towers over the fields and forests of the Connecticut River valley. The beginnings of this 407-mile-long river tumble southward, quick and shallow at first, then slow through S curves across broad floodplains before filling the 7-mile-long Moore Reservoir. The Connecticut River and its environs provide critical bird habitats and are an important bird-migration flyway. Herons and mergansers are common along the edges, while ospreys, various hawks, and bald eagles fish the river's waters. Common loons occasionally visit the river but are more likely to be spotted swimming in the Kingdom's many ponds and lakes.

The view from Mount Pisgah's southern slopes includes a distant Burke Mountain.

52
BURKE MOUNTAIN

This remote trail passes through a stand of enormous ash and maple trees on its way to spectacular views from the summit of a popular skiing and mountain-biking destination.

DIRECTIONS

From VT 114 in East Burke Village, follow Mountain Road 1.1 miles to Sherburne Lodge Road on the right. Ample parking for the trailhead is at the far end of the large lower lot. *GPS coordinates:* 44° 35.25' N, 71° 55.08' W.

TRAIL DESCRIPTION

Burke Mountain (3,267 feet) rises steeply from the gently sloping Passumpsic River valley. Its northern slopes and summit are a beehive of activity during ski season, but the challenging hiking trail up its western ridge is surprisingly insulated.

From the trailhead kiosk, Red Trail follows a dirt two-track into the woods and curves through tamarack, maple, and overgrown log landings as it gently rises. After 0.6 mile, Red Trail turns left, departing the two-track. In 500 feet, the trail turns right, joining Kirby Connector, a mountain-bike trail. The two trails coincide for 0.2 mile; be aware of bikers and give them room to pass. The open understory here allows for long views beneath the canopy, a rare treat in eastern forests. At a register box, turn left off Kirby Connector and continue up Red Trail, entering Darling State Park.

Enormous tree trunks make this section of trail interesting. The largest are ash and maple, while larger than usual yellow and paper birches also make an appearance. Look for jumbo-sized shelf mushrooms growing off the huge trunks. The undergrowth thickens as the slope steepens. Red Trail turns sharply left to climb alongside a steep

LOCATION
Burke, VT

RATING
Strenuous

DISTANCE
6.2 miles

ELEVATION GAIN
2,080 feet

ESTIMATED TIME
4.5 hours

MAPS
USGS Burke Mountain

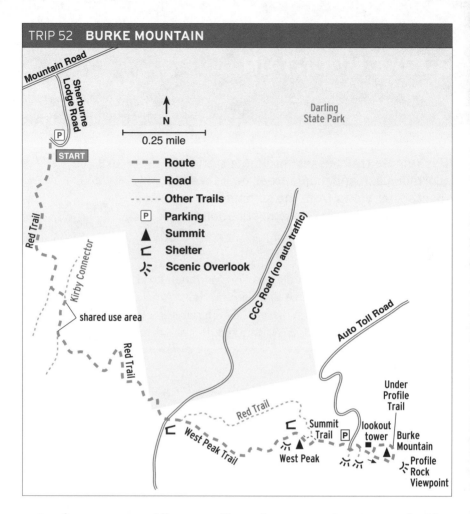

ravine then crosses a saddle up top. The path now ascends onto a maple ridge, heading straight up the fall line. After passing through a dark spruce-fir stand, Red Trail crosses the Civilian Conservation Corps (CCC) Road, which no longer bears vehicle traffic, at 1.7 miles. Straight ahead, Red Trail intersects with West Peak Trail in a clearing that's home to a CCC-era lean-to and a stone fireplace still used by campers and skiers. Turn right in this clearing and head up the scenic blue-blazed West Peak Trail.

Climb steeply through paper and yellow birches for 0.2 mile then enter a shallow ravine thick with bushy chokecherries and maples. West Peak Trail ascends through stunted birch trees and mountain ashes, traverses the gully, and climbs out. Now on a high ridge, the hiking alternates between scrambling up ledges draped in thick moss and crossing level areas where small pockets of fern glades open between fragrant softwood thickets. After several rising switchbacks, West Peak Trail emerges from the tree canopy, passes along the bottom of a steep rock face, and climbs up the far side. On top of this promontory, views extend west across the broad Passumpsic Valley and south, over the shoulder of nearby Kirby Mountain (2,750 feet). The wooded summit of West Peak (3,150 feet) is just 0.1 mile farther and is marked by another log lean-to. Go right, staying on West Peak Trail, which ends at a five-way junction.

Stay right to follow Summit Trail along the undeveloped south edge of the mountaintop, passing remnants of CCC campsites and shelters. After passing the top edge of a ski trail and a parking lot, reenter the woods and find two successive spur trails leading to viewpoints. Summit Trail continues to wind through the forest to the junction with Under Profile Trail (a.k.a. Profile Trail). Summit Trail heads left to the fire tower, but go right, continuing along the ridge to pass beneath the jutting rock overhang before circling to climb on top of Profile Rock (via the Profile Vista spur trail) for the most expansive views yet. (*Caution:* Surrounding trees can disguise cliff edges.) To the northeast, East Haven Mountain (3,070 feet) rises in the foreground. Beyond it, an abandoned Cold War-era radar station is visible on East Mountain (3,420 feet).

Ski trails on Burke Mountain provide breaks in the treeline that allow hikers to spy Willoughby Gap, a National Natural Landmark made up of Mount Pisgah's cliffs on the east and Mount Hor's on the west.

Leaving Profile Rock, continue on Profile Trail west across the rocky open area of Burke's true summit. Just beyond it, climb the metal tower for 360-degree views, including Willoughby Gap to the northwest, a remarkable notch formed by Mount Hor on the west and Mount Pisgah on the east. From the tower, follow Summit Trail downhill and return the way you came. An alternate route down is via Toll Road and Mountain Road, 3.6 miles from the summit to the trailhead.

DID YOU KNOW?

Burke Mountain is one of several Vermont monadnocks, isolated mountains that, due to their erosion-resistant rock, rise abruptly from gently sloping surroundings.

MORE INFORMATION

Darling State Park is managed by Vermont Department of Forests, Parks and Recreation (FPR), 1229 Portland Avenue, Saint Johnsbury, VT 05819; 802-751-0110; vtfpr.org. Trails are maintained by Burke Mountain Resort, 223 Sherburne Lodge Road, East Burke, VT 05832; 802-626-7300; skiburke.com; in partnership with Vermont FPR and local conservation organizations.

NEARBY

East Burke's Kingdom Trails Association is a renowned mountain-biking center, with trails open to hiking, running, skiing, and snowshoeing as well. Groceries and dining options are found on VT 114 in East Burke or on US 5 in Lyndonville, 5.7 miles southwest.

53

BARR HILL

More sightseeing ramble than hike, this short loop treats you to a collection of scenic vistas from several perspectives as you circle the wooded summit of Barr Hill.

DIRECTIONS

From the center of Greensboro Village, follow East Craftsbury Road north 0.2 mile and bear right onto Laurendon Road. Go 0.6 mile and bear left onto Barr Hill Road. Drive 1.7 miles to a circle turnaround and park alongside the woods (space for 6 cars). (In winter, expect to park at the end of the plowed section of Barr Hill Road and hike into the trailhead.) *GPS coordinates*: 44° 36.52′ N, 72° 17.27′ W.

TRAIL DESCRIPTION

Barr Hill (2,110 feet) is a locally loved little bump and a favorite sunset destination given its wide southwestern views and a stone fire ring that encourages you to settle down and stay awhile. The 256-acre preserve has a variety of woods, fields, ledges, and a ravine, which make the short, undulating loop trail feel chock-full of experiences. You certainly can walk the 0.8 mile in less than 45 minutes, but with so much to see, why hurry? This mellow trail is appropriate for kids of all ages; dogs are not allowed in Barr Hill Preserve. In winter, the nearby Craftsbury Outdoor Center grooms trails into the preserve (although not along this hiking loop), so you can ski here from the center.

The parking area has a register box that may or may not contain self-guided nature-hike brochures, with descriptions corresponding to numbered signposts along the route. The chances of finding directional signage at Barr Hill are slim to nonexistent, so go with a sense of exploration. The hilltop is small enough that you're never too far from the trailhead.

LOCATION
Greensboro, VT

RATING
Easy

DISTANCE
0.8 miles

ELEVATION GAIN
120 feet

ESTIMATED TIME
45 minutes

MAPS
USGS Caspian Lake

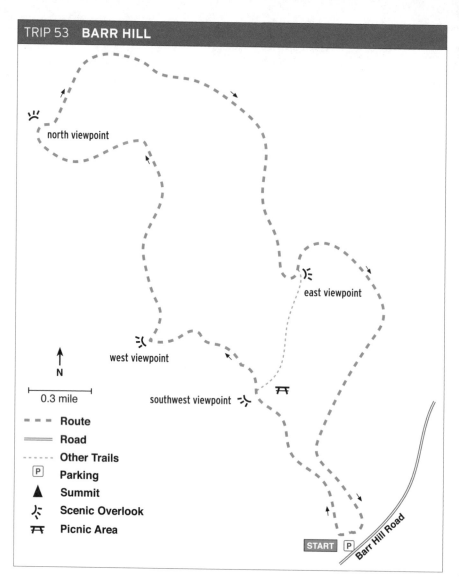

The trail begins inconspicuously, in an opening in the trees to the right of the register box. But you can be forgiven for simply wandering past it onto the open hillside and starting uphill toward the obvious lookout point. The proper trail pops out of the woods onto this hillside after 200 feet and crosses to the lookout spot, where a weathered signboard names the many peaks and ranges spread across the horizon. From Spruce Mountain (Trip 30) in the south to the massive, rocky bulk of Mount Mansfield (Trips 45 and 46) in the west, you can pick out Vermont's most recognizable and well-loved peaks—Breadloaf Mountain (3,835 feet), Mount Abraham (Trip 25), Camel's Hump (Trip 27), and Mount Hunger (Trip 41)—and fill in your knowledge of some of the lesser known summits, such as Woodbury Mountain (2,471 feet) and Mount Worcester (Trip 39).

When you turn your back on the view and continue uphill on the path, you'll spot the picnic knoll in the top-right corner of the meadow and the trail loop's departure into the woods on the left (0.1 mile). Follow the trail into the woods and immediately descend a staircase, cross a small ravine, and climb out the other side. Mount a gentle slope through maples to a spur trail (0.2 mile) on the left and walk its few steps to a view of Caspian Lake. This 789-acre lake has crystal-clear water—and an active local association working diligently to keep it that way. Loons frequent the lake, as do writers, artists, and others seeking refuge and inspiration. Wallace Stegner set several of his novels here.

Returning to the main trail, continue to the left and cross ledges and soft, needle-covered ground as you circle the summit. Chunks of white quartz rest alongside the trail amid patches of thick club moss. Reach the far side of the loop at 0.4 mile, where an opening in the trees affords a view northwest. The chocolate-kiss summit of Jay Peak (Trip 51) perches near the Canadian border, and wind turbines in the foreground spin atop the long ridge of Lowell Mountain (2,641 feet). The trail U-turns at this viewpoint, heading north through large spruces before curving east. A stone wall and privately owned camp are visible downhill through the trees.

Barr Hill's circumferential trail hits one spectacular viewpoint after another. Photo by Kip Roberts.

Continue on the curving, rolling trail, with large patches of moss and fern spreading between the conifer trunks. A small window in the foliage gives a preview of the panorama just around the next bend, where the trail climbs onto a knoll and arrives at a junction, 0.6 mile from your start. Straight ahead, a 200-foot shortcut returns you to the picnic area.

Turn left to continue on the loop trail, entering a clearing that slopes downhill in front of you, opening a broad view east. A signboard provides a guide to the peaks that stretch across the horizon. In the northeast, Wheeler Mountain (Trip 56), Mount Pisgah (Trip 54), and Mount Hor (Trip 55) cluster together around the high, pointy peak of Bald Mountain (3,310 feet) in Westmore. To the southeast, Burke Mountain (Trip 52) is recognizable by the towers on its ridge and the north-facing ski trails. Continue beyond the signboard, following the rock ledge across the top of the clearing before curving downhill to cross the bottom of the field. The trail curves south and west now, descending into a wooded ravine on its final leg before returning to the trailhead.

DID YOU KNOW?

Every summer circus performers ages 10 to 18 train at the Circus Smirkus campus in Greensboro then hit the road for a two-month tour of New England. Their amazing stunts will knock your socks off. Make sure to catch a show if you're visiting in season.

MORE INFORMATION

Barr Hill Nature Preserve is maintained as a sanctuary for all wildlife. No dogs other than service animals; no camping, hunting, or trapping. Please picnic only in the designated area. The Nature Conservancy, 575 Stone Cutters Way, Montpelier, VT 05602; 802-229-4425; nature.org.

NEARBY

Swim in and paddle on beautiful Caspian Lake from the public beach and boat launch at its south end. Lodging and food are available in Greensboro, with more options in Hardwick, 9 miles south. Craftsbury Outdoor Center maintains cross-country ski trails that extend around Caspian Lake and to Barr Hill. Mountain biking is at Craftsbury Outdoor Center, 9 miles northeast.

IS THE WATER CLEAN?

Pristine waters are part of the allure of hiking and one of the signs we're away from the garbage and pollution of developed areas. But is the water tumbling over rocks in clear mountain streams along the trail and in high-mountain lakes really clean?

The answer depends on why you're asking. If you're looking to swim or fish, chances are that the answer in Vermont will be yes, the water is clean enough. (Check healthvermont.gov for specific warnings.) If you're wondering about the health of the ecosystem, the answer is more complex. If you simply want to refill your water bottle, the answer is that "clean" may not mean, "OK to drink."

New England's waterways suffered historically from industrial uses involving mills and dams and from erosion caused by extensive tree clearing. Today, most waterways have recovered significantly due to decreased manufacturing and logging, as well as to pollution-control standards, such as the Clean Water Act of 1972. Selected industrial-era dams have been dismantled, increasing the amount of free-flowing water that is crucial in the life cycles of some fish.

But even with these improvements, Vermont's water quality is threatened. Power plants and factories emit chemicals that blow over New England and descend as acid rain or snow, altering the chemistry and thus the biology of streams, rivers, and lakes. Closer to home, chemicals have seeped into the ground at manufacturing plants, while fertilizers that wash into the water from farms and residential areas cause excessive algae growth. Algae blooms are especially problematic in Lake Champlain, where

Refilling water bottles along the trail is important to keeping a hard-working body hydrated—just make sure to treat the water before quenching your thirst.

they degrade habitats and limit boating and swimming opportunities. Lake Champlain receives water from so many feeder streams and rivers that any pollution problems upstream affect the big lake as well.

So, those clear, high streams and ponds are the place for you to refill your water bottle—but don't mistake clean water with healthy-for-you water. You still need to sterilize any surface water before you chug it down. Clean water has lots of microscopic organisms swimming around, and some of them—notably the protozoan *Giardia lamblia*, which enters the water from the waste of animals or from hikers not up to speed on the principles of Leave No Trace (see page xxiv)— can ruin your vacation and leave you sick for several weeks afterward.

There are lots of ways to make clean surface water safe to drink, from boiling, filtering, or adding iodine, to the latest technology that zaps microorganisms with electrically charged brine or ultraviolet light. Staying hydrated is important to staying healthy while hiking, so head upstream with your treatment method of choice and enjoy the clean water.

54
MOUNT PISGAH

Outlooks atop Mount Pisgah's cliffs, which drop precipitously into scenic Lake Willoughby, provide sweeping views across the Northeast Kingdom.

DIRECTIONS

From the junction of US 5 and VT 5A in West Burke, travel north on VT 5A for 5.7 miles. Mount Pisgah's South Trail parking lot (space for about 15 cars) is on the right. An additional parking lot (space for about 12 cars) is on the left, at the bottom of the CCC Road. *GPS coordinates:* 44° 42.65′ N, 72° 01.44′ W.

TRAIL DESCRIPTION

Hikers climb Mount Pisgah not for its wooded summit, which you can pass over without realizing you're on it, but for the dramatic views from its western-facing ledges. The dark, deep waters of Lake Willoughby fill the narrow gap between Pisgah and its cliffy cousin, Mount Hor (Trip 55). Together, these mountains and the lake make up a National Natural Landmark. Mount Pisgah's cliffs are spectacular, but there are no restraints on them—not a railing or even a warning sign. Use caution.

South Trail begins in the far-right corner of the parking lot, from which it descends several rock steps and enters the woods. A short distance from the road, you reach the first of two wide boardwalks that cross a beaver pond. Watch for great blue herons standing quietly amid the dead tree trunks and lily pads. Cross the swamp and head north along a low ridge, passing a register box and beginning to climb gradually through a deciduous forest. Purple-flowering raspberry spreads its maple-like leaves

LOCATION
Westmore, VT

RATING
Moderate

DISTANCE
4.8 miles

ELEVATION GAIN
1,395 feet

ESTIMATED TIME
3 hours

MAPS
USGS Sutton

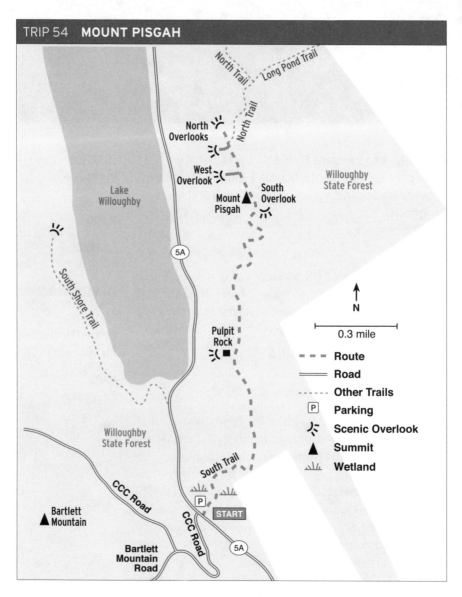

alongside the steepening trail. Hobblebush also thrives here, its flexible stems bending and taking root again where they touch the ground.

Glimpses of Lake Willoughby appear at intervals as South Trail follows the edge of the steep western hillside. Be wary of this drop when exploring any of the informal footpaths that lead to lookout points alongside the trail. Pulpit Rock, a small overlook almost 700 feet above the lake, appears on your left at 0.9 mile. This popular destination provides a striking, if more limited, view of the south end of Willoughby and the cliffs of Mount Hor. After passing an interesting tangle of two tree trunks leaning toward the precipice, the trail turns away from the ledges and heads into the woods, starting up the most sustained part of the climb. As you huff and puff up it, admire the artistry of many rock staircases built by the local youth crews of the NorthWoods Stewardship Center. The forest changes here to firs and short, thick paper birches.

Just below the summit, South Trail emerges from the forest onto South Overlook, a rocky bald spot with a view of Burke Mountain's ski trails, which appear to be just a stone's throw away. The trail returns to the woods and, without any fanfare, passes over the summit of Pisgah en route to the ledges. From the summit to the overlooks, you are on Mount Pisgah's North Trail. If you haven't already put a leash on your dog, do so now.

Three ledge overlooks provide three slightly different angles from which to view the surrounding landscape, and each rocky sitting area is a little more spacious than the last. Spur trails to the ledges are marked with brown signs.

Below the ledges, the landlocked fjord of Lake Willoughby stretches long and narrow, its far shore an oddly straight line lacking coves or inlets. It's easy to imagine how southward-creeping glaciers of the last ice age pushed through this narrow valley, gouging the trough that eventually became the deepest lake (308 feet) within Vermont's borders. Look northwest over the woods to the cliffs of Wheeler Mountain (Trip 56) for another example of that grinding ice sheet's

Pulpit Rock, overlooking the south end of Lake Willoughby, provides a scenic rest stop midway up Mount Pisgah or a worthwhile destination on its own merits.

power. Beyond Wheeler Mountain, the spine of the Green Mountains etches the western horizon, with Mount Mansfield to the southwest and the distinctive point of Jay Peak to the northwest. In the far northwest, Lake Memphremagog stretches into Quebec.

Climb back up the overlook spur trail and turn right on North Trail to return to the summit. Descend the way you came up.

DID YOU KNOW?

Mount Pisgah's nineteenth-century name was Mount Annance (or variants of that), after a local Wabanaki chief. When settlers of European descent began hosting tourists on the lake, the mountain was renamed, perhaps as clever marketing, to refer to the biblical Promised Land. This south side of Pisgah has had a trail up it since at least 1857, when a local innkeeper cleared a route to the views.

MORE INFORMATION

Willoughby State Forest is managed by Vermont Department of Forests, Parks and Recreation, 103 S. Main Street, Waterbury, VT 05671; 802-241-3670, or the Saint Johnsbury District Office, 802-751-0110; vtfpr.org. Mount Pisgah trails are maintained by the NorthWoods Stewardship Center, P.O. Box 220, East Charleston, VT 05833; 802-723-6551; northwoodscenter.org.

NEARBY

Camping and swimming areas are located at both ends of Lake Willoughby. Some dining options can be found along the lake, with many more in East Burke or Lyndonville, each 20 miles south, or Newport, 20 miles north. Outdoor outfitters are in East Burke and Newport.

THE PSYCHOLOGY OF TRAIL MAINTENANCE

When you pause—panting—at the top of a flight of rock steps, are you more inclined to curse the steps or to appreciate their flat surfaces? How you answer may indicate your awareness of erosion and trail-maintenance techniques. Although some trail features are put in place to ease the way for hikers, such as a ladder up a rock face or a railing on a bridge, the goal of most trail work is preventing erosion.

Soil erosion is the single biggest threat to the life of a trail. If you've ever hiked up a gullied path with tree roots suspended in midair, you know what the effects of erosion look like. Although erosion is a natural process of soils wearing away, it becomes a problem when it prompts hikers to seek alternate routes, trampling plants and causing further damage. Trails that become too badly eroded have to be relocated, and relocation is an expensive, time-consuming activity that results in additional impact on the forest.

Trail maintainers assessing an eroded stretch of trail have two thoughts: "How can I drain the water off this trail and stabilize the soil?" and "How can I convince hikers to walk on the more durable path?"

There are many ways to drain and harden a trail—that is, to make it more durable. You've stepped in and out of countless shallow, rounded troughs that cross the trail; these dips direct downstream currents off the path. Dips reinforced with a slippery skinned log or a row of rocks are called water bars.

Step stones and bog bridges (also called puncheons) provide dry footing across persistently muddy areas while protecting soils and plants.

Log or rock steps stabilize steep trails and provide a durable and relatively flat surface for footsteps. Many hikers avoid steps and climb the dirt slope beside them, causing that to erode and undermine the stability of the staircase. To make the steps more appealing than the hill beside them, trail maintainers plant pointy, less stable-looking rocks called scree alongside the staircase.

You won't look at trails the same way after you start noticing the subtle methods maintainers use to guide your footsteps and prevent erosion. That log ladder helping you up a ledge controls erosion by keeping you on durable rock rather than on erodible soil around the edge. A railing makes the durable bridge route the most appealing way across a ravine. Trail maintainers focus on protecting the trail and its surrounding environment, benefiting hikers in the long term, even if occasionally making life a little more challenging on the way up the mountain.

55

MOUNT HOR

A short hike through a lovely hardwood forest leads to lookouts with long views, including dramatic Lake Willoughby and the cliffs of Mount Pisgah.

LOCATION
Sutton, VT

RATING
Easy to Moderate

DISTANCE
2.9 miles

ELEVATION GAIN
601 feet

ESTIMATED TIME
1.5 hours

MAPS
USGS Sutton

DIRECTIONS

From VT 5A at the southern end of Lake Willoughby, go 0.5 mile south to the height of land and turn right onto the dirt CCC Road. After 0.5 mile, bear right at the fork and continue uphill. The unmarked parking area (space for 6 cars) is on the right at 1.7 miles. (The CCC Road is not maintained in winter; snowshoers should park at the bottom and add 3.4 miles round-trip to the hike.) *GPS coordinates: 44° 42.53′ N, 72° 02.83′ W.*

TRAIL DESCRIPTION

Mount Hor (2,648 feet) is one of two peaks that make up the National Natural Landmark of Willoughby Gap. Mirroring Mount Pisgah on the opposite side of the gap, Hor's cliffs rise 1,000 feet from narrow Lake Willoughby, forming a fjord-like landscape. Although the hiking is appropriate for kids roughly ages 6 and older, children and dogs need to be carefully monitored at the outlook points.

Herbert Hawkes Trail begins up the road a short distance beyond the parking area. The wide path climbs briefly, following an old road, then flattens out through an airy hardwood forest. After 0.4 mile, Herbert Hawkes Trail turns left off the old road and climbs steadily on a narrow path. At 0.6 mile, you will arrive at a ridge-top T junction: To the left, the trail skirts Mount Hor's summit, offering a view southwest; to the right, it's a little more than 0.5 mile to the vistas north and east over Lake Willoughby. Go left on Summit Spur, ascending over rocks until the low curve of the summit appears above you on your right, at which

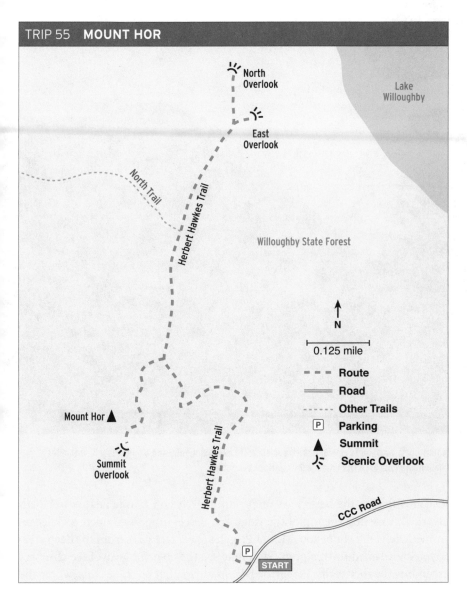

North Overlook

East Overlook

Lake Willoughby

North Trail

Herbert Hawkes Trail

Willoughby State Forest

N

0.125 mile

- - - Route
=== Road
······ Other Trails
P Parking
▲ Summit
🔆 Scenic Overlook

Mount Hor ▲

Summit Overlook

Herbert Hawkes Trail

CCC Road

P

START

point the trail flattens and curves around it. Straight ahead, down a short slope, a hole in the forest frames a view over numerous small ponds to Norris Mountain (2,292 feet). The ponds are part of the 30-acre Marl Pond and Swamp Natural Area, a northern-white-cedar swamp with several rare plants.

Return to the trail junction and pick up Herbert Hawkes Trail again, continuing straight along the ridgeline. The 0.6 mile to East Overlook is mostly flat, passing the junction of North Trail on your left and crossing muddy areas where you're likely to see moose prints, if not the hump-shouldered ungulate itself. A spur trail leads right down a short, eroded slope to a vista with limited views of the south cove of Lake Willoughby and the end of the Mount

Mount Hor's viewpoints reveal a dramatic slice of Lake Willoughby and Mount Pisgah, with a less-challenging approach than most other outlooks require.

Pisgah cliffs. For the best views on Mount Hor, head 0.1 mile farther to North Overlook, crossing the top of the ridge and descending to an open rock ledge. Immediately in front of you, Mount Pisgah's sheer face rises from the deep lake. If you snowshoed to this point, you may see the colorful gear of ice climbers ascending the rock walls. Peregrine falcons also gather on these cliffs, where the combination of horizontal ledges that support nests (called aeries) and vertical drops for hunting dives makes this an ideal raptor habitat.

Lake Willoughby stretches 4 miles northwest from here, with the comparatively gentle slope of Goodwin Mountain (2,900 feet) rising from the water north of Pisgah. The village of Westmore sits along the lake beneath Goodwin, where the shoreline curves into the mountainside. The Westmore Association has long maintained an active role in developing trails, including Herbert Hawkes Trail, which is named for the Trails Committee chair who proposed building it in 1971.

Mount Hor sits at the heart of the approximately 8,000-acre Willoughby State Forest, which was established in 1928 with an initial 1,700 acres. The forest is managed for multiple uses, meaning some areas are conserved for ecological reasons, such as Marl Pond and Swamp; some areas are maintained for recreation, such as the mountain summits; and some areas are managed for public timber harvest through a program that allows residents to cut wood for home heating. The forest also has a long history of work by various conservation corps programs (see "From the CCC to the VYCC: Conservation Corps in Vermont," page 257).

Return to the trail junction and go left, descending on Herbert Hawkes Trail to the parking lot the way you came up.

DID YOU KNOW?

The peregrine falcon is the fastest animal in the world. These birds achieve horizontal cruising speeds of 40 to 65 MPH, and their hunting dives, called stoops, have been recorded at more than 200 MPH.

MORE INFORMATION

Willoughby State Forest is managed by Vermont Department of Forests, Parks and Recreation, Saint Johnsbury District Office, 374 Emerson Falls Road, Suite 4, Saint Johnsbury, VT 05819; 802-751-0110; vtfpr.org. Mount Hor trails are maintained by the NorthWoods Stewardship Center, P.O. Box 220, East Charleston, VT 05833; 802-723-6551; northwoodscenter.org.

NEARBY

Camping and swimming areas are located at both ends of Lake Willoughby. Some dining options can be found along the lake, with more in East Burke or Lyndonville, each 20 miles south, or Newport, 20 miles north.

56

WHEELER MOUNTAIN

Wheeler Mountain's cliff-top vistas give panoramic views of the Northeast Kingdom landscape, including the spectacular and fjord-like Lake Willoughby.

LOCATION
Sutton, VT

RATING
Moderate

DISTANCE
4.1 miles

ELEVATION GAIN
870 feet

ESTIMATED TIME
3.5 hours

MAPS
USGS Sutton

DIRECTIONS

From the junction of VT 16 and US 5 in downtown Barton, head south on US 5 for 4.7 miles. Turn left onto the dirt Wheeler Mountain Road (Sutton Town Road 15). Go 1.4 miles to a large parking area on the right (space for 16 cars). *GPS coordinates: 44° 43.23′ N, 72° 06.00′ W.*

TRAIL DESCRIPTION

The hike up Wheeler Mountain (2,371 feet) begins with a ridge ascent and culminates in a cliff-top walk with many viewpoints over the great forest of the Northeast Kingdom. The hike was historically a quick scramble onto the cliffs from directly beneath them, but in 2016 the trail was rerouted from private land into Willoughby State Forest. Before hiking, check with Audubon Vermont (vt.audubon.org) for peregrine falcon activity here. The cliffs may be closed between March 15 and August 1 to protect falcon chicks.

Wheeler Mountain Trail begins downhill from the parking area and crosses Wheeler Mountain Road. Follow blue blazes to a register box then begin the steady climb over rocky ground. At times you will scramble over and around mossy ledges and boulders. At 0.6 mile, you will arrive at a T junction. To the right is a view of the cliffs of Wheeler Mountain; go left to stay on Wheeler Mountain Trail and continue heading uphill.

As you gain elevation, you will cross streams and clusters of rocks that provide tricky, often slippery footing. Mature birches and maples shelter the undergrowth of

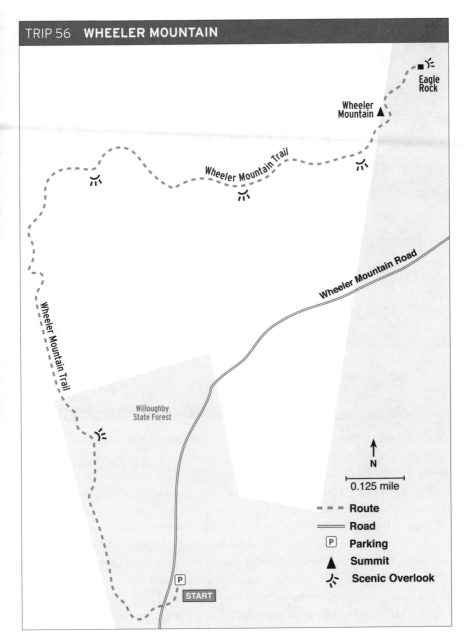

striped maples and hobblebushes. The trail zigzags as it climbs alongside a ravine then leads across the hillside, entering a high spruce-fir forest. At 1.2 miles, a double blue blaze marks a spur trail to a limited view of Wheeler Pond, as well as the wind turbines on Granby Mountain (2,393 feet) and Libby Hill. Return to Wheeler Mountain Trail and descend 0.2 mile into a pine forest, passing the now-closed junction of the old trail. From here, you will meander through patches of thick forest and open rock as you approach Wheeler's cliffs, arriving

Wheeler Mountain's cliffs offer endless views as hikers follow the crest around its summit.

at the first of many lookout points at 1.6 miles. A broad, smooth expanse of bare rock gives a magnificent view of the valley below, with Wheeler Pond and Granby Mountain in the near distance.

From here, the trail crosses open ledges and reenters the woods, climbing gradually. Along this top part of Wheeler Mountain, look for blazes on rocks, as well as on trees, as you weave through forests and over open areas. At 1.9 miles, Wheeler Mountain Trail emerges on open cliffs. Use extreme caution here as you scramble up a rock spine, with trees on the left and a drop on the right opening to wide views north, east, and south that get wider as you climb. From the panoramic views on top of the spine, Wheeler Mountain Trail heads back into a thick, mossy spruce-fir forest that edges around the summit proper. Descend gradually to the terminus of the hike at Eagle Rock, a ledge that feels like it's floating above the Northeast Kingdom landscape. Lake Willoughby shines beneath the cliffs of Mount Pisgah (Trip 54). Beyond the lake, Bald Mountain (3,310 feet) is the noticeably conical peak. To the southeast, Burke Mountain (Trip 52) is also distinct in its tall solitude.

Return to the trailhead the way you hiked up.

DID YOU KNOW?

Peregrine falcons are still recovering from the devastating effects of DDT and other chemicals used over the past century. Vermont's peregrine population is stable but remains susceptible to disturbance—particularly when hikers or rock climbers disturb the birds' cliff-side aeries during nesting season. The falcons may respond to disturbance by sounding a loud *cack, cack, cack* alarm call or displaying aggressive flight behavior. If the birds appear agitated, retreat from the overlook.

MORE INFORMATION

Wheeler Mountain Trail is managed by Vermont Department of Forests, Parks and Recreation, 1229 Portland Street, Suite 201, Saint Johnsbury, VT 05819; 802-751-0110; fpr.vermont.gov.

NEARBY

Food is available in Barton, 6 miles west. Crystal Lake State Park, also 6 miles west, is good for swimming and paddling. Closer by, Wheeler Pond has a nice loop walk around it, and the Green Mountain Club rents two cabins on its shore. The epicenter of Vermont mountain biking is 15 miles southeast, at Kingdom Trails. The Fairbanks Museum has natural history exhibits and a planetarium in Saint Johnsbury, 26 miles south.

57

CONTE REFUGE

Explore the banks and woods of the remote Nulhegan River as it meanders through this conserved basin full of water, wetlands, woods, and boreal species.

DIRECTIONS

To Nulhegan River Trailhead

From Island Pond, head west on VT 105 for 10.7 miles to the Silvio O. Conte National Fish and Wildlife Refuge Visitor Center, on the left (space for 20 cars). *GPS coordinates: 44° 46.05′ N, 71° 42.18′ W.*

To North Branch Trailhead

From Island Pond, head west on VT 105 for 7.3 miles to a small parking area on the left (space for 4 cars). *GPS coordinates: 44° 46.75′ N, 71° 45.36′ W.*

TRAIL DESCRIPTION

The Nulhegan Basin is a lowland in a highland: a 10-mile-wide depression in a cold, high corner of Vermont's Northeast Kingdom. With an average of 100 inches of snow and only 100 frost-free days each year, this rugged, forested, waterlogged landscape is ideal for migratory songbirds and moose (who need all the help they can get in Vermont; see "Moose in Peril," page 251). The basin also harbors rare plants, beavers, black bears, wintering deer herds, coyotes, fishers, bobcats, the state-endangered spruce grouse, and the federally endangered Canada lynx. At one time heavily logged, the basin is now a 26,000-acre National Fish and Wildlife Refuge, part of the bigger conservation effort for the whole Connecticut River watershed that was named for its champion in the U.S. Congress, Silvio O. Conte.

Because this area is managed for wildlife diversity and not necessarily for recreation, trails are few, although old

NULHEGAN RIVER TRAIL:
LOCATION
Brunswick, VT

RATING
Easy

DISTANCE
1.1 miles

ELEVATION GAIN
120 feet

ESTIMATED TIME
45 minutes

NORTH BRANCH TRAIL:
LOCATION
Ferdinand, VT

RATING
Easy

DISTANCE
3.9 miles

ELEVATION GAIN
90 feet

ESTIMATED TIME
2.5 hours

MAPS
USGS Bloomfield, USGS Spectacle Pond

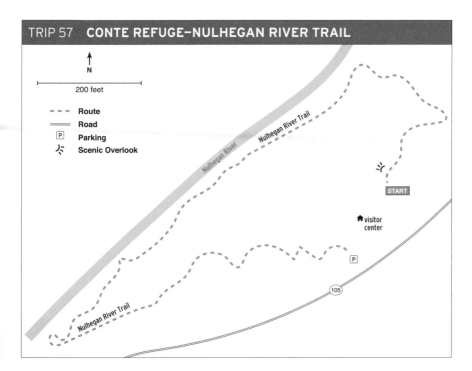

logging roads are plentiful. Exploring the wilder areas of the vast refuge is easier to do in the heart of winter, when the soupy ground solidifies, but if you visit during the brief warm season, two hiking trails give you a taste of this special area. The short, self-guided, interpretive loop called Nulhegan River Trail visits the banks near the visitor center and is appropriate for kids as young as 3. The longer, more leisurely North Branch Trail features beaver dams, swimming holes, and a more remote experience that would appeal to kids 6 and older. Additionally, if you're up for a meandering drive or a bicycle ride into the heart of the refuge, get directions at the visitor center to Mollie Beattie Bog, where a 200-foot, wheelchair-accessible boardwalk keeps your hiking boots dry as you enter a black-spruce woodland bog.

Nulhegan River Trail

This hillside loop begins and ends at the roadside visitor center, where you will find restrooms, maps, and excellent exhibits. An interpretive pamphlet provides a guide to the trees and other vegetation along the route. Begin at the granite outlook behind the visitor center, where a gap in the trees allows a view northwest over the basin's woods to Gore Mountain (3,332 feet). Beneath those trees, the North, Black, Yellow, and East branches of the Nulhegan River flow southward to join the main stem at the bottom of the hill below you.

Head across the grass, away from the visitor center, to find the top of the wide trail into the woods. Descend alongside a stream to an opening, with a bench beside an apple tree. The narrow course of the Nulhegan River cuts through the forest, shallow and gurgling in summer but roaring and swollen in spring with snowmelt from its tributaries. Turn left and follow the river upstream on a rolling, winding path through spruces, firs, yellow birches, and cedars for 0.5 mile. Tree foliage screens the river from sight much of the time, but occasional openings give views of small islands, as well as opportunities to wade out into the chilly current favored by brook trout.

The trail bends in a wide U-turn and begins a gentle climb uphill. Look for blue-bead lilies, with their small, wispy yellow flowers in early to midsummer, followed by round blue fruits perched on top of their stalks as the season winds down. The trail mounts a couple of switchbacks as it crests the hill and follows the audible but not visible road back to the visitor center, emerging at the west end of the parking area.

Two riverside loop trails in Conte Refuge provide plenty of opportunities to play along the tumbling, tannic North Branch of Nulhegan River.

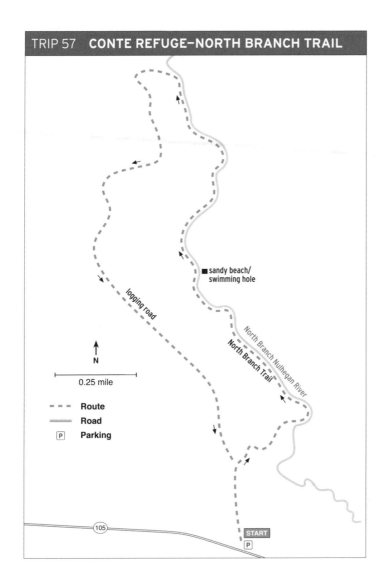

■ sandy beach/
swimming hole

North Branch Nulhegan River

North Branch Trail

logging road

N

0.25 mile

- - - Route
═══ Road
P Parking

105

START

P

North Branch Trail

This lollipop loop has a pretty eastern half, following the bank of the North Branch of the Nulhegan River, and a relatively featureless green tunnel of a return on its western half. I prefer this hike as an out-and-back, following the river both directions, but the old road has its benefits: It provides good terrain for cross-country skiing and wildlife viewing, and its width allows conversational, side-by-side hiking.

From the trailhead kiosk, go around a metal gate and follow the two-track 0.2 mile north, away from the road, to a junction where the loop begins. Go right and then quickly right again, leaving the road for a single-track. White blazes lead you through mossy woods with bunchberries and balsam firs, bending around a switchback and crossing bog bridges as you approach the river at

0.6 mile. For the next 1.5 miles, you will walk upstream along the North Branch, sometimes next to it and sometimes curving a short distance into the woods. Watch for beaver activity both on the river and among the trees and stumps along the trail. In places, the river riffles around rocks and pours over small ledges, but mostly it is smooth and flat.

Halfway along your riverside trek (mile 1.3), a lovely sandy spot appears next to a relatively deep hole, inviting a swim on a hot day. As you walk, watch for snakes warming themselves and patches of blackberries in the sunnier, open spots. Listen for the drumming of ruffed grouse and don't be surprised—if you can keep from startling—if one explodes out of the brush in a flurry and does a good impression of being injured to distract you from its young.

At 2.2 miles, the trail leaves the river and curves west, passing through dense woods before arriving in a meadow where tall joe-pye weed blooms with clusters of fuzzy pink flowers in late summer. Although there aren't clear signs, the only obvious way to go (if you aren't turning around to return via the river route) is across the meadow and onto a two-track. The old road enters the woods and rolls along, climbing gently to the hike's highest point at 2.8 miles before gradually descending the rest of the way to the loop junction. Go straight and follow the old road out the way you came in.

DID YOU KNOW?

Beavers give birth to litters of kits between mid-May and early June, and the young take to these frigid waters when they're only a few days old.

MORE INFORMATION

The Nulhegan Basin Division of the refuge is closed to vehicle access during mud season but remains open to foot travel. The refuge conducts habitat-management activities, including logging; signs will alert visitors to current operations. Hunting, fishing, and snowmobiling are permitted, and car travel is not allowed on roads while they are open to snowmobile traffic. Bicycles are allowed on refuge roads. Camping and campfires are not allowed anywhere in the refuge. Silvio O. Conte National Fish and Wildlife Refuge, 5396 Route 105, Brunswick, VT 05905; 802-962-5240; fws.gov/refuge/Silvio_O_Conte.

NEARBY

Camp, paddle, and swim at Brighton State Park in Island Pond, 10 miles west. Island Pond is also the best bet for restaurants, groceries, and shops. The Northern Forest Canoe Trail follows the Nulhegan River on its 740-mile path between the Adirondacks and northern Maine; trail kiosks are on the lakeshore in Island Pond and at the Nulhegan's confluence with the Connecticut River.

MOOSE IN PERIL

There aren't many big animals that have adapted to the Green Mountains as well as the comically majestic moose. These gangly creatures spend winters sheltering in the protective boughs of mountainside evergreens, munching twigs and using their teeth to scrape bark from balsam fir, maple, aspen, and ash trunks. In summer, they head for the leafy shade of lower-elevation forests and cool off in beaver ponds and lakes. Those long legs help them to navigate deep snow and downed trees and to propel themselves surprisingly well in the water, where they can dive more than 15 feet down in search of delicious aquatic plants.

But wooded hillsides aren't so useful to humans intent on farming, and Vermont's nineteenth-century settlers logged and cleared and slashed and burned with fervor. Forests became sheep pastures and cropland. The moose vacated, along with many other native residents, and when Vermont's legislature caught up with the situation and banned moose hunting in 1896, it was a moot point: The hump-shouldered, long-nosed beasts were nowhere to be found. As it turned out, farming Vermont's rocky slopes wasn't a wildly successful endeavor. Over time, forests retook abandoned pastures, beavers returned from their own

Although gangly in appearance, the moose is surprisingly graceful and adept in water, feeding on aquatic vegetation as deep as 15 feet below the surface. Photo by Jerry Monkman.

hiatus and began creating swampy wetlands again, and eventually the moose wandered back in from the forests of northern New Hampshire and Quebec.

You might not expect such big animals to be as quick as rabbits at reproducing, but moose excel at this activity. According to Vermont's Fish and Wildlife Department, almost all adult moose breed every year, and half of the pregnancies result in twins. Additionally, half of the yearling females breed and give birth to single calves. When the situation is ideal—that is, without natural predators, as was the case in the Green Mountains when the moose returned—moose populations can increase by as much as 25 percent per year. In 1965, there were about 25 moose in Vermont; 40 years later, in 2005, the population was a healthy 4,800 individuals.

It sounds like a success story, but a new combination of threats is quickly laying waste to the population gains of the late-twentieth century. Between 2005 and 2015, Vermont's moose numbers plummeted to 2,070, well below the 3,000 animals the state considers a sustainable population. What is bringing down the mighty moose? There are several culprits. Humans with cars and rifles kill a percentage of the moose population each year. Modern moose must combat new, tiny predators, as well: Brainworms and winter ticks are parasites that aren't particularly harmful to their traditional hosts, white-tailed deer, but are hugely destructive to moose. (Previously, moose and deer didn't mix much, but deforestation and reforestation provided landscapes that support both, and they now share habitats.) Recent warm winters have allowed ticks to flourish, with tens of thousands feeding on a single moose, causing anemia and blood loss that kills calves and weakens adults.

Even if moose survive all of their current challenges, a larger problem threatens to push them from Vermont once again. Climate change has been hard on these big creatures of the cold north. They are adept at surviving long, frigid winters but not well equipped to shed heat as the mercury rises. If forecasted temperature increases come to pass, Vermont may be mooseless once again.

58

MONADNOCK MOUNTAIN

This isolated peak combines a remote hiking experience with extensive views of far northern New Hampshire and Vermont.

DIRECTIONS

From the Lemington–Colebrook bridge across the Connecticut River, travel about 0.1 mile north on VT 102 to a gravel pit on the left. Hiker parking is on the far left side of the working quarry in an open lot; use caution and do not block access for trucks. *GPS coordinates:* 44° 54.06′ N, 71° 30.43′ W.

TRAIL DESCRIPTION

Monadnock Mountain (3,130 feet) is a true geologic monadnock: a peak standing alone because its rocks are more resistant to erosion than the surrounding landscape. This hike ascends a rocky drainage between steep ridges on the mountain's east side. While rugged, the trail is well maintained and easily navigated, treating hikers to a journey through a remote and wild-feeling forest.

From the parking area, head 0.1 mile up a gravel road to a sign-in box in an open field. Following yellow markers, start along the left edge of the clearing then turn right through a brushy meadow, popping over a low ridge halfway across. Departing the meadow, Monadnock Mountain Trail climbs into a recently reestablished forest of small fir, birch, and spruce. Along with the gravel pit, timber has long been harvested from Monadnock's slopes.

In a short distance, pass through an open, slightly older softwood plantation. Following a stream on your left and a tall, mossy ledge on your right, duck under a rock overhang and enter an older mixed forest. A short, steep pitch leads to a stream crossing and a junction with an old fire road at 0.7 mile. Monadnock Mountain Trail turns right

LOCATION
Lemington, VT

RATING
Moderate to Strenuous

DISTANCE
5 miles

ELEVATION GAIN
2,108 feet

ESTIMATED TIME
3.5 hours

MAPS
USGS Monadnock Mountain

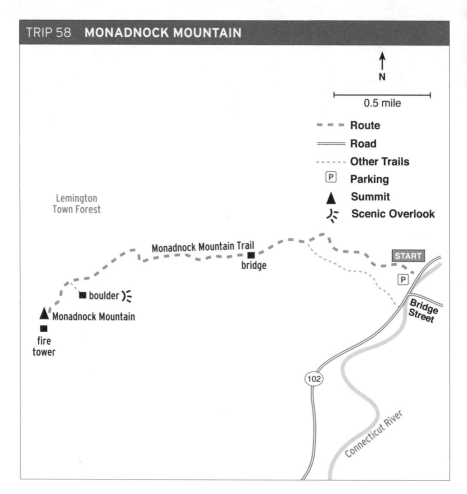

N

0.5 mile

- - -   Route
====   Road
- - - -   Other Trails
P   Parking
▲   Summit
)⟨   Scenic Overlook

Lemington
Town Forest

Monadnock Mountain Trail
bridge

START
P

Bridge
Street

■ boulder)⟨
▲ Monadnock Mountain
■
fire
tower

102

Connecticut River

and follows this road for the next steep 0.3 mile. (On your return trip, a loose pile of rocks resembling a cairn marks this junction.)

As you head up the rocky road, the footing occasionally will be difficult over loose rocks. When the road becomes more of a trail again, it crests a hill and swings right to cross the stream on a plank bridge at 1 mile. Be careful; algae and spray make the surface slippery. The mossy cascade beneath the bridge and a couple of seat-sized rocks create a scenic resting spot.

From the bridge, Monadnock Mountain Trail climbs steadily and moderately over ledges, rocks, and drainage gullies. Climb through a stand of paper birch then into the spruce-fir zone of the upper mountain. Red spruce, balsam fir, mountain ash, and paper birch are particularly suited to the thin, acidic soils and cold temperatures of mountaintops in New England. You can easily tell spruce and fir apart by shaking their hands: A spruce bough is spiny and sharp when you grip it, while a fir is flat and friendly.

At 2 miles, a short dead-end spur trail on the left leads to a boulder with a view east. Staying right, ascend to the final, flat walk through a dense stand of conifers covered with old-man's beard and arrive at the base of the fire tower. Monadnock's height made it an obvious location for a lookout tower, which was built during the Great Depression by the Civilian Conservation Corps (see "From the CCC to the VYCC: Conservation Corps in Vermont," page 257). The foundation and chimney of the Monadnock fire warden's cabin remain just beyond the tower.

Over the pointed tips of Monadnock's thick summit forest, the Connecticut River meanders south through a glacially scoured valley, forming the Vermont–New Hampshire border. The White Mountains push up against the eastern shore of the river, most notably the Nash Stream mountains to the southeast. On a clear day, the tall ridge of the Presidential Range can be seen in the southeast, and Magalloway Mountain (3,350 feet) in the northeast. To the southwest, Nulhegan Basin is a sort of geologic opposite of Monadnock, in which the center of a high land eroded more quickly than its edges, leaving a 10-mile-wide depression surrounded by a ring of hills, part of the Conte Refuge (Trip 57). To the northeast, Averill Mountain (2,240 feet) and Brousseau Mountain (Trip 60) back the two Averill ponds on the Quebec border.

Retrace your path to the trailhead.

Puffball mushrooms, like these on Monadnock Mountain, issue a puff of spores when disturbed.

Monadnock Mountain Trail follows a stream that cascades over ledges. Boardwalks aid hikers in navigating the slippery terrain and stream crossings on this outpost mountain.

DID YOU KNOW?

Gold has been mined in Vermont—but not very successfully. A reputed gold mine was on Monadnock Mountain, and small amounts of placer gold, or pieces eroded from their source, are present in many streams in Vermont. Hand-panning for gold is allowed on state and federal lands without a permit.

MORE INFORMATION

Monadnock Mountain Trail is partly on private land and partly on town forest-land. Please respect the generosity of the landowners: Do not kindle fires, camp, or use motorized vehicles on the trail; carry out all trash. The trail is maintained by the NorthWoods Stewardship Center, P.O. Box 220, East Charleston, VT 05833; 802-723-6551; northwoodscenter.org.

NEARBY

The Connecticut River Paddlers Trail and the Northern Forest Canoe Trail maintain access and campsites along the river. The Nulhegan Basin Division of the Silvio O. Conte National Fish and Wildlife Refuge has a visitor center and trails 18.5 miles southwest on VT 105. Food is along US 3 in Colebrook, New Hampshire, 0.8 mile east.

FROM THE CCC TO THE VYCC: CONSERVATION CORPS IN VERMONT

Vermont has almost as many trails as it has citizens. OK, maybe that's an exaggeration, but think not only of the hiking trails that cobweb the whole state but also the cross-country and alpine ski trails, the mountain-bike and paddling trails, the all-terrain-vehicle and snowmobile trails, the rail trails and horseback-riding trails, and the birding trails and town-park trails. How did one of this country's smallest states, with one of the smallest populations, come to be so covered with trails?

It would be too simple to say the Civilian Conservation Corps (CCC) is responsible, but in a way it's true. The Depression-era program, part of Franklin Delano Roosevelt's New Deal, harnessed the energies of unemployed young men to accomplish environmental conservation projects across the nation. The federal government originally allotted Vermont four CCC camps, but Perry Merrill, then the state forester, had a long list of planned projects, and he lobbied successfully for additional men and funding to complete them.

Vermont eventually hosted 30 CCC camps that supported more than 40,000 men, including more than 11,000 Vermonters, as they constructed hiking and ski trails, state-park facilities, fire towers, and mountain roads. They hand built massive earthen flood-control dams and bridges. They fought forest fires and tree diseases, and they planted thousands of trees. Their legacy is not only the physical infrastructure that enables people to actively enjoy Vermont's landscape but also the promotion of a culture of outdoor recreation and conservation that today values all manner of trails.

Another CCC legacy is its many offspring. The first and one of the most successful descendants is the Student Conservation Association (SCA), which began in 1957 to save national parks from being "loved to death" and continues in a broader capacity today. In the 1970s, the federally funded Youth Conservation Corps followed SCA's lead and employed hundreds of thousands of young Americans. When federal funding was cut in 1981, many states, including Vermont, picked up the tab to keep these programs running. The Vermont Youth Conservation Corps (VYCC) was born in 1985.

Today VYCC is a private nonprofit organization that hires young people to complete conservation projects in the service of its mission: "to teach individuals to take personal responsibility for all their actions." The NorthWoods Conservation Corps, founded separately to serve the Northeast Kingdom, hires young people as part of its mission: "to help local youth become stewards of their natural and community resources."

If you come across a youth crew laboring on the trail in brightly colored hard hats, offer them some encouragement. The state's trails and recreation facilities depend on their hard work today—and on their attitudes and values in the decades to come.

59

BLUFF MOUNTAIN

Steep rock outcrops provide exciting hiking and a bird's-eye view of Island Pond, as well as the expanse of forested peaks beyond it.

DIRECTIONS

From the junction of VT 105 and VT 114 in the middle of Island Pond, go east on VT 105 for 0.2 mile and turn left on South Street. Take the second right onto Mountain Street and drive 0.6 mile to the trailhead parking lot (space for about 6 cars) on the left. *GPS coordinates:* 44° 49.52′ N, 71° 52.57′ W.

TRAIL DESCRIPTION

Bluff Mountain (2,450 feet) is a north–south ridge with three high points, the middle being the proper summit. The Community Trail–Lookout Trail loop climbs the steep-sided southern summit (2,380 feet) overlooking Island Pond. Lookout Trail traverses a very steep pitch with the aid of iron handles affixed to the rock; children, dogs, and people who aren't comfortable with that level of exposure can use Bluff Mountain Community Trail to ascend and descend, or to make a loop with the middle-of-the-mountain trail that goes between Lookout Trail and Community Trail. If you skip the ladders and ascend via Community Trail, be sure to go past the treed summit of Bluff and continue 0.1 mile to the magnificent overlook. The steep section of Lookout Trail is best as an ascent—and best avoided altogether in wet or icy conditions. But for hikers who appreciate variety and challenge, Lookout Trail provides a fun, memorable experience.

Bluff Mountain Community Trail starts in a plantation of red pine, following blue blazes uphill through tidy rows of tall trees. At 0.1 mile, a register box marks the transition into a more natural forest of maple, birch, and fir.

LOCATION
Island Pond, VT

RATING
Moderate

DISTANCE
3.3 miles

ELEVATION GAIN
1,110 feet

ESTIMATED TIME
2.5 hours

MAPS
USGS Island Pond,
USGS Spectacle Pond

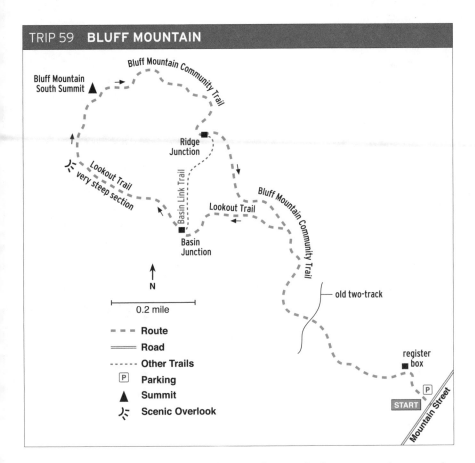

Bluff Mountain Community Trail

Bluff Mountain
South Summit ▲

Ridge
Junction

Lookout Trail
very steep section

Basin Link Trail

Lookout Trail

Bluff Mountain Community Trail

Basin
Junction

↑
N

0.2 mile

- - - **Route**
=== **Road**
----- **Other Trails**
P **Parking**
▲ **Summit**
⅄ **Scenic Overlook**

old two-track

register
■ box

P

START

Mountain Street

Ferns and the glossy, dark green leaves of partridgeberry spread across the forest floor. Climbing moderately, the trail crosses a bushy swath at 0.2 mile where blackberries and raspberries thrive. At 0.4 mile, you cross an old, eroded two-track in the forest and continue snaking up the hill through a stand of big cedars. At 0.7 mile, you arrive at the junction of Lookout Trail. Bluff Mountain Community Trail goes right and will be your downhill route. Go left onto the yellow-blazed Lookout Trail, crossing the hillside for 0.2 mile then descending another 0.1 mile to reach Basin Junction at 1 mile. Basin Link Trail heads uphill here 0.3 mile to join Bluff Mountain Community Trail, providing an alternate route to the summit that avoids the ladders of Lookout Trail.

From Basin Junction, Lookout Trail rises at a pleasant rate at first, crossing a couple of wet swaths filled with ferns then crossing the hillside. A rock staircase marks the beginning of the steep section of trail. Steep becomes very steep, and for the final 0.1 mile of the climb, you'll need your hands to help you ascend several sets of metal rungs attached to the ledges. At the top, a small view of the shining waters of Island Pond rewards your efforts. Continue a short distance up Lookout Trail to a grassy clearing with a bigger overlook and a more stable place to stand while viewing it.

Bluff Mountain's outlook gives hikers a well-deserved view of Island Pond.

The village of Island Pond and its namesake lake are the highlights of this view. Island Pond sits in an interesting position on a watershed divide. From the pond, the Clyde River flows northwest, descending to Lake Memphremagog, which drains north into the Saint Lawrence River. Just on the other side of Island Pond, the Nulhegan River rises from Nulhegan Pond and flows the opposite direction, southeast to the Connecticut River, which drains south into Long Island Sound.

Look closely at the ridge beyond Island Pond's waters to spot the blocky, Cold War-era radar building on East Mountain (3,420 feet). The summit of Burke Mountain (3,267 feet) curves against the sky behind the Seneca Range to the south. New Hampshire's White Mountains are in the distant south, with the pointed summit of Mount Garfield (4,500 feet) east of the big hump of Mount Lafayette (5,260 feet).

From here, follow Lookout Trail's yellow blazes across the clearing and into the woods. A rolling, mossy path leads through a boreal forest to a short spur trail at 1.5 miles. The south, or lower, mountain summit is here, on a large rock surrounded by trees. From the spur-trail junction, the blue blazes of Bluff Mountain Community Trail begin, leading through a damp, flat-bottomed ravine at 1.7 miles then to the Ridge Junction of Basin Link Trail at 2.1 miles. Stay left and continue downhill on Bluff Mountain Community Trail, returning to the Lookout Trail junction at 2.6 miles. Follow Bluff Mountain Community Trail out the way you hiked in.

DID YOU KNOW?

Paddlers on the Clyde River steer their boats through a tunnel under the Essex House and Tavern as they leave Island Pond.

MORE INFORMATION

Bluff Mountain's trails are maintained by the NorthWoods Stewardship Center, P.O. Box 220, East Charleston, VT 05833; 802-723-6551; northwoodscenter.org.

NEARBY

Northern Forest Canoe Trail's 740-mile route passes through Island Pond; a kiosk with more information is downtown in Pavilion Park, 1 mile south, which is also a nice place to picnic and swim. Camp, paddle, and swim at Brighton State Park, 3.5 miles east. Food, lodging, and shops are in Island Pond, 1 mile south.

60

BROUSSEAU MOUNTAIN

A short, pretty climb over the summit of this small northern peak leads to dramatic cliffs and a wide view south over lakes and mountains.

DIRECTIONS

From the junction of VT 114 and VT 147 in Norton, near the border-crossing station, follow VT 114 east 3 miles. Turn right on Brousseau Mountain Road and follow it 1.3 miles to its end at a gate. Park alongside the road (space for about 5 cars), being careful not to block the gate or driveways. (This road is not maintained in winter; depending on the conditions, snowshoers may need to park at the bottom and add 2.6 miles round-trip to the hike.) *GPS coordinates:* 44° 58.61' N, 71° 44.47' W.

TRAIL DESCRIPTION

Brousseau Mountain (2,723 feet), just south of the Quebec border, is off the beaten path of most hikers; consequently, its incredible views and lovely forests are often quiet. Approaching this inconspicuous forested bump from the north, you don't see the dramatic cliffs on its south face until you arrive on top of them. Peregrine falcons have sometimes nested on these crags, and if they are there, the overlook may be closed to hikers between March 15 and August 1 to protect chicks; check with Audubon Vermont (vt.audubon.org) for current information. The short, steady climb is appropriate for kids ages 5 and older.

Go around the gate and follow the extension of Brousseau Mountain Road about 400 feet, where Brousseau Mountain Trail goes left into the woods and passes a register box just inside the treeline. Climbing gradually through the thin trunks of a young forest, you will pass an old apple tree and brushy openings on both sides of the

LOCATION
Norton, VT

RATING
Easy to Moderate

DISTANCE
1.6 miles

ELEVATION GAIN
590 feet

ESTIMATED TIME
1 hour

MAPS
USGS Averill

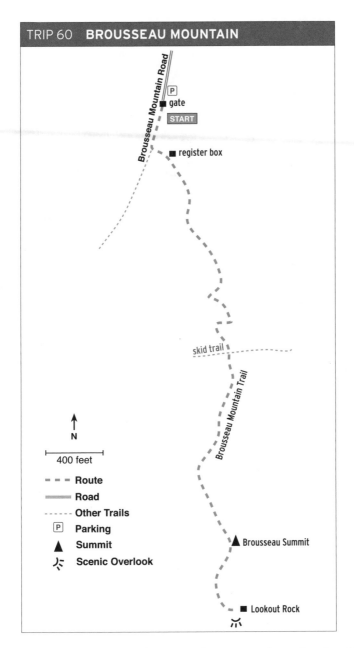

Brousseau Mountain Road

P

■ gate

START

■ register box

skid trail ■

Brousseau Mountain Trail

↑
N

|——————|
400 feet

- - - **Route**

═══ **Road**

----- **Other Trails**

P **Parking**

▲ **Summit**

乄 **Scenic Overlook**

▲ Brousseau Summit

■ Lookout Rock

乄

trail that hint at the land's recent history. After passing through a dim fir stand, the trail angles up the mountainside.

At 0.4 mile, Brousseau Mountain Trail crosses a narrow swath cut across the mountain: the remains of a skid trail used to remove logs. From here, the forest becomes more boreal: a beautiful mix of fir, spruce, mountain ash, and paper birch. These trees are older than those below, and the thick trunks are spaced far enough apart to give a view through the forest. The treadway is often solid

So far north it's almost in Canada, Brousseau Mountain gives hikers a view south across Little Averill Lake and the mountainous, immense forests of the Northeast Kingdom.

bedrock, lined with moss, blueberries, and ferns as Brousseau Mountain Trail makes its way back and forth and sometimes directly up the slope. Occasional rock steps and bog bridges break up the long stripes of rock trail.

The pitch lessens as you enter a tunnel of tight saplings near the top of the mountain. Curving left, cross the forested summit at 0.7 mile. The trail drops to the right, descending through spruce and fir for 0.1 mile before arriving at the open rocks of the lookout. Leash dogs here and keep children close by.

Little Averill Pond spreads across the valley beneath the cliffs, its inlet stream zigzagging through a marsh to the west. Sable Mountain (2,725 feet) is the little solo peak south of the pond, and Green (2,700 feet) and Black (2,800 feet) mountains form the high ground beyond the inlet marsh. The expanse of forest beyond Little Averill Pond is largely Kingdom and Victory state forests. Monadnock Mountain (Trip 58) rises beyond ridges to the southeast, its fire tower discernible against the sky. Turbines visible on the ridges north and south of Monadnock are in New Hampshire, as are the White Mountains spread across the southern horizon, including Mount Garfield (4,500 feet) and Mount Lafayette (5,260 feet). Jay Peak (3,830 feet) pokes above closer ridgelines to the west.

Return downhill the way you climbed up.

DID YOU KNOW?

Norton, Vermont, and Stanhope, Quebec, developed together, as did many other border towns in this rural area, where the lay of the land often influenced communities more than political lines did. A general store was situated on the international border for years, with doors on both sides, so residents of either country could enter to shop.

MORE INFORMATION

Brousseau Mountain Trail is maintained by the NorthWoods Stewardship Center, P.O. Box 220, East Charleston, VT 05833; 802-723-6551; northwoodscenter.org.

NEARBY

Little Averill and Great Averill ponds have placid paddling around the base of Brousseau Mountain. Pack your passport to mountain bike at Hereford Mountain in East Hereford, Quebec, 19 miles northeast. Paddle, camp, and swim at Brighton State Park, 23 miles south. A general store in Norton provides some food; for more options, head to Island Pond, 20 miles south.

APPENDIX
MOUNTAIN BIKING

The popularity of mountain biking has grown rapidly in Vermont over the past two decades and so have the number of trails specifically for bikes. The Vermont Mountain Bike Association (VMBA) is a central organizer and promoter of mountain biking, with chapter organizations heading up regional trail work. Some mountain-bike areas charge riders a fee to help defray maintenance expenses; other places are free to ride, with trail maintenance dependent on volunteers, memberships, and donations. Although not listed here, some ski areas maintain mountain-bike trails, and the many rail trails throughout the state offer beginner-friendly off-road riding experiences.

Here is a partial list of some of the best mountain biking in Vermont, with the caveat that more options exist than can be listed, and more trails are being added each season, all across the state. For the most up-to-date information, consult local bike shops and VMBA chapters (vmba.org).

Kingdom Trails: The award-winning Kingdom Trails in East Burke has everything from beginner-friendly farm roads to fast-flowing single-track to technical free-ride trails. With more than 100 miles of well-maintained, interconnected cross-country trails and a lift-served downhill and free-ride area, this trail system is the leader in mountain biking—not just in Vermont but in the Northeast. Near Burke Mountain (Trip 52); kingdomtrails.com.

Moosalamoo National Recreation Area: The U.S. Forest Service has joined forces with VMBA and various other groups to develop mountain biking in this diverse section of the northern Green Mountain National Forest. Trails range from dirt roads to technical single-track. Near Rattlesnake Cliffs (Trip 20), Robert Frost Trail (Trip 22), and Mount Horrid's Great Cliff (Trip 21); moosalamoo.org.

Vermont Ride Center: One of only five U.S. sites approved by the International Mountain Bike Association as a model in mountain-bike development, the Vermont Ride Center is a work in progress. Centered in the Waterbury–Stowe area, it radiates to include trail systems in Bolton, Cambridge, and Jericho. All levels and all types of riding (cross-country, free ride, and downhill) will be featured by the time the project is complete. Near Camel's Hump (Trip 27) and Mount Hunger (Trip 41); vmba.org.

Trapp Family Lodge: High on the mountain above Stowe, this iconic resort's trail system offers 40 miles and counting of double- and single-track riding that connects to a network of local trails, accommodating all abilities of riders. Near Wiessner Woods (Trip 43), Stowe Pinnacle (Trip 44), and Sterling Pond (Trip 47); trappfamily.com.

Mad River Valley: This central Vermont area has both steep technical riding and flowy, beginner-friendly single-track at Blueberry Lake. Near Sunset Ledge (Trip 24), Mount Abraham (Trip 25), and Burnt Rock Mountain (Trip 26); madriverriders.com.

Millstone Hill: Circumnavigating old, scenic granite quarries on the hill above Barre, more than 35 miles of trails provide tons of technical riding, as well as loops for beginner and intermediate riders. Near Spruce Mountain (Trip 30) and Owl's Head (Trip 31); millstonetrails.com.

Chittenden County: With more than 100 miles of trails in a dozen locations not far from Burlington, Chittenden County offers options for all levels of riders. Near Colchester Pond (Trip 35) and Mount Mansfield (Trips 45 and 46); fotwheel.org.

Sleepy Hollow: This inn in Huntington offers more than a dozen miles of intermediate and advanced single-track that connects to a network of multiuse trails in Hinesburg Town Forest. Near Camel's Hump (Trip 27); skisleepyhollow.com.

Catamount Outdoor Family Center: These multiuse trails in Williston accommodate trail runners and hikers, in addition to mountain bikers. Popular camps, races, and other events make the center a hub of local outdoor activity. Near Mount Mansfield (Trips 45 and 46); catamountoutdoorfamilycenter.org.

Norwich University's Shaw Outdoor Center: The hillside that historically hosted alpine ski trails is now crisscrossed with single-track; a skills park at the base helps beginning and intermediate riders get up to speed before tackling the trails. Near White Rock Mountain (Trip 40), Spruce Mountain (Trip 30), and Burnt Rock Mountain (Trip 26); lifeat.norwich.edu/shaw-outdoor-center.

Green Mountain Trails: Twenty-five miles of multiuse single-track in Pittsfield, Stockbridge, and Chittenden offer all levels of riding on a variety of terrain. Near Pico Peak (Trip 16), Deer Leap (Trip 17), and Mount Horrid's Great Cliff (Trip 21); greenmountaintrails.com.

Pine Hill Park: Within Rutland, a 300-acre preserve of wooded hills and ravines hosts 16 miles of multiuse single-track trails. The majority is intermediate level, but there are beginner-friendly routes and some technical aspects for advanced riders. Near White Rocks Ice Beds (Trip 13), Pico Peak (Trip 16), Deer Leap (Trip 17), and Buckner Preserve (Trip 18); pinehillpark.org.

Sports Trails of the Ascutney Basin: The western flank of Mount Ascutney is covered with 30 miles of multiuse trails looping through woods and fields, accommodating all abilities. Near Okemo Mountain (Trip 14) and Mount Ascutney (Trip 15); stabvt.org.

INDEX

ABOUT THE AUTHOR

Jen Lamphere Roberts loves to explore all kinds of trails and landscapes. Her professional pursuits include helping develop the Northern Forest Canoe Trail and teaching backcountry skills clinics with organizations such as Vermont Works for Women. She lives with her family in Montpelier, Vermont.

AMC BOOK UPDATES

At AMC Books, we keep our guidebooks as up-to-date as possible to help you plan safe and enjoyable adventures. After publishing a book, if we learn that trails have been relocated, or that route or contact information has changed, we will post an update online. Before you hit the trail, check outdoors.org/bookupdates.

While hiking, if you notice discrepancies with a trail description or a map, or if you find any other errors in this book, please submit them by email to amcbookupdates@outdoors.org or by letter to Books Editor, c/o AMC, 10 City Square, Boston, MA 02129. We verify all submissions and post key updates each month.

We are dedicated to making AMC Books a recognized leader in outdoor publishing. Thank you for your participation.

APPALACHIAN MOUNTAIN CLUB

At AMC, connecting you to the freedom and exhilaration of the outdoors is our calling. We help people of all ages and abilities to explore and develop a deep appreciation of the natural world.

AMC helps you get outdoors on your own, with family and friends, and through activities close to home and beyond. With chapters from Maine to Washington, D.C., including groups in Boston, New York City, and Philadelphia, you can enjoy activities like hiking, paddling, cycling, and skiing, and learn new outdoor skills. We offer advice, guidebooks, maps, and unique lodges and huts to inspire your next outing. You will also have the opportunity to support conservation advocacy and research, youth programming, and caring for 1,800 miles of trails.

We invite you to join us in the outdoors.

YOUR CONNECTION TO THE OUTDOORS

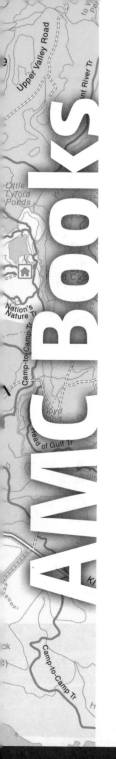

Quiet Water New Hampshire and Vermont, 3rd Edition

John Hayes & Alex Wilson

Great for families, anglers, canoeists, and kayakers of all abilitie this guide features 90 of the best calm-water paddling trip in New Hampshire and Vermont. Explore the many ponds c Pillsbury State Park, paddle Chocorua Lake with breathtakin views, and rediscover Vermont's scenic Lake Champlain.

$19.95 • 978-1-934028-35-3

White Mountain Guide, 30th Edition

Compiled and Edited by Steven D. Smith

Now in print for 110 years, AMC's comprehensive *White Moun tain Guide* remains hikers' most trusted resource for the Whit Mountain National Forest and surrounding regions. New in thi thoroughly updated 30th edition are at-a-glance icons for sug gested hikes and easier-to-follow statistics for all 500-plus trails

$24.95 • 978-1-934028-85-8

White Mountain National Forest Map & Guide, 3rd Edition

AMC Books

If you only have one trail map of the White Mountains, mak it this one, featuring the entire national forest. Waterproof anc tear-resistant, this newly revised third edition is significantl larger scale and easier to read, with updated before-you-gc safety, planning, and packing tips; plus, a 4,000-footer checklis and 24 recommended hikes for all skill levels.

$9.95 • 978-1-62842-093-7

Best Backcountry Skiing in the Northeast

David Goodman

Earn your turns with this definitive guide to backcountry skiing in New England and New York, covering the 50 best spots fo off-slope adventures, including Tuckerman Ravine, Katahdin and the historic Thunderbolt Ski Trail, with descriptions, eleva tions, topographic maps, and directions for each trip.

$19.95 • 978-1-934028-14-8

Find these and other AMC titles, as well as ebooks, through ebook stores, booksellers, and outdoor retailers. Or order directly from AMC at **outdoors.org/amcstore** or call **800-262-4455**